THE POETRY OF SAYING

LIVERPOOL ENGLISH TEXTS AND STUDIES, 45

THE POETRY OF SAYING

British Poetry and its Discontents 1950–2000

ROBERT SHEPPARD

LIVERPOOL UNIVERSITY PRESS

First published 2005 by
Liverpool University Press
4 Cambridge Street, Liverpool L69 7ZU

British Library Cataloguing-in-Publication Data
A catalogue record for this book is available from the British Library

Library of Congress Cataloging-in-Publication Data applied for

14 13 12 11 10 09 08 07 06 05 10 9 8 7 6 5 4 3 2 1

ISBN 0 85323 8197

Edited and typeset by
Frances Hackeson Freelance Publishing Services, Brinscall, Lancs
Printed in Great Britain
by MPG Books, Bodmin, Cornwall

Contents

Contents

Preface

This book has been many years in the making, the critical counter word to my development as a poet. It includes nearly everything I wanted to say about British Poetry in the second half of the twentieth century up until its completion in manuscript in 2001. Before that time innumerable reviews and short articles have shaped my thinking, including those collected in *Far Language: Poetics and Linguistically Innovative Poetry 1978–1997* (Exeter: Stride Research Documents, 1999), which is, in many ways, a companion volume to *The Poetry of Saying*. My cannibalized dry-runs, earlier versions, variant readings, and parallel out-takes or after-thoughts include: 'Recognition and Discovery in the 1980s', *Fragmente* 2 (1990); 'The Necessary Business of Allen Fisher', in *Future Exiles* (London: Paladin, 1992); 'De-Anglicizing the Midlands: The European Context of Roy Fisher's *City*', *English*, vol. 41, no. 169 (Spring 1992); 'British Poetry and its Discontents' in Moore-Gilbert, B. and Seed, J., eds., *Cultural Revolution? The Challenge of the Arts in the 1960s* (London: Routledge, 1992); 'Lee Harwood and the Poetics of the Open Work' in Hampson R. and Barry P., eds., *New British Poetries*, (Manchester: Manchester University Press, 1993); 'Artifice and the everyday world: poetry in the 1970s', in Moore-Gilbert, B., ed., *Arts in the 1970s: Cultural Closure?* (London: Routledge, 1994); 'Negative Definitions: Talk for the Sub Voicive Colloquium, London, 1997', *Sulfur* 42 (1998); '"Elsewhere and Everywhere": Other New (British) Poetries', *Critical Survey*, vol. 10, no. 1 (1998); 'A thing or two upon the page', in Upton, L. and Cobbing, B., eds., *Word Score Utterance Choreography in verbal and visual poetry* (London: Writers Forum, 1998); 'The Poetics of Poetics: Charles Bernstein, Allen Fisher and "the poetic thinking that results"' in *Symbiosis*, vol. 3, no. 1 (April 1999); 'Making Forms with Remarks', in Kerrigan, J. and Robinson, P., eds., *The Thing About Roy Fisher*, (Liverpool: Liverpool University Press, 2000); 'A Bloating Bubble A', in Upton, L., ed., *For Bob Cobbing* (London:

Mainstream Press, 2000); 'The Performing and the Performed', on *How2*, 2002: www.scc.rutgers.edu/however/v1_6_2001/current/in-conference/sheppard.html; 'Poetics and Ethics: The Saying and the Said in the Linguistically Innovative Poetry of Tom Raworth', *Critical Survey*, vol. 14, no. 2 (2002); and '"Whose Lives Does the Government Affect?": Looking Back at *West Wind*', in Dorward, N., ed., *Removed for Further Study: The Poetry of Tom Raworth* (Toronto: The Gig, 2003); and in various postings on *Pages* blogzine, www.robertsheppard.blogspot.com.

I gratefully acknowledge the assistance of funds made available by various research committees of Edge Hill College of Higher Education in the completion of this volume, and meeting the costs of permissions. The earliest traces of this work may be found in my doctoral thesis 'Some Aspects of Contemporary British Poetry', PhD thesis, University of East Anglia, 1988 – particularly the first few chapters – and I would like to offer belated thanks to my supervisor, Professor Victor Sage, for his exacting encouragement and to dedicate this volume to him.

Acknowledgements

Anvil Press Poetry Ltd, for extracts from 'Poet for Our Times' taken from *The Other Country* by Carol Ann Duffy, published by Anvil Press Poetry in 1990.

Bloodaxe Books for extracts from Simon Armitage, *Zoom!* (1989); from Roy Fisher, *The Dow Low Drop: New and Selected Poems* (1996); and from Geoffrey Hattersley's 'Minus Three Point Six' and 'Religion, Insanity, Suicide', and from Barry MacSweeney's *Wolf Tongue: Selected Poems 1965–2000* (2003).

Faber and Faber for extracts from Sylvia Plath's 'Lady Lazarus' from *Collected Poems* (1981); from Seamus Heaney's *Selected Poems 1990* (1990); and from Philip Larkin's *The Whitsun Weddings* (1964).

To Gordon Dickerson, literary agent, for permission to quote Tony Harrison, from 'Long Distance', *Selected Poems*, Penguin, 1987.

The following poets also kindly granted me permission to quote copyright material:

Gilbert Adair; Caroline Bergvall; cris cheek from 'stranger'; Adrian Clarke; the late Bob Cobbing; Andrew Crozier; Ken Edwards; Allen Fisher for various texts from *Place* and *Gravity as a consequence of shape*; Roy Fisher from *The Cut Pages*, 'Dudley from the Castle Keep', 'On the open Side' and 'Handsworth Liberties'; Ulli Freer; Bill Griffiths; Lee Harwood; Ian McMillan; Drew Milne; Maggie O'Sullivan; J.H. Prynne for copyright material from *Poems* (Edinburgh and London: Agneau 2, 1982) and from *Her Weasels Wild Returning* (Cambridge: Equipage, 1994), which appears in *Conductors of Chaos: a poetry anthology*, ed. Iain Sinclair (London: Picador, 1996); Tom Raworth; Denise Riley; Peter Riley from *Alstonefield* and *Excavations*; Iain Sinclair; John Wilkinson from 'Cabling the Suburbs'; and Aaron Williamson.

It has not proved possible to locate a copyright holder for the work of the late Mark Hyatt.

Abbreviations

CA   *Children of Albion: Poetry of the 'Underground' in Britain,* ed. Michael Horovitz (Harmondsworth: Penguin, 1969)

CC   *Conductors of Chaos: a poetry anthology,* ed. Iain Sinclair (London: Picador, 1996)

CFR   Lee Harwood, *Crossing the Frozen River: selected poems* (London: Paladin, 1988)

CBP   *The Penguin Book of Contemporary British Poetry,* eds. Blake Morrison and Andrew Motion (Harmondsworth: Penguin, 1982)

CP86   Roy Fisher, *The Cut Pages* (second edition) (London: Oasis Books/Shearsman Books, 1986)

DLD   Roy Fisher, *The Dow Low Drop: new and selected poems* (Newcastle upon Tyne: Bloodaxe Books, 1996)

NP66   *The New Poetry,* ed. A Alvarez (second edition) (Harmondsworth: Penguin, 1966)

NP93   *The New Poetry,* eds. Michael Hulse, David Kennedy and David Morley (Newcastle upon Tyne: Bloodaxe Books, 1993)

P55–87   Roy Fisher, *Poems 1955–1987* (Oxford: Oxford University Press, 1988)

TS88   Tom Raworth (second edition) *Tottering State: selected poems 1963–1987* (London: Paladin, 1988)

TS2000   Tom Raworth (third edition) *Tottering State: selected early poems 1963–1983* (Oakland: O Books, 2000)

INTRODUCTION
Technique: Dialogue: Saying

While this work offers a unifying theory of the poetry studied, I am cautioned by what has become increasingly clear to me after writing about (and writing) this verse for the last twenty years: the overriding virtue of its diversity. I am aware, therefore, that any theoretical approach needs to emphasize the particularity of this heterodoxy, to allow its otherness to speak.

This is partly why *The Poetry of Saying* is also a history. The story of this poetry has hardly begun to be told, particularly given the influence of an alternative narrative of a poetic orthodoxy that has dominated the period 1950–2000, and which is the focus of two summary chapters. The necessary context the larger story offers both supports and balances my choice of authors to whom whole or substantial parts of chapters are dedicated.

In this introduction, I argue that this poetry – I use the terms British Poetry Revival and Linguistically Innovative Poetry for its two, not entirely distinct, phases – may be seen with regard to a tripartite theory that informs my individual chapters. This work may be analysed at three levels: the technical, the social, and the ethical.

The technical level concerns techniques of indeterminacy and discontinuity, of collage and creative linkage, of poetic artifice and defamiliarization.

The social level concerns itself with a reading of the necessary dialogic nature of all utterance, including the kinds of poetry offered here. This builds on the technical devices described, ones which animate the reading process into necessary dialogue.

The ethical level of analysis extends from the first two levels into an understanding of the varieties of openness to the other implied by the techniques and social orientation of the work.

Technique: The Poetics of Form

At the level of technique the work of the British Poetry Revival and the Linguistically Innovative Poetry that followed, differs from that of the Movement and its dominant orthodoxy, one whose adventures I will summarize in Chapters 1 and 5. As an orthodoxy it operates as a variety of poetic unconscious, a socio-literary norm that does not exist in a pure form, but which has had a lasting and limiting effect on the world of letters (often through the polemic of the poetry anthologies I will examine in this book).

The Movement Orthodoxy, or its norm, privileges a poetry of closure, narrative coherence and grammatical and syntactic cohesion, which colludes with the processes of naturalization, that is, with the 'attempt to reduce the strangeness of poetic language and poetic organization by making it intelligible, by translating it into a statement about the non-verbal external world', as Veronica Forrest-Thomson puts it.[1] Its poetry favours an empirical lyricism of discrete moments of experience. Its insistence upon tone, and the speaking voice, strives to maintain the effect of a stable ego, present in the discourse as the validating source of the utterance. The principle of the orthodoxy's metrical practice, although used with greater laxity through the decades, has largely relied upon the iambic pentameter to level the tone, which both controls, and assists in the maintenance of, a coherent 'voice'.

As I shall show the orthodoxy has changed its attitude towards, and its uses of, figurative language: from a distrust of any figurative distortion of the empirical in its originating moment in the 1950s; to a rhetorical use of images to circumscribe psychological disruptions in the 1960s; to a reliance upon ornamental simile to mediate a world and confirm the presence of the author-subject in the 1980s. In the 1990s its supposed pluralism – even a 'postmodernism' – authorized a wider range of techniques, often under pressure from identity politics to allow spaces for 'marginalized' voices to be heard, but just as often concurred with the civilities of the orthodoxy. But this apparent consensus still excludes a vaster range of poetry, with a wider set of poetic practices, which is the main focus of this study.

Postmodernism is a term I wish to use exclusively in Lyotard's sense of a defined condition, a generalized philosophical worldview, one that is useful to introduce my particular poetics of technique. Knowledge, scientific knowledge in particular, is not so much the result of the recording of empirical investigation but involves a permanent condition of exploratory and incomplete process. Rules are not normative prescriptions but are produced coterminously with the event or process they regulate. Lyotard's formulation of the now famous resistance to grand narratives also involves a commitment to exploratory techniques that are spelt out precisely in terms of poetics:

> A postmodern artist or writer is in the position of a philosopher: the text he writes, the work he produces are not in principle governed by preestablished rules ... Those rules and categories are what the work of art itself is looking for. The artist and the writer, then, are working without rules in order to formulate the rules of what *will have been done*.[2]

Any activity will be 'producing not the known, but the unknown'.[3] In a purely literary sense, this suggests a mode of writing which acknowledges that its only possible condition is one of technical development, a process of working towards new, and initially difficult, meanings, and suspending naturalization. It cannot be the formulation of a product from prior assumptions of meaning. Philip Larkin's insistence on poetry as empirical reconstruction:

> if you've seen this sight, felt this feeling, had this vision, and have got to find a combination of words that will preserve it by setting it off in other people

is clearly inadequate.[4]

The poetics of the British Poetry Revival and of Linguistically Innovative Poetry stresses the centrality of the notions of discontinuity and indeterminacy as technical elements of poetics, notions which Umberto Eco, writing of certain musical compositions in 1959, recognized were derived from science: 'indeterminacy as a valid stepping-stone in the cognitive process' and discontinuity as 'an essential stage in all scientific verification procedures'.[5] Perception (Eco also has in mind the phenomenology of Merleau Ponty) is an indeterminate process, both for the writer writing and for the reader reading. There is in the work discussed in this study a preference for, an imperative towards, various forms of indeterminacy: structural, syntactic, semantic and metrical; the effects of these difficulties will be to emphasize the activation of the reader so that he or she has to enter into the artwork to complete it.

Techniques of indeterminacy and discontinuity range from the avoidance of narrative naturalization in Roy Fisher's *The Cut Pages* and the referential and perceptual uncertainties of his short lyrics, to the invitation of

Lee Harwood's open syntax and collage structures. The development of collage into what I call techniques of creative linkage (where the linking is more radical) is a central device in the works of Tom Raworth, Allen Fisher, Adrian Clarke and Ulli Freer.

Considerations of metrics reveal the paucity of descriptive terms for new poetic experiments, which demonstrate the inadequacy of the dated term 'free verse', particularly in the case of the sound and visual poetry of Bob Cobbing, which is a precursor of the new non-linear poetry found in the radical collage of Maggie O'Sullivan. In both these cases, and in certain later texts of Allen Fisher, the transformation of materials plays upon their instability in order to produce new meanings. In the case of performance texts their realizations may be unique, different each time they are attempted.

Indeterminacy should not be assumed to imply randomness, but a process of working with contingency in a conscious fashion, even in the procedural and processual works of a writer like Allen Fisher, where a dialogue between choice and chance, a precisely stochastic process, ensures that systems are subject to disruptive interventions by the poet. Clarke's isoverbalist metrics (counting numbers of words per line, per poem) is an instance of a closed system which is at one level an affront to traditional metrics, but one that is arguably as demanding, a modern constraint rather than a convention authorized by tradition, to borrow a distinction from the Oulipo movement. At another level it also works as a vehicle for the hinging of phrases in an indeterminate syntactic practice, a practice which is arguably stronger because of the tension between its systems.

British Poetry Revival and Linguistically Innovative poets foreground the fact of the artificiality of the forms and discourses they employ. In Harwood's narratives a self-conscious narrator is often presented, while Roy Fisher's lyrics often make 'the poem' a counter in its own argument. Allen Fisher deliberately adopts techniques of 'process-showing' in his work. Cobbing's processual pieces develop out of previous texts. By foregrounding artifice or construction, the poem suspends the inevitable act of naturalization; it can be said additionally to be de-automatizing the reader's habitual responses, defamiliarizing them, in that deferral.

When, in the famous definition of defamiliarization as device, Shklovsky says 'the purpose of art' is 'to impart the sensation of things as they are perceived not as they are known', he is not merely arguing for a freshness of perception, a seeing as though for the first time.[6] He founds 'the technique of art' on its attempt 'to make objects unfamiliar', the famous 'making strange' of the more colloquial translation of the Russian *ostrananie*. It is often forgotten that, in order to effect an increase in 'the difficulty and length of perception', it is necessary not just to admit an estranging 'content', but to 'make forms difficult'.[7] This is not a question of likening a flowerpot to a fez, as in a poem by Craig Raine, but of using the variety of *formal* techniques of indeterminacy and discontinuity, of foregrounding artifice and construction, outlined here.

A poem is an object, but it is also part of the reader's responses, since he or she must complete it; any reader, in Umberto Eco's words 'is bound to supply his own existential credentials'.[8] This is, as the theoreticians of reception aesthetics have noted, an active fact of interpretation of both structurally closed works, and of the kinds of work examined here. However, in certain kinds of open work offered by some writers of the British Poetry Revival and Linguistically Innovative persuasions, who work in deliberate collusion with this fact, this is crucial. Eco calls artworks with such radical structural indeterminacy and discontinuity 'works in movement' which he characterizes as involving 'the possibility of numerous different personal interventions.'[9] Eco defines this limit case of an 'open work' as one that is 'literally "unfinished": the author seems to hand them to the performer more or less like the components of a construction kit'.[10] Harwood at times conceives of his work in this way, as leaving textual lacunae for a reader to complete.

Allen Fisher has most fully theorized this position in relation to his own poetics. Poetry, he argues, is at its most pertinent when fresh significations are produced by an active reader. A text is judged on its ability to escape the writer and invigorate the reader's engagement. It is assumed that this is effected by means of technique: modes of creative linkage are utilized to present a plurivocal text to which a reader brings his or her existential credentials, which are, like the text itself, the results of historical and social processes.

This emphasis upon the activity of reading brings us to Forrest-Thomson's notion of naturalization to focus upon and emend the distinctions she makes between 'good' and 'bad' naturalization. Bad naturalization is defined as an attempt to reduce 'the strangeness of poetic language … by translating it in to a statement about the non-verbal external world, by making the Artifice appear natural', whereas

> Good naturalization dwells on the non-meaningful levels of poetic language, such as phonetic and prosodic patterning and spatial organization, and tries to state their relationship to other levels of organization rather than set(ting) them aside in an attempt to produce a statement about the world.[11]

Charles Bernstein augments Forrest-Thomson's taxonomy to remind us that *all* levels of poetry, any discernable device, linguistic or not, should be regarded as meaningful.[12] (This could include stutters in a verbal performance, or choices of typeface on the page, as recent performance writers argue.) The whole of a literary text signifies for the engaged reader, as he or she enters it; 'Whatever else I may get from a work of art,' argues Allen Fisher, 'because its dominant function is aesthetic it requires my engagement to create it, to produce it.'[13] Its artifice may not be willed away, in all its particularity and, even, in the case of some of the work I will be examining, its peculiarity; its artifice has to be read because no 'paraphrase' is accurate or full enough, or, in some cases, possible. Forrest-Thomson's general account of artifice and naturalization reminds the reader always of the strangeness of technique, and that to only read 'formal features' as 'noteworthy components of the poem' if they 'can be shown to contribute to a thematic synthesis that is stated in terms of the external world', is a denial of poetry's singularity.[14] She quotes Wittgenstein's minatory aphorism: 'Do not forget ... that a poem, even though it is composed in the language of information is not used in the language-game of giving information.'[15]

The Social Poetics of Form: Dialogue

That the various entries of various readers into actual texts is represented as its affirmative moment by such a theory points towards why the work of the reception theorists is only hinted at by Allen Fisher and others. The poets' notions of readership are *actual* rather than *ideal*. When Harwood speaks of leaving an object (the poem) in the room for others to use, or when Roy Fisher similarly talks of the poem being used as a subversive catalyst by potential readers, they are thinking of a clear social authorization for their work, but not one that can be predicted, codified or regulated.

Such a view distances itself from conventional discussions about the social and political functions of poetry. While agitprop and propagandist verse are not critically approved, the empirical lyricism of the Movement Ortho-doxy will as often as not be negotiated in class terms. A poem such as Tony Harrison's 'Them and [uz]', with its use of class solidarity, pride in non-RP forms of English, and educational alienation, demands naturalization in the same social terms as Larkin's 'Mr Bleaney' written twenty years earlier, where the significance of souvenir saucers, 60 watt light bulbs and holidays in Frinton serve to delineate fallen middle-class gentility.

There is a clear difference here between a practice that sees a social di-mension for poetry *embedded in* its artifice, and a poetry that has as its chief dimension *mimesis of* a recognizable social world. The implication of the former position is at once more radical and more general: no poem is more 'social' than any other since all poems are social facts open to social comprehension (or even completion in the case of open works). Indeed *all* utterances are social, in this sense. The accessibility of an utterance is not a determinant of its sociality. A mathematical formula that is understood only by three experts is no less dialogic than the TV sports news watched by millions.

The sociality of all language derives from its essential dialogic nature, a determining factor of language and literature first noted by the Bakhtin circle of critics, and explicitly developed as a *social* theory in the work of Vološinov, who states: 'The utterance is a social phenomenon'.[16] The indi-vidual speech act is therefore a contradiction in terms.

> Life begins only at the point where utterance crosses utterance, i.e., where verbal interaction begins, be it not even 'face-to-face' verbal interaction, but the mediated, literary variety.[17]

This crossing emphasizes an essential instability and dynamism not ac-counted for by synchronic and static models of language, such as Saussure's abstract system.

There is no escape from this process of dialogue. 'A word is a bridge thrown between myself and another,' writes Vološinov; '*Word is a two-sided act* ...As word, it is precisely *the product of the reciprocal relation-ship between speaker and listener, addesser and addressee.*'[18] Even thinking, or inner speech, is conceived as a dialogue with the world. 'There is no such thing as thinking outside orientation toward possible expression' in the socio-ideological sphere.[19] Thought itself resembles 'the *alternating lines of a dialogue*'.[20]

While this is of the utmost importance, it is in the extension of these concepts that confirmation of the dialogic nature of *literary* practice is found.

> But dialogue can also be understood in a broader sense, meaning not only direct, face-to-face, vocalized verbal communication between persons, but also verbal communication of any type whatsoever. A book, i.e., *a verbal performance in print*, is also an element of verbal communication.[21]

This formulation also makes a text an event rather than an object, and one that engenders further social events.

> It is something discussable in actual, real-life dialogue, but aside from that, it is calculated for active perception, involving attentive reading and inner responsiveness, and for organized, *printed* reaction in the various forms devised by the particular sphere of verbal communication in question (book reviews, critical surveys, defining influence on subsequent works and so on).[22]

That some of the poetry discussed in this book has not been part of many such discussions of British poetry points to the timely nature of this study, and indeed to this book's function in developing its poetics. But, more importantly, the presumption of any reader's active perception of a literary text is evidence of its dialogic intention. The *potentiality* of response is more important than the *actual* response which cannot be forced and cannot be predicted, as Roy Fisher and Harwood realize in their poetics. But as Bakhtin writes: 'The living utterance ... cannot fail to brush up against thousands of living dialogic threads' in the consciousnesses of actual readers, receptively positive, hostile or neutral.[23] Vološinov states:

> A verbal performance of this kind also inevitably orients itself with respect to previous performances in the same sphere, both those by the same author and those by other authors. It inevitably takes its point of departure from some particular state of affairs involving a ... literary style. Thus the printed verbal performance engages, as it were, in ideological colloquy of large scale: it responds to something, objects to something, affirms something, anticipates possible responses and objections, seeks support, and so on.[24]

At one level this approaches comprehension of the field of cultural production in a systemized way, akin to that of the theorizing of Pierre Bourdieu, and as such is a reminder of the value of the sociological and historical mappings of poetries in later chapters. It reminds us: '*Any utterance ... is only a moment in the continuous process of verbal communication.*'[25] While the poetry I am analysing here contests the socio-literary delineations of the

Movement Orthodoxy, more importantly it develops its own terms, in dialogue with its own past, and that of other poetries eclipsed by that orthodoxy.

Through its technical resources of openness, indeterminacy and artificiality this poetry demands social completion. The insistence that 'attentive reading' is necessary reminds us that 'to understand another person's utterance means to orient oneself with respect to it.'[26] The comprehension of a literary text involves the kind of engaged reading described by Allen Fisher; it demands focused acts of participation from its readers. As Vološinov says,

> *Any true understanding is dialogic in nature.* Understanding is to utterance as one line of a dialogue is to the next. Understanding strives to match a speaker's word with a *counter word.*[27]

The structures of these texts work in conformity with social dialogic utterance, even if they do not emphasize social realism. The poetics described here refutes such comprehension, as a counter word itself, in favour of a comprehension of form itself in social and historical terms.

This social dynamic has been described here in terms of Vološinov's explicitly Marxist work, *Marxism and the Philosophy of Language*, but this insistence upon the dialogic nature of all acts of language is famously present in the work of his colleague Bakhtin. His work on the polyphonic novel and the heteroglossic text might be said to be equivalent to the plurovocity Allen Fisher identifies in his poetics. They both agree that a text itself is a dialogue in which discourses clash and contest, even beyond the intentionality of its author, although Fisher and others favour techniques of creative linkage to achieve this.

However, at this point of the argument, it is interesting to note the philosophical and ethical implications of 'dialogue' in Bakhtin's thinking. Language 'directed towards its object' (by which Bakhtin means towards its theme),

> enters a dialogically agitated and tension-filled environment of alien words, value judgements and accents, weaves in and out of complex interrelationships, merges with some, recoils from others, intersects with yet a third group; and all this may crucially shape discourse, may leave a trace in all its semantic layers, may complicate the expression and influence its entire stylistic profile.[28]

Not only is the alien word (an invasion of new or unusual material, which will effect language change) waiting there; the encounter with the counter word is anticipated. 'Every word is directed toward an *answer* and cannot escape the profound influence of the answering word that it anticipates.'[29] Linguistic exchange (and that must include performances in print) is a question of answerability, an encounter with an other, and one in which response entails responsibility. Usefully for my argument, Hwa Yol Jung identifies

> an affinity between the structural requirement of 'answerability' ('response-ability') in Bakhtin's dialogical principle and Emmanuel Levinas's ethics of proximity, which privileges the face and epitomizes human co-presence and interhuman presence in terms of the structural primacy of the other.[30]

The Point of Poetry: Ethics, Dialogue and Form

Levinas might be thought a strange philosopher to use in a defence of poetry, since he has stated categorically that art can only be a 'shadow' that dimly represents reality. 'The artist has given the statue a lifeless life, a derisory life which is not master of itself, a caricature of life.'[31] As *representation*, art remains wholly within the realm of perception, whereas criticism, or philosophy proper, is a superior discourse, because it remains conceptual. 'The most lucid writer finds himself in the world bewitched by its images,' whereas 'the interpretation of criticism speaks in full self-possession, frankly, through concepts, which are like the muscles of the mind.'[32] Levinas' very rhetoric here, in this 1948 essay 'Reality and Its Shadow' (which had to carry an editorial disclaimer when first published in the flagship of literary commitment, *Les Temps Modernes*) reveals a bitterness about, perhaps even a sense of betrayal by, an activity which he warned was 'not the supreme value of civilization ... having its place, but only a place, in man's happiness.'[33] But even this formulation suggests that there is a modest role for art; to recover art for Levinas' ethical project one needs to redefine art, not as stale representation of bewitching imagery, or as something without a conceptual dimension, but as something capable of being open to a dialogue with the other.

The face of the other, Levinas argues, presents an immediate, non-negotiable, ethical demand, one that transforms an individual, as he or she is obliged to respond and answer. This encounter is the foundational moment for ethics, which, for Levinas, is 'first philosophy'.[34] He is not concerned to define a particular morality or law, the theological or social codification of these precepts, but of a basic ethical *condition,* which Derrida has called 'an Ethics of Ethics', one embodied in actual interhuman situations.[35] Levinas writes:

> The proximity of the other is the face's meaning ... The other becomes my neighbour precisely through the way the face summons me, calls for me, begs for me, and in so doing recalls my responsibility, and calls me into question ... It is the responsibility of a hostage which can be carried to the point of being substituted for the other person and demands an infinite subjection of subjectivity.[36]

As proof, and example, of the last point, of the essential asymmetricality of the relationship between self and other, even when the other seems not to reciprocate, or when the other has died and the individual persists as a survivor (the analogy with the Jews after the Holocaust is intended), Levinas is fond of quoting from an artwork, Dostoyevsky's *The Brothers Karamazov,* one he should condemn for its umbrageous illusoriness rather than utilizing its conceptual acuity: 'We are all responsible for everyone else – but I am more responsible than all the others'.[37]

Tim Woods' article 'Memory and Ethics in Contemporary Poetry' traces an important theoretical perspective within the work of the British Poetry Revival and Linguistically Innovative Poetry by theorizing a Levinasian 'ethics of form' to supplement the more familiar 'politics of form'. Woods argues

> Language attesting to the 'heard word' of the other in sound, becomes the basis for an ethical poetics ...an ethics of the voice is attention to what interrupts. That 'alternative' other is partly what much contemporary British ... 'experimental' poetry is seeking; to release the Utopian other in writing.[38]

I shall return to the interruptions of literary experimentation, to this interaction of technique and ethics.

Woods' use of 'voice' here instead of 'face' points to Levinas' later thought, one partly caused by the linguistic turn his work took in the 1960s, whose result was the theory of *Otherwise than Being, or Beyond Essence* of 1974. The central element of this ethics, for my purposes, is the distinction between the saying and the said.

Levinas' most fruitful remark for this ethics of form is contained in a series of assertions made in a 1981 interview that draws on this pair of terms.

> Man can give himself in saying to the point of poetry – or he can withdraw into the
> non-saying of lies. Language as *saying* is an ethical openness to the other; as that
> which is *said* – reduced to a fixed identity or synchronized presence – it is an
> ontological closure of the other.[39]

Saying is the call of, the call to, the other, the fact of the need and obligation
to respond to, and become responsible for, the other, as Levinas had always
maintained. It is a quasi-transcendental state beyond being, yet it is also 'a
performative doing', as Simon Critchley puts it, 'that cannot be reduced to
a constative description'.[40] It is the site and performance of ethics because
of this obligation to respond. It is public, yet it does not communicate
anything but the desire to communicate. Thus explained it seems like a
philosophical version of interhuman phatic communion that precedes, or
in comfortable circumstances replaces, actual informational communication. Indeed Levinas has indicated that passing the time of day about the
weather may embody such a gesture. As he explains: 'Saying opens me to
the other before saying what is said.'[41] We cannot, as in his everyday example, but not reply (even with silence). Yet importantly, Levinas recognizes difference as a corollary of such proximity, one which avoids the violence of assimilation, or even the need to express unity with the other. Levinas'
earlier sense of the individual as a hostage, committed to response, as a
permanent possible substitute for the other, even as a sacrifice to the act of
proximity, is re-introduced in this linguistic recasting: saying is a metaphor
for what cannot be said; saying makes *us* into signs of significations without
content. It is the gift of openness that is the very ethicality Levinas posits.
Yet this cannot be painlessly achieved.

   This saying can be defined apart from, but is not found other than inter-
woven with, the said. There is a price to pay; for the saying to *appear* it has
to undergo a betrayal, a 'subordination of the saying to the said', to the
linguistic system, in Levinas' terms, to ontology.[42] As Robert Eaglestone
explains:

> It is impossible to say the saying because at the moment of saying it becomes the
> said, betrayed by the concrete language which is the language of ontology. The
> saying, which is unthematizable, impossible to delimit, becomes limited, thematized,
> said.[43]

Yet the saying is what interrupts the said, ruptures the said. The saying
'appears' as a knot catching in the thread of the said, its necessary condition

of falling into essence in language. Indeed, without this knottiness it would not have its being or effectivity. Conversely, 'The said ... arises in the saying'.[44] It is the point at which 'clarity occurs, and thought aims at themes'.[45] The said and the saying both support, yet react against, one another, hence the tragic lifting towards poetry and the fateful thematization in what Levinas regards as ontological solidity. The 'otherwise than being' which is found in the act of saying is 'betrayed in the said which dominates the saying which states it'.[46]

This outline suggests that uncovering the saying in the said is the task of philosophy; it seems to suggest, in an echo of Levinas' early theory, that art would belong to the realm of essences, 'in which the said is reduced to a pure theme – to absolute exposition)[47] and that only criticism (by which he meant philosophy) could uncover the saying. But it is Eaglestone's argument, and Levinas' own belief, if we take seriously the notion that 'man can give himself in saying to the point of poetry', that the qualities of saying occur in art.[48] Eaglestone reminds us that 'the poem must interrupt in the name of the saying ... as literary texts, they work as "prophecy", fracturing the said.'[49] They must open to the other; they are saying as well as said. Indeed he sees Levinas' own *Otherwise than Being* structured like a literary work, 'especially self-reflexive contemporary postmodern poetry and prose'.[50] It is precisely its foregrounded artifice that makes it so, that attempts to keep the saying, the interruption, open in the text we read. According to Eaglestone: 'In his style of writing and choice of metaphors Levinas performatively foregrounds language in order to disrupt the said.'[51]

This description of Levinas' literary practice recalls Woods' similar assertion about the *interruptive* nature of the technical devices of the British Poetry Revival and Linguistically Innovative Poetry. The technically defamiliarising poetry that imposes such a task of dialogue on any reader may indeed approach a poetry of an open saying rather than of a closed saidness. The recent self-interruptive texts of Tom Raworth, with their lateral shiftings, or the neologistically resistant materiality of Maggie O'Sullivan's poems, are works which court the refusal of a saidness.

Writing as saying is ethical, processual, interhuman, dialogic in Bakhtin's sense. Writing as said is ontological and fixed, even violent; a closure of the other, monologic in Bakhtian terms. However, there cannot be a poetry of pure saying; the saying must exist in the said, as ghost to its host. A text in very physical terms needs to be printed, the order of words (usually) fixed. The openness that is its gesture must go hand in hand with some thematic or semantic fixity, however that is resisted by what Forrest-Thomson calls suspended naturalization. For the saying to be witnessed at all, it must be naturalized, be turned into the said. Suspension is always temporary.

Conversely, there cannot be a poetry of the pure said, since only active reading, the *performance* of saying, could body forth the said on the page, and as it does it both supports and disrupts the said.

'Saying makes signs to the other, but in this sign signifies the very giving of signs', argues Levinas.[52] The text is a gift that may be brought to a thematized rest only after having been given or taken to the point of poetry. The text and its other, which is the act of reading, are brought together. When this poetry is successful it is arguably able to articulate that saying in the said of the dialogic performance of the book. A successful reading will be one that exposes the saidness of the text to an openness of performance since saying, Critchley reminds us, is a 'performative doing'.[53]

(Another way of valorising active reading is to suggest that there must exist a corollary of the interdependence of the saying and the said in a reader's act of *reading*, as against the reader's sense of the *read*, as the already read, the thematized said, completed. Indeed Derek Attridge defines an act of innovative 'reading as an attempt to respond to the otherness of the other', working performatively with the text and 'working against the mind's tendency to assimilate the other to the same, attending to that which can barely be heard', in ways which remind us of the ethical asymmetricality a reader must face with a text.) [54]

Terms from speech act theory, such as Critchley's, are often used to describe the relation between the saying and the said. Jill Robbins, for example, echoes Critchley, and writes:

> The Saying and the Said is a correlative relation … that marks the difference between a conative speech, oriented towards the addressee, interlocutionary and ethical, and a speech oriented towards the referent, more like a speaking *about* than a speaking *to* the other.[55]

The necessity of saying arises before self-identity, and indeed breaks up the sense of identity, emphasizes the approach of the undeniable other. Interruption brings forth dialogue. In a text, where the face-to-face has been replaced, the responsibility is more acute, from reader to writer, and from writer to reader. As the author is responsible to the reader, then the reading is responsible to the writing to preserve *reading* as an act of saying, as the reader responds, participates in the text's structural indeterminacies, as it ruptures the said, interrupts by effects of defamiliarization, or suspends like Forrest-Thomson's good naturalization, through its textual opacities. These preserve the saying in the said, since they compel the reader to dwell on the devices of the utterance rather than reducing them, or closing them, to dead paraphrasable fixities. They preserve reading as an activity, resist closing it in a summary. This recognizes that the text maintains its differences as well as its proximity, through its technical devices, its social dialogism. Appropriation must be countered by distanciation. Open works are, in a sense, always open books.

A reading which operates as a paraphrase (and writing which works in collusion with such readings) is an appropriation of, a fearful taming of, the otherness of the text. In Levinasian terms, it judges the other in terms of the same; it closes. It attempts to be (or more colloquially we would say have) the last word.

Each successive level of my argument becomes less demonstrable, is precisely theoretical, and implies an increasing faith in the effects of writing and reading.[56] Arguments about the second and, particularly, the third level, will be implied by the chapters that follow, but will not be continually reiterated. The ethics of form will be assumed in the descriptions of form.

One must remain vigilant to the possibility that the concern that writing may do violence to the other, possibly by a fake 'saying' that is simply a gesturing of responsibility in the thematized language of the said, or in a non-saying that Levinas identifies as lying. Robbins, in her study of Levinas' theoretic of literature, stresses,

> We should not take for granted that we know what we mean by the saying. This is precisely what is seized upon by Levinas's readers hoping to extend his positive evaluations of art to an ethical poetics.[57]

This would never so much be the case than if the techniques used by poets were applied for technique alone, for an empty performance, or for a competitive stylistic escalation, what has been called 'placebo experimentalism'.[58] This is why a formalist approach to this work is inadequate. A social level of motivation for those techniques demands a social comprehension of form. Both the technical and the social levels contribute to the effects of making the point of poetry its saying, an interruption, and not its said. To read is to be proximate to, to face alterity as distance, and be implored to *answer*, as Bakhtin would say. To write of this work, or of any work, is also to attempt to do justice to alterity and diversity.

Notes

Italics in quotations in this book are original unless otherwise stated.

1   Veronica Forrest-Thompson, *Poetic Artifice* (Manchester: Manchester University Press, 1978), p. xi. For a general account of Forrest-Thomson as poet and writer of poetics, see Alison Mark, *Veronica Forrest-Thomson and Language Poetry* (Tavistock: Northcote House, 2001).

2   Jean-Francois Lyotard, *The Postmodern Condition* (Manchester: Manchester University Press, 1984), p. 81.

3   *Ibid.* p 60.

4   Philip Larkin, *Required Writing* (London: Faber and Faber, 1983), p. 58.

5   Umberto Eco, 'The Poetics of the Open Work', in *The Role of the Reader* (London: Hutchinson, 1981), pp. 47–66, at p. 58.

6   Viktor Shklovsky, 'Technique as Device', in *Russian Formalist Criticism*, ed. Lee T. Lemon and Marion J. Reis (Nebraska: University of Nebraska Press, 1965), p. 12.

7   *Ibid.* p 12 .

8   Eco, 'Poetics of the Open Work', p. 49.

9   *Ibid.*, p. 62.

10 *Ibid.*, p. 19.

11 Forrest-Thomson, *Poetic Artifice*, p. xi.

12 See Charles Bernstein, 'The Artifice of Absorption' in *A Poetics* (Cambridge MA: Harvard University Press, 1992), pp. 9–17. Allen Fisher, *Necessary Business* (London: Spanner, 1985), p. 165. For a further contrast with Bernstein, see Mark, *Veronica Forrest-Thomson and Language Poetry*, pp. 111–20. See also my 'The Poetics of Poetics: Charles Bernstein and Allen Fisher', in *Symbiosis*, vol. 3, no. 1 (April 1999), pp. 77–92. Chapter 2 will present an historical reading of Forrest-Thomson's piece as poetics.

13 Fisher, *Necessary Business*, p. 165.

14 Forrest-Thomson, *Poetic Artifice*, p. x.

15 *Ibid.*, p. x.

16 V.N. Vološinov, *Marxism and the Philosophy of Language* (Cambridge, MA: Harvard University Press, 1973), p. 82.

17 *Ibid.*, p. 145.

18 *Ibid.*, p. 86.

19 *Ibid.*, p. 90.

20 *Ibid.*, p. 38.

21 *Ibid.*, p. 95.

22 *Ibid.*, p. 95.

23 *The Bakhtin Reader*, ed. Pam Morris (London, New York, Sydney, Auckland: Edward Arnold, 1994), p. 76.

24 Vološinov, *Marxism and the Philosophy of Language*, p. 95.

25 *Ibid.*, p. 95.

26 *Ibid.*, p. 102.

27 *Ibid.*, p. 102.

28 *The Bakhtin Reader*, ed. Morris, pp. 75–76.

29 *Ibid.*, p. 76.

30 Hwa Yol Jung, 'Bakhtin's Dialogical Body Politics', in *Bakhtin and the Human Sciences*, eds. Michael Mayerfield Bell and Michael Gardiner (London, New Delhi: Sage, 1998), pp. 95–111, at p. 102. See also Michael Eskin, *Ethics and Dialogue in the Works of Levinas, Bakhtin, Mandel'shtam, and Celan* (Oxford: Oxford University Press, 2000) for an account of similarities between Bakhtin and Levinas in terms of dialogue and ethics.

31 *The Levinas Reader*, ed. Sean Hand (Oxford: Blackwell Publishers, 1989), p. 138.

32 *Ibid.*, pp. 142–43.

33 *Ibid.*, p. 142.

34 Emmanuel Levinas, 'Ethics of the Infinite', interview with the editor in *Dialogues with Contemporary Continental Thinkers*, ed. Richard Kearney (Manchester: Manchester University Press, 1984), pp. 47–69 at p. 65.

35 Jacques Derrida, 'Violence and Metaphysics', in *Writing and Difference* (London and Henley: Routledge and Kegan Paul, 1978), pp. 79–153, at p. 111.

36 *The Levinas Reader*, ed. Hand, pp. 82–84.

37 Quoted in Levinas, 'Ethics of the Infinite', p. 67. It is differently translated in *The Levinas Reader*, p. 182, and in Emmanuel Levinas, *Otherwise than Being, or Beyond Essence* (The Hague: Martinus Nijhoff, 1981), p. 146. It may be found in Volume 2, Book VI, IIa of Dostoyevsky's novel.

38 Tim Woods, 'Memory and Ethics in Contemporary Poetry', *English*, vol. 49, Summer 2000, pp. 159–60.

39 Levinas, 'Ethics of the Infinite', p. 65.

40 Simon Critchley, *The Ethics of Deconstruction* (Oxford: Blackwell, 1992), p. 7.

41 *The Levinas Reader*, p. 183.

42 Levinas, *Otherwise than Being*, p. 6.

43 Robert Eaglestone, *Ethical Criticism, Reading After Levinas* (Edinburgh: Edinburgh University Press, 1997), p. 147.

44 Levinas, *Otherwise than Being*, p. 46.

45 *Ibid.*, p. 46.

46 *Ibid.*, p. 7.

47 *The Levinas Reader*, p. 40.

48 Levinas, 'Ethics of the Infinite', p. 65.

49 Eaglestone, *Ethical Criticism*, p. 161.

50 *Ibid.*, p. 162.

51 *Ibid.*, p. 162.

52 *The Levinas Reader*, p. 183.

53 Critchley, *The Ethics of Deconstruction*, p. 7.

54 Derek Attridge, 'Innovation, Literature, Ethics: Relating to the Other', *Proceedings of the Modern Language Association* (*PMLA*), (January 1999), pp. 20–31, at p. 25.

55   Jill Robbins, *Altered Reading: Levinas and Literature* (Chicago and London: The University
      of Chicago Press, 1999), p. 144.
56   In 'Innovation, Literature, Ethics: Relating to the Other,' Attridge argues that 'The ethical
      force that conditions the creative act is ungrounded – here Levinas's difficult thinking is
      valuable – because that force is prior to any possible grounds ... It is necessarily
      undemonstrable.' (p. 28.)
57   Robbins, *Altered Reading*, p. 144. There have been at least three other attempts to construct
      a Levinasian *poetics*, apart from Tim Woods' 'Memory and Ethics in Contemporary Poetry'
      (and, to a lesser extent, Derek Attridge's 'Innovation, Literature, Ethics'): two critical projects,
      the other the poetics of a contemporary Canadian poet, and it seems only just, in the light
      of Robbins' warning, to reflect on them here and contrast them to my own.
         Krzysztof Ziarek's *Inflected Language: Toward a Hermeneutics of Nearness* (Albany: SUNY
      Press, 1994), attempts to 'rethink the ontological and ethical dimensions of language by re-
      reading Heidegger's work, more specifically his reflection on poetry, and by engaging Levinas'
      ethics and contemporary poetics' (p. 1). It reads Levinas in Heideggerean terms, which,
      while useful for tracing the 'hermeneutics of nearness' of the book's title, is less useful for
      drawing out an ethical poetics. This is evident in his tracing of the relationship of the saying
      and the said to Heidegger's usages.

      > As Heidegger clarifies in his essays on language, the 'essence' (*Wesen*) of human beings is to be the
      > speakers, to say after Being, where this saying means thinking toward Being in such a way as to
      > voice the saying of Being (*Sage*). (p. 86)

      However he concedes, 'While Heidegger can be said to focus mostly on the arranging,
      on the gathering of *Sage*, Levinas's primary concern lies with the direction in which the
      gathering of saying ... gathers – the other' (pp. 88–89). An insistence upon the technical
      basis of linguistic disruption or interruption, for the relation of the saying to the said,
      surfaces in two masterly chapters on the work of Paul Celan, which recognize that 'Celan's
      poetics can be characterized as ethical in the Levinasian sense.' (p. 160). He explains:

      > The ethical here has no cognitive or normative sense but rather a linguistic one: it indicates a
      > singular curve of language, a direction that inflects language toward the other. (p. 160)

      Ziarek outlines the *technical* means of poems which

      > unmistakeably point them toward the other: either by opening a ceasura inside words, by severing
      > and separating them into two different lines, or by directly relating it to one of the 'names'
      > indicating the other. (p. 172)

      To this might be added the characteristic practice of neologism, that Maggie O'Sullivan,
      for example, shares with Celan. Finally Ziarek reminds us that Levinas was directly in-
      debted to Celan and doubtless it was partly his experience of Celan's work that led to his
      late recognition of the 'point of poetry'.
         In Michael Eskin's *Ethics and Dialogue* a 'semethics' of language and a 'poethics' of poetry
      combine to trace an ethical reading of the dialogic, intertextual, aspects of particular poetry.
      Eskin also finds Celan crucial to Levinas (and vice versa) and traces resemblances to Bakhtin's
      thinking. Closely argued, meticulously referenced, and using previously un-translated work,
      this account argues that,

      > As the interruption of ethics, poetry replicates ethics as the interruption of politics, and semethics

as the interruption of Being, which in turn informs both ethics and politics; poetry – being socio-politically interruptive par excellence – exemplarily accomplishes the critical task of ethics and thereby, ironically, reveals its deeply political significance.' (p. 61).

Eskin's sense that the realm of the said stages witnessability has had some influence upon my notion of the said. In his conclusion he poses the question of whether his 'metapoethics' might be of service to the intertextual reading of poets other than Levinas' favoured Celan and Celan's brother-poet Mandelstam.

> This approach would be predicated on the interpretation of poetry in the light of its singular responsiveness, in the light of the particular ways in which an author's responsiveness to and answerability to and for another text and its author organizes his or her poetic response'. (p. 269)

He leaves his question open.

The creative work treated by Steve McCaffery in his essay 'The Scandal of Sincerity; towards a Levinasian poetics', in *Pretexts: studies in writing and culture,* vol. 6, no. 2 (1997), pp. 167–90, is consonant with work I discuss: works by Cage, Antin, Burroughs and Tom Phillips. His question is 'What constitutes a Levinasian ethical poetics within the ontological adventure?' (p 167) and his answers present some useful additions to my own thinking (particularly in his conceptualizations of the neighbourly aspects of the writer–reader relationship, to which I would otherwise have paid too little attention). Whereas Ziarek reads Levinas through Heidegger, MacCaffery reads Levinas – distantly – through Derrida. 'Ultimately the other to whom I am responsible, like Derridean "presence", is not there' (p. 170). His outline of the distinction between the saying and the said is a singular and useful one:

> a transcendental signification of sincerity, obligation and immediacy to the other carried by a language of the Saying, and a Saussurean-style system of differential and oppositive signs constituting a language of the Said. (p. 172)

Ultimately the poetics (perhaps like mine) is also that of his own work as a poet (and the above quotation reinforces borrowings from his thinking I have made in Chapter 9): a desire for a readership who will be proximate and receptive, without feeling the need for an interpretative function that might be thought to be ethically violent. But it is here, where the passive face to face rejects dialogue, that my theorising differs from McCaffery's. 'This community of the other and the others is not one of dialogue and interaction but of a solidarity gained precisely by taciturnity and prelingual receptivity' (p. 173). Nevertheless, his readings, particularly of Antin's talk poems which he writes, 'evoke the proximity required of the Levinasian obligation', (p. 181) is most impressive and suggestive.

58   The term is used by Christopher Middleton in *Jackdaw Jiving* (Manchester: Carcanet, 1998), pp. 149–50.

I

The Movement Poets and the Movement Orthodoxy in the 1950s and 1960s

New Lines

The official literary history of the period 1950–2000 has also been the history of its most strident poetry anthologies. Their introductions supply a set of criteria for a uniform reading or re-reading of their selective contents, and some (in the words of one I shall examine in Chapter 5) claim to discern 'decisive shifts of sensibility'.[1] Often they present themselves as the petulant heirs to, and revisionists of, a previous anthology, with claims for a monolithic or diverse poetic of the decade or a particular generation. Some of these anthologies were produced in cheap editions by Penguin Books, which ensured maximum distribution of their contents; this alone could make such anthologies canonical, often via the medium of various teaching syllabuses. The extent to which extra-literary concerns impinge upon the reception of contemporary literature, and upon this analysis of the persistent orthodoxy of the Movement, should not be underestimated.

The orthodoxy itself is a literary-polemical construct from which individual writers can deviate, following the diversities of their individual sensibilities, only at the cost of leaving the confines of what is most acceptable. This is because innovation is narrowly conceived as mere modulation of its norm, a norm which has proved both persuasive and durable. Therefore full development is often sacrificed to the orthodoxy, and only partial readings of some poets' works become acceptable; this summary history chapter and Chapter 5 deal with *readings* of writers' works which, through the powerful media of anthologies, have come to consolidate both the reputations of the poets and the axioms of the Movement Orthodoxy, even when they are exceeded. The orthodoxy thus operates as an unlocatable, often denied, invisible, but pervasive, centre, a poetic unconscious of the age, which offers an often ideal model of poetic discourse and artifice. Its increasing flexibility enabled its survival until the end of the century, in diluted form.

The original moment of the Movement, though, was real enough. Robert Conquest's anthology, *New Lines*, was published in July 1956 in the clear belief 'that a genuine and healthy poetry of the new period has established itself'.[2] The anthology contained the work of nine poets: Kingsley Amis, Robert Conquest, Donald Davie, D.J. Enright, Thom Gunn, John Holloway, Elizabeth Jennings, Philip Larkin and John Wain. That it was a commercial success, being reprinted within months and once more the following year, is not entirely surprising. Articles in *The Spectator* and elsewhere had announced the advent of this new generation. Two series of BBC Radio poetry programmes, edited by John Lehmann and John Wain, had been receptive to the new writers; recently published and widely acclaimed books by Amis, Gunn and Davie, had prepared the ground. What Ian Hamilton called 'advance promotion' became self-fulfilling prophecy.[3]

The lower middle class Oxbridge origins and attitudes of the Movement define a certain social instability that appealed to the age, but it is also important to examine the narrowly literary context of the early 1950s, to demonstrate how the Movement was able to gain its unassailable dominance. During the Second World War, there had been an unexpected poetry boom, but this brief commercialization of culture did not endure peacetime reconstruction and austerity. The following case history is typical:

> The re-designed twenty-seventh number of 'Penguin New Writing', published in 1946, had an initial print order of 100,000. A year later, that figure had declined to 80,000. By 1949 it was down to 40,000. Allen Lane wound up the series in 1950 after forty numbers.[4]

The poetry nexus had shrunk to a limited circle (with many writers ceasing to publish), and the Movement poets had to rely upon little presses – particularly the Fantasy Press – for publication. This form of production was not, however, an avant-garde or 'underground' activity (as it had been before the war, even in Britain, and would become again in the 1960s). Despite the publication of an alternative anthology, *Mavericks*, edited by Howard Sergeant and Dannie Abse in 1957, there was little opposition to the claims of novelty made for the work of the *New Lines* poets.

Possibly the gravest criticism of the Movement came – significantly enough, in the absence of much external critique – from an eventually repentant member of the Movement itself, Donald Davie.

All of us in the Movement had read the articles in *Scrutiny* about how the reputations of Auden and Spender and Day Lewis were made by skilful promotion and publicity and it was to placate *Scrutiny* readers that we pretended ... that the Movement was not being 'sold' to the public in the same way ... I remember nothing so distastefully as the maidenly shudders with which I wished to know nothing of the machinery of publicity even as I liked publicity and profited from it.[5]

This reveals the curious ambivalence of the Movement poets; they rebuked Auden and his contemporaries while simultaneously creating the taste by which they themselves were to be valued by a small public, in Davie's *Purity of Diction in English Verse* and *Articulate Energy*, in Wain's and Amis's *Spectator* reviews, as well as in the polemic of *New Lines* itself.

Half of the poems in the *New Lines* anthology use the first person plural. The principal question this raises is: what model of community, if any, is being invoked, and who is included in the embrace of 'we'? Blake Morrison candidly observes that in Movement poetry 'we' is often used 'in the sense of "our generation", or even "the group of us"'.[6] At other times the first person plural may form a bridge from the narrow poetry circle to a wider community of readers (witnessed in Davie's sense of the Neo-Augustan common reader); in one case,

while the confidence which enables Amis to use the pronoun 'we' stems from his sense of belonging to a specific group, the pronoun itself is intended to reach and represent a much wider and more nebulous audience – 'we (all of us)' or, at any rate, 'we men'.[7]

While some Movement pronominal generalizations claim to speak of common humanity, as when Larkin tells 'us' that the part that will survive of 'us' is love, in other cases, as Andrew Crozier has noted, with reference to Davie's work, the community implied can equally be an elect circle, a lower middle-class clericy: 'a few others who can be imagined as sharing the moments of privileged contemplation'.[8] Davie's 1952 critical work, *Purity of Diction in English Verse*, ostensibly a study of the diction of the poets of the Augustan period, during which time Davie supposed a genuine poetic community to have existed, was, he admitted, a thinly disguised manifesto for the Movement: 'The merest whiff of art for art's sake, and we panicked, shouting ... I declare myself indifferent to any poem or poetic effect that cannot be shown to be "moral".'[9] The use of the first person plural is one such effect, a moralistic embrace. This is not to be confused with a Levinasian ethics, since it effects a rhetorical assimilation of the reader, which is in many ways unethical.

The literary status of the Movement, and its persistence, was enhanced by a fortuitous accident. The 1950s, Crozier states,

> saw something like the establishment of a new kind of literary professionalism, utilizing the cultural prestige of poetry to diversify into new markets – universities, the media, the secondary education syllabus.[10]

The Movement poets, particularly Larkin, remained a substantial part of syllabuses for schoolchildren sitting examinations in 'modern' English Literature. What had begun as the poetic manner of a selective group became the privileged national poetic discourse.

It is by general consent that the work of Philip Larkin is taken to be exemplary. 'Mr Bleaney', from Larkin's second mature volume, *The Whitsun Weddings* (1964), tells of a prospective boarder inspecting, and finally taking, an insufficient room with a landlady who continually reminds him of the former occupant. Thus Mr Bleaney remains both a presence and an absence in the poem. Its plot is reducible to paraphrase, its details demand naturalization in social terms. It is a poem that atomizes the world into discrete, recognizable 'experiences':

> This was Mr Bleaney's room. He stayed
> The whole time he was at the Bodies, till
> They moved him.[11]

This apparent speaking voice delineates the narrator as an individualized personality: typical, exemplary. His calamities are banal, as he foresees himself battling with the noise from the television Mr Bleaney persuaded the landlady to buy, even if the poem does end in a dismissive epiphany on the valueless life of the removed Mr Bleaney; the elegiac tone is perhaps what makes some readers imagine the hero of the poem is dead, rather than vocationally relocated. Ironical judgement and moral questioning slide effortlessly from the personal to the generalized third person plural as the poem contends that 'how we live measures our own nature'.[12]

As Davie confessed in 'Remembering the Movement',

> Just consider … how difficult we find it to conceive of or approve of any 'tone' that isn't ironical in a limited way, defensive and deprecating, a way of looking at ourselves and our pretensions, not a way of looking at the world.[13]

Crozier, in his essay 'Thrills and Frills: poetry as figures of empirical lyricism', writes that he detects in the Movement poet's 'authority a relentless determination of poetic discourse and foreclosure of its intended audience'.[14] This is true of Larkin's poem. The irony shields the author-subject, as one may refer to the poet here, yet projects him – and his moral attitudes and social codes – onto the empty room, its vanished inhabitant (it will never be anything other than 'Mr' Bleaney's room). Indeed, as Crozier has demonstrated, 'Occasions are not felt to be trustworthy'; experiences are presented as discrete, and always 'wrap around their author-subject'.[15] Charles Tomlinson similarly complained of the *New Lines*' poet's presentation of 'his mental conceit of himself' as against 'a poet's sense of objectivity', of seeing the world as a continuum, not as a useable function of the perceiving ego.[16]

The rhythm of the poem and the dominant metrics of nearly all Movement poets (with the exceptions of Enright and Gunn), is the iambic pentameter, traditionally regarded as the 'natural' English metre; Conquest extolled its virtues in his introduction. In his book *Poetry as Discourse*, Anthony Easthope devotes a chapter to the linguistic, subjective and ideological implications of this favoured prosodic structure, and finds it to be as deeply value-laden as more semantic aspects of poetry, such as its irony. Although Larkin is dismissed by Easthope, and his comments directed at the entire discourse of English poetry, Easthope's analysis is particularly relevant to the work of the Movement.

Easthope proves erroneous the claim that iambic rhythm 'arises naturally from the English language itself', by demonstrating that pure stress metrics would seem, historically, to have at least an equal claim.[17] Nevertheless, iambics allow a great deal of variation, of deviation from a metrical norm, which is not possible in pure stress metres. Larkin sees his work as a dialectical struggle between the freedom of speech and the determinism of poetic structure. 'Writing poetry is playing off the natural rhythms and word order of speech against the artificialities of rhyme and metre.'[18] Actual performance of such a poem as Larkin's is neither controlled by the monotony of the norm nor by the freedom of non-poetic intonation, but is a variable 'function' of the two. This can be observed in the abrupt enjambement of the opening three lines of 'Mr Bleaney'.

Easthope's book traces the ideological construction of the iambic pentameter 'not as a neutral form of poetic necessity but a specific historical form providing certain meanings and acting to exclude others'.[19] There is one effect which is a specific result of the tension between metre and intonation: the iambic beat becomes concealed behind a varied speech. 'Through counterpoint,' Easthope explains, 'the abstract norm is relatively backgrounded.'[20] This results in a paradox: the Movement will towards transparent discourse, of 'backgrounded' form, suppresses the artifice of its construction, draws the reader's attention away from the form towards content, in this case the all-important speaking origin of the poem. The reader is supposed to admire this lyrical monologue as if it were 'a spontaneously generated *product*'.[21]

Although intonation is the exertion of a limited freedom within the poetic context, metre can serve to specify a particular accent for spoken performance, that must also affect silent reading. Iambics demand that 'vernacular elision' is suppressed in favour of a 'clipped, precise, and fastidious elocution', because of its inherent tendency to require full and slow pronunciation of each syllable in the foot and line.[22] Listening to Movement poets reading one notes the predominance of received pronunciation. One reviewer writes of Larkin's recording of his volume *The Less Deceived*, with 'its hesitant, ironic quality, in which certain words are ... singled out for pejorative mention'.[23]

This notion of 'voice' brings the argument to the question of subjectivity and text. Wordsworth praised metre for its restraints upon the passions; iambics even out the natural emphatic intonation patterns of English.[24] Movement metrics 'promote the "realist" effect of an individual voice "actually" speaking',[25] a process which colludes with the Movement's avowed aims (again in Davie's confession) to produce 'writing considered as self-adjustment, a getting on the right terms with our reader (that is, with our society), a hitting on the right tone and attitude towards him'.[26] It is partly the poetry's 'voice' – educated but ordinary, versified yet spoken – that enables its social comprehension as a rational discourse.

An essential part of *New Lines* 'empiricism' consists of a distrust of figurative language, which is, in part, a rejection of modernism. The distrust was a reaction against what Conquest called 'the debilitating theory that poetry *must* be metaphorical' found among the poets of the 1940s, particularly writers of The New Apocalypse, such as Nicholas Moore and J.F. Hendry.[27] The 1940s poets, Conquest writes, 'were encouraged to produce diffuse and sentimental verbiage, or hollow technical pirouettes'.[28]

The death of Dylan Thomas in 1953 seemed to signal to the young writers the end of an era. The poetry of the 1940s characterized itself as a utopian synthetic neo-Romanticism; it argued a plea for freedom in the machine age, a plea for validating myth and for 'a dematerializing of Surrealism'.[29] The

New Apocalypse published in journals such as Tambimuttu's *Poetry London*, and were collected in anthologies like *The White Horseman* (1941), and were blamed for the decline in the popularity of poetry since the War. Conquest wrote, 'Without integrity and judgement enough to prevent surrender to subjective moods or social pressures, all the technical and emotional gifts are almost worthless.'[30] Conquest did not, therefore, deny Thomas' technical proficiency, but stated that in the poetry of the previous decade the 'mistake was made of giving the Id … too much of a say'.[31] Integrity would have been defined by the Movement as the maintenance of an empirical, conscious and sober discourse, as opposed to Thomas' supposedly unconscious, impacted figurative language.

All of this reveals more about the Movement preferences than about Thomas and his procedures. Donald Davie's investigation of the syntax of English poetry, *Articulate Energy*, published a year before *New Lines*, is particularly harsh on the looseness of Thomas' 'pseudo-syntax' and states censoriously that 'the articulation and spacing of images is done by rhythm instead of syntax'.[32] The images themselves seem suspect, part of Thomas' vatic persona, the objects of the world turned into groundless metaphors. As Davie writes of Thomas' work, 'When concrete things are crowded upon each other, they lose their concreteness … The things will not stand still, but fluctuate and swim like weeds in a stream.'[33]

Faced with the metaphorical crowding of Thomas' work, it is not surprising that metaphor was distrusted, or that, when the *New Lines* poets did employ elaborate figures, it should have been for purposes of defining the empirical Movement version of textual subjectivity all the more clearly. There is a hardly a figure in 'Mr Bleaney' that does not belong to the category of demotic or dead metaphor. As Morrison writes, 'The Movement poetry of Larkin and Davie can also be thought of as Realist in tendency because of its marked preference for metonymy over metaphor', which is a trait of nearly all anti-modernist writing.[34]

The Movement poets were deliberately working against the radical function of metaphor (as the modernists, and even Dylan Thomas, understood it). Wain demanded that Thomas' metaphors be subject to paraphrase. Ricoeur argues that metaphors are not 'translatable'; indeed, they 'create their meaning'.[35] Metaphor, Ricoeur argues, 'has more than an emotive value, because it offers new information. A metaphor, in short, tells us something new about reality.'[36]

The Movement favoured a poetry of closure, narrative coherence and grammatical and syntactic cohesion: a poetry of 'backgrounded' form rather than a poetry of foregrounded artifice. Its emphasis upon the demotic, upon 'tone' and upon the speaking voice, posited the existence of a stable ego, an author-subject, as the unifying principle of the poem; its rhetoric operated at a social level. The iambic pentameter prevalent in the work was another example of the will to invisible form, which foregrounded and yet controlled the speaking origin. Its metaphors were generally neither embellishments nor perceptual instruments, but figures which supported the attitudes (and, often, morality) of the author-subject, and served to circumscribe him or her. The world was atomized into discrete areas of experience, although the use of the first person plural suggests an ambiguous sense of community. Its discourses were carefully constructed in collusion with the saidness of language, and with a social naturalization of content rather than of form. Variations of this mode constructed the poetic unconscious that permeated British poetry for the next half century.

The New Poetry: and so on …?

The polemic of A. Alvarez's anthology *The New Poetry* (1962), attempted to delineate and define the potentialities of a new 'depth' poetry, although such work did not then exist, and with only the hint of his desired poetic revolution to come. By the second edition of 1966 (which remained in print for 35 years), with its inclusion of the work of Sylvia Plath – among others – it seemed as if the editor's earlier prophecy had been fulfilled. An apparent reaction against the Movement and its poetic values had been effected. However, I wish to show that this 'reaction', although real enough in terms of psychological focus, is conducted upon common ground with the Movement. The 'new poetry' can be seen as of a piece with the representative work of the 1950s, however much it steps beyond its heavily criticized 'gentility principle'.[37]

It is in terms of 'reactions' that the literary history of the twentieth century is presented by Alvarez, through a modish metaphor derived from cybernetics. Each decade, or rather each decade represented as an hermetic capsule of unified literary style, defines itself in reaction against the previous decade, through a restless dialectic of 'reactions' and 'negative feedbacks'

(*NP66*, p. 21). This historicist schema dictates that each subsequent decade – and it has been operating since modernism – produces its own appropriate stylistic 'feedback'. The reaction to the 1930s poets (who had themselves replaced the aesthetic modern with the politicized contemporary) 'took the form of anti-intellectualism', and Alvarez shares Conquest's dismissal of the New Apocalypse: 'The war brought with it a taste for high, if obscure, rhetoric' (*NP66*, p. 23).

More fulsome is Alvarez's critique of the *New Lines* poets, and his attack is one of the most cogent. The Movement style is equated with the occupations of the nine featured poets. 'It was … academic-administrative verse, polite, knowledgeable, efficient, polished, and, in its quiet way, even intelligent' (*NP66*, p. 23). The social focus of his criticism engages the Movement on its own terms; they formed 'the third negative feed-back: an attempt to show that the poet is not a strange creature inspired; on the contrary, he is just like the man next door' (*NP66*, p. 25). The thrust of Alvarez's whole polemic is away from questions of style towards psychologism and subjectivity.

The irony of *The New Poetry*, in its first edition, was that, since it claims to be a selective anthology of poetry published between 1952–62, the book was forced to contain predominantly Movement work: thus Enright, Davie, Larkin, Amis, Wain and Gunn are found within its pages, Larkin represented by 'Mr Bleaney'. As such the anthology did more than *New Lines* to bring that work to the attention of the public, to establish the more generalized orthodoxy; this Penguin anthology was a canonical schoolroom text for at least a quarter of a century. This must be remembered in tracing the orthodoxy's normative effect on poetic taste, despite the fact that Alvarez's polemical introduction berates these writers collectively for their 'gentility'. Indeed, by selecting lines from his own anthology Alvarez is able to synthesize an identikit poem to demonstrate a lamentable evenness of tone among the Movement writers, the 'unity of flatness' of such verse (*NP66*, p. 24). He notes a 'considerable similarity in the quality both of the language and of the experience' (*NP66*, p. 24). Alvarez is right in stating that such rationality held psychological stress in check (even the verse form and metre assist in this). In Alvarez's terminology, the Movement believed, 'that life is always more or less orderly, people always more or less polite, their emotions and habits more or less decent and more or less controllable …' (*NP66*, p. 25). Such gentility, Alvarez argues, is historically and intellectually untenable. The Movement wished to preserve parochial civilities as a bulwark against 'evil' or 'libido' – the various 'forces of disintegration which destroy the old standards of civilization' – present in twentieth-century history and revealed by modern psychology (*NP66*, p. 26). 'Their public faces are those of two world wars, of the concentration camps, of genocide, and the threat of nuclear war' (*NP66*, p. 26). Although these themes are not, in fact, untouched by the Movement, their limited, often domestic, empiricism did fall short of Alvarez's debatable contention that, 'a mass evil outside us has developed precisely parallel with psychoanalysis; that is, with our recognition of the ways in which the same forces are at work within us' (*NP66*, p. 27). It is clearly this dual dimension of psychology – both intensely personal and conspicuously social – that interests Alvarez. The latter part of his introduction becomes a manifesto. The experience of the self – in extremity – comes to be seen as identical to the unbearable objective social reality. The poet's self is the sole guarantor of that reality; he or she need not mediate it, tame it, need not assume communal, commonsense civilities.

Before turning to the poetry, it is important to examine the fate of modernism – 'Eliot and the rest' to use Alvarez's vague terms – that had been rejected by the Movement (*NP66*, p. 21). Alvarez's parochialism is little better than Larkin's famous literary xenophobia when he announces that experimentalism 'never really took on in England because [it was] an essentially American concern' (*NP66*, p. 21). The Americans featured in *The New Poetry* – Berryman and Lowell in the first edition – had 'assimilated the lesson of Eliot', as theorist, rather than as a poet (*NP66*, p. 28). This 'lesson' involved a general emphasis upon technique and skill: the poet had to be 'very skilful, very original, very intelligent' (*NP66*, p. 28). Eliot's theories of impersonality were bypassed by American writers who had used Eliot's 'lesson' to write technically proficient verse on highly personal themes: the so-called 'confessional' writers. When Berryman, in particular, adopted the apparently modernist technique of the persona, in the 'Dream Songs', it was for purposes of performed self-disclosure. Modernism has been rendered invisible, part of the literary background for the 'new' poetry.

Alvarez argues the need for 'a new seriousness' defined 'simply as the poet's ability and willingness to face the full range of his experience with his full intelligence', avoiding both the 'conventional response' of the 1950s and the 'choking incoherence' of the 1940s: maintaining a traditional balance between intellect and feeling while remaining attuned to the modern world

and its evils (*NP66*, p. 28). At the end of his essay he posits a possible model
for this 'new depth poetry' (a term which mimes depth psychology): the
'psychological insight and integrity of D.H. Lawrence' would be 'creatively
reconciled ... with the technical skill and formal intelligence of T.S. Eliot'
(*NP66*, p. 32). Eliot, divested of any 'experimentalism', is a shadowy figure
here: the meditative poet of *The Four Quartets*, as well as the incumbent of
the Faber poetry chair, the publisher of Larkin and Hughes. However, this
creative reconciliation is irrelevant since it is obvious, from Alvarez's comparative analysis of poems by Larkin and Hughes, that this contemporary
pair effectively replaces Eliot and Lawrence (respectively). Larkin's poem is
'more skilful but less urgent' than Hughes', while Hughes' is 'less controlled
than Larkin's' (*NP66*, p. 30–31).

  With the 1966 second edition of *The New Poetry*, Alvarez was able to
repackage his (unrevised) polemic as description and no longer prescription. A fusion of Larkin and Hughes would no longer suffice. The anthology had been expanded slightly, most notably to include the work of another American, Sylvia Plath, who had died three years previously. In her
work, the empirical rationality of the Movement is exchanged for the empirical irrationality of the 'confessionals', such as Lowell, who had taught
her to deal with 'peculiar private and taboo subjects' within a controlling
style.[38] Later, however, as if chiming with the polemic of Alvarez (whom she
knew at the time of this British Council interview extract), Plath said, 'I
think that personal experience shouldn't be a kind of shut box and a mirror-
looking narcissistic experience. I believe it should be generally relevant, to
such things as Hiroshima and Dachau, and so on.'[39]

  However, Plath, I shall show, was no Paul Celan (in his 'Todesfuge'), or
Reznikoff (in *Holocaust*), the one with subjective and agonized experience
of Romanian labour camps, which he transmuted into metaphorical structures that inspired Levinas to speak of his interruption of 'the ludic order of
the beautiful';[40] the other working with the grisly, but objectified, US Government documentation of the Nuremburg Tribunal and records of the
Eichmann trial.[41] The social and psychological – Alvarez's poles – only merge
in Plath's work insofar as the social is suffused by the subjective; it shares
with sentimentality the same subjective annexation of that which is other.

  Alvarez anthologizes one of Plath's last poems, 'Lady Lazarus'. The subject matter of the text is recovery (some would say rebirth) from a suicide
attempt and there are some lines which are clearly autobiographical, taken

in isolation, admissions of suicide attempts at ten-year intervals since the age of ten, for example. The plain facts are verifiable, but it is contemplation of a redemptive third suicide attempt that is the focus of the poem (written weeks before her death). But the poem, rather than being naturalizable in terms of biography – which is the way it is too often read – adopts high artifice and a mythic persona: Lady Lazarus rises from death (or, at least, attempts to) and the self's voice is carried, not by a Movement style iambic base, but by jerky internal rhymes (that hint at nursery rhymes and music-hall songs), in short nervy lines that suffuse the grave subject matter with an hysterical levity.

> Dying
> Is an art, like everything else.
> I do it exceptionally well.
>
> I do it so it feels like hell.
> I do it so it feels real.
> I guess you could say I've a call...
>
> It's the theatrical
>
> Comeback in broad day ...
>
> 'A miracle!'
> (*NP66*, pp. 62–63)

The variety of rhetorical styles – the medical, the religious, the pornographic, the fairground, the concentration camp – need not detain this analysis. What is important, for an analysis of the dominant ethos, is to see that the depth of the new depth poetry lies in its circumscription of self, whether empirical or mythical, the repeated 'I' that anchors the discourse. In her use of this concentration camp imagery, and of genetic experimentation and extermination, Plath has – in the words of Peter Ackroyd – let 'the experience of a false subjectivity generate a false world of objects'.[42]

It is at this point that the empirically bound orthodoxy of the Movement might be supposed to have been surpassed. However, Crozier has succinctly identified a major unifying principle. Both Movement verse and Plath's highly artificial development beyond 'confessional' poetry share a discourse which operates through the form of the personal lyric, though Plath's is often dramatic or mythic in presentation, and employs an elaborate figurative language to draw together the self and its objects.[43] Thus the death camp details relate to the psyche of the persona, and the poem ends with multiple metaphors, all of which serve to define and emphasize the centrality of the surviving suicide. (The narrator can only achieve the semblance of authenticity by dying.) The concentration camp commandant (or doctor) becomes simultaneously God and Lucifer in an ontological confusion; the narrator is Lazarus, but she rises from the ash of the incinerator; she takes her revenge on men (like a vampire's victim). Metaphor and analogy serve to define the subjectivity and bind it to its false world of invented objects. Far from coming to terms with widespread 'evil', it allows only the phantoms of that 'evil' any vitality.

Despite the apparent reaction against the 'gentility' of the Movement, the *New Poetry* readings of Plath still left unchallenged its major tenets: the mentally unstable ego, however artificial and dramatized, is still a stable textual entity, still the unifying principle of the poem. To speak of unspeakable horror is to remain firmly in the realm of the said, whose ontological violence was conceived by Levinas to be precisely analogous with the Holocaust. The longing for the realm of the saying is an act of resistance to both those horrors and to the discourse that would attempt to prescribe it, to the chilling generalizing thematics of Plath's 'Hiroshima and Dauchau, and so on'.

Plath's poetry – and that of her husband Ted Hughes – is thus only a partial exception, a limit case, for the orthodoxy as it developed away from the actual examples of the 1950s Movement, to become the ideal poetic unconscious that defined acceptability in the 1960s and beyond. Indeed, despite the exertions of Plath, Alvarez's identikit poem remained the standard default mode of the era, as evinced by the contents of lesser anthologies than his own.

Notes

1   *The Penguin Book of Contemporary British Poetry*, eds. Blake Morrison and Andrew Motion (Harmondsworth: Penguin, 1982), p. 11.
2   Blake Morrison, *The Movement* (Oxford: Oxford University Press, 1980), p. 240.
3   Ian Hamilton, 'The Making of the Movement' in *A Poetry Chronicle* (London: Faber, 1973), p. 127.
4   Eric Homberger, *The Art of the Real* (London and Toronto: Dent, 1977), p. 70.
5   Quoted in Hamilton, 'The Making of the Movement', p. 129–30.
6   Morrison, *The Movement*, p. 11.

7   *Ibid.*, p. 124.

8   Andrew Crozier, 'Thrills and Frills: poetry as figures of empirical lyricism' in *Society and Literature 1945–1970*, ed. Alan Sinfield (London: Methuen, 1983), p. 205.

9   Donald Davie, *Purity of Diction in English Verse* (London: Routledge and Kegan Paul, 1952 (second edition, with postscript 1974), p. 198.

10 Crozier, 'Thrills and Frills', p. 207.

11 Philip Larkin, *The Whitsun Weddings* (London: Faber and Faber, 1964), p. 10.

12 *Ibid.*, p. 10.

13 Donald Davie, *The Poet in the Imaginary Museum* (Manchester: Carcanet, 1977), p. 74.

14 Crozier, 'Thrills and Frills', p. 204.

15 *Ibid.*, pp. 204–06.

16 Quoted in John Press, *A Map of Modern English Verse* (Oxford, Oxford University Press, 1969), p. 259.

17 Antony Easthope, *Poetry as Discourse* (London and New York: Methuen, 1983), p. 53.

18 Philip Larkin, *Required Writing* (London: Faber and Faber, 1983), p. 171.

19 Easthope, *Poetry as Discourse*, p. 25.

20 *Ibid.*, p. 25.

21 *Ibid.*, p. 67.

22 *Ibid.*, p. 69.

23 Quoted on dust jacket of Philip Larkin, *The Less Deceived* (London: The Marvell Press, 1955).

24 Easthope, *Poetry as Discourse*, p. 72.

25 *Ibid.*, p. 76.

26 Quoted in Morrison, *The Movement*, p. 268.

27 *New Lines*, ed. Robert Conquest (London: Macmillan, 1956), p. xii.

28 *Ibid.*, p. xii.

29 Francis Scarfe, *Auden and After* (London: Routledge, 1942), p. 158.

30 Conquest, *New Lines*, p. xiii.

31 Morrison, *The Movement*, p. 159.

32 Donald Davie, *Articulate Energy* (New York: Harcourt, Brace and Company, 1958), pp. 126–27.

33 *Ibid.*, p. 127. See also Morrison, *The Movement*, p. 149.

34 Morrison, *The Movement*, p. 14.

35 Paul Ricoeur, *Interpretation Theory: Discourse and the Surplus of Meaning* (Texas: Christian University of Texas Press, 1976), p. 52.

36 *Ibid.*, pp. 52–53.

37 *The New Poetry*, ed. A. Alvarez (Harmondsworth: Penguin, 1966 (second edition)), p. 21. Subsequent reference to this volume will be cited in the text as *NP66*.

38 *British Poetry since 1945*, ed. Edward Lucie-Smith (Harmondsworth: Penguin, 1970) p. 391.

39 *Ibid*, p. 391

40 Quoted in Jill Robbins, *Altered Reading: Levinas and Literature* (Chicago and London: The University of Chicago Press, 1999), p. 145.

41 See Paul Celan, *Selected Poems*, trans. Michael Hamburger (Harmondsworth: Penguin, 1990) ('Todesfuge'/Death Fugue' is found on pp. 60–61); and Charles Reznikoff, *Holocaust* (Santa

Barbara: Black Sparrow Press, 1977).

42   Peter Ackroyd, *Notes for a New Culture* (London: Vision Press, 1976), p. 122.

43   See Crozier, 'Thrills and Frills', p. 217.

2

The British Poetry Revival 1960–1978

The British Poetry Revival

... the 'British poetry revival': an exciting growth and flowering that encompasses an immense variety of forms and procedures and that has gone largely unheeded by the British literary establishment ... and it may be that one day (probably when we're all long gone, or our work lapsed into repetition and genre ...) some bright critic, as usual too late, will discover this to have been a kind of golden age.

Ken Edwards, 1979[1]

While some conventional accounts of British poetry have colluded with Morrison and Motion's contention that the 1960s and 1970s formed a 'stretch ... when very little – in England at any rate – seemed to be happening',[2] this study offers the counter-view, presented by Ken Edwards above, and spelt out in oppositional terms by another poet-critic, Gavin Selerie:

As various reviewers have pointed out, the 1960s and 1970s actually witnessed an explosion of poetic activity, which was in itself a reaction against the full common-sense politeness of the 'Movement' poets of the 1950s. After a period dominated by such figures as Philip Larkin, qualities of inventiveness, passion, *intelligence* entered once again into British verse. Poets as diverse as Lee Harwood, Tom Raworth, Roy Fisher, and Tom Pickard exhibited a toughness and also a splendour that were entirely absent from the writing collected in the Movement anthology *New Lines* (1956).[3]

This chapter will define this serious, but heterogeneous literary movement. The term I use to describe it, the British Poetry Revival, was first proposed by Tina Morris and Dave Cunliffe in the eighth issue of their underground magazine *Poetmeat* around 1965, which presented an anthology of such work. It was subsequently used as the title of a 1974 Polytechnic of Central London conference: 'The British Poetry Revival (1960–1974)', and of its conference essay, by Eric Mottram. Ken Edwards and Barry MacSweeney have both adopted this term.[4] Mottram also used the term in his revised essay 'The British Poetry Revival, 1960–75', an important survey, published in 1993.[5] Significantly, it proposes a limit to the years of 'revival', to which I shall return. Given the dominance of the Movement Orthodoxy during the period 1955–2000, the Revival can be seen as a counter-movement. Yet it looks less of a 'reaction' than Selerie suggests, when it is set in its own, still largely uncharted, context, to emphasize its own positive qualities.

The 1950s and 1960s

Although Roy Fisher began to write seriously at the age of 23, in 1953, some of his first attempts, other than a spoof sonnet, which he submitted to the BBC, were the pieces published as *Three Early Pieces* in 1971. Fisher has described them as 'verbally automatic', and there is a general debt to surrealism, although the images strain for a cosmic significance, which suggests the influence of Thomas and the New Apocalypse:

> As laden slaves sweat upwards
> lash hums like a fly about
> God in his ebony ark.[6]

Although it was a style Fisher was quick to reject, it avoided the empirical lyricism of the Movement, which Fisher regarded as exhibiting 'all sorts of misanthropy and resignation, both social and artistic'.[7] By this time he had found a viable avenue to European modernism, which he knew he 'strangely wanted to re-visit', via the new American writers of the time to whom he had been introduced by fellow poet Gael Turnbull (who was himself an influence).[8] These writers – Charles Olson, Robert Creeley, Robert Duncan and Denise Levertov, the Black Mountain school – were 'still showing allegiance to the claims of early twentieth century modernism, claims which to my mind had been far too hastily abandoned', particularly by the stridently anti-modernist Movement.[9]

Turnbull was an important publisher of British and American work. Between July 1959 and September 1960, he and Michael Shayer edited eight issues of *Migrant* magazine; design and production were spartan: stencil and mimeograph. The print run was 250 and the distribution uneven. A note inserted in the first issue gives a telling summary of its ethos:

> Dear Reader, MIGRANT will be published irregularly ... For it to pretend to be a 'magazine' with a 'public' would be absurd. There is no such public ... What

subscription rate could there be? And so, it will be sent to anyone who wishes to receive it. That is, to anyone interested to read it. Thus our ambition will be to have a minimal number of readers; but for those readers to be maximally interested.[10]

Additionally, Turnbull published an impressive list of publications between 1957 and the mid-1960s, including books by Creeley and Edward Dorn, Ian Hamilton Finlay's pre-concrete poetry collection, *The Dancers Inherit the Party*, and in 1961, Fisher's *City*, with a foreword by Shayer, and later Turnbull's own impressive improvisation *Twenty Words, Twenty Days*, the title of which describes its time-based form and the lexical nature of the starting material. In 1965, by which time Fisher was helping to run the press, Migrant published Basil Bunting's *The Spoils*, in association with Modern Tower in Newcastle. By 1965 Migrant was no longer an isolated venture, and the Americans Turnbull had introduced were more generally well-known within the larger alternative network.[11]

In that year an issue of a university magazine, *Cambridge Opinion*, was dedicated to the subject of 'Carlos Williams in England' – that is, the influence the work of Williams and the Black Mountain poets were having. Bunting's example of influence, 'The Oratova Road' dated back to 1935, but Fisher's 'Seven Attempted Moves' is described as having evolved from a recent experiment with Williams' famous triple line.[12] 'A Gesture to be Clean', in which Turnbull praises Williams for his Objectivist presentation of 'the things themselves, however absurd, however limited', for avoiding the impulse to 'symbolize' found in the dominant modes of modernism, accompanied his own poems.[13] This magazine was also one of the earliest gatherings of what has come to be called 'Cambridge' poetry which derives as much from the example of J.H. Prynne, then, as now, a fellow of Caius College, as it does from American influences, particularly the projective theories of Olson. This group's own journals included the *English Intelligencer*, a privately distributed poetry and discussion sheet, which was issued to a mailing list of around 30 between February 1967 and April 1968, edited by poets Peter Riley and Andrew Crozier, with Prynne's assistance. Simon Perril has recently described the open exchange of *The English Intelligencer* as 'the constitution of trust through the establishment of a "community of risk"'.[14] Crozier's magazine *The Park*, moved from the University of Essex to Keele where Crozier became a teaching colleague of Roy Fisher.[15] In 1968 a further two poets, John Riley and Tim Longville, edited the *Grosseteste Review*, and the largely 'Cambridge' oriented Grosseteste Press.[16]

Swinging the Duplicator Handle

The sudden but confusing profusion of networks of little magazines and presses, and the spontaneity of this community of exchange for writer-editors, is noted by Jeff Nuttall in his valuable account of the 1960s, *Bomb Culture*. When he and his friends, including Bob Cobbing, were 'swinging the duplicator handle throughout the long Saturday afternoons of 1963 we had no idea that the same thing was happening all over the world'.[17] Bob Cobbing, an indefatigable arts and workshop organizer and publisher, had intermittently operated under the name Writers Forum since 1954. From 1963 the press became a model of radical consistency, tirelessly producing cheap mimeo pamphlets of concrete and experimental poetry, much of it his own (see Chapter 9). Often he presented young talent, as in the case of Lee Harwood's *title illegible* in 1965, which contained beat and surrealist work that had been first aired at Cobbing's workshops, which, like the press, continued running throughout subsequent decades.[18] Cobbing became manager of Better Books, an important venue for London readings and happenings, and an unofficial resource centre.

These sorts of personal contact were vital in order to sustain a poetry different from established forms and unwelcome at conventional institutions: from performances at Better Books in London through to those at Tom Pickard's Morden Tower bookshop and venue in Newcastle, where Basil Bunting first read to his new young audience, an experience which encouraged him to pen *Briggflatts*. Visiting Americans, whether Robert Creeley talking to a teenage Barry MacSweeney in Newcastle, or Edward Dorn, resident at the University of Essex for a number of years, where he befriended writers as various as J.H. Prynne and Tom Raworth, broadened horizons by their presence, readings, information, and (in the above two cases) their poetry written out of their experiences of visiting Britain. Lee Harwood went further, and visited the Dadaist poet Tristan Tzara, whose work he would translate throughout the 1960s, in Paris in 1963.[19] This was a visit to modernism at its source; Tzara's rooms, decorated with Picassos, Miros and Klees, must have made an appropriate backdrop for Harwood's first translations to be approved. In 1966 Harwood made his first trip to experimental modernism's second home, New York, where he mixed with John Ashbery and other New York writers, who had adapted surrealist imagery to a discursive mode. Harwood's own adaptation of this style led to his second book, *The Man with Blue Eyes,* being published in New York and receiving the prestigious Poets' Foundation Award. The United States was equally receptive to Tom Raworth, who has been an intermittent resident and visitor to this day.

Throughout the 1960s, Harwood was also the publisher of an irregular magazine. Like Turnbull, in a refusal to produce monuments and to negate the consistency of a subscription list or bookshop distribution (other than at outlets like Better Books), each issue had a different title: one was, predictably, *Tzarad.* It introduced a small nexus of readers that Harwood had built up through correspondence to new English, American and French work. Tom Raworth's *Outburst,* and hundreds of other fugitive magazines, were organized on the same vital, evanescent principle, in this time of relatively easy and cheap mimeo and litho printing. The ethos is perhaps neatly summed up by the title of Jeff Nuttall's magazine: *My Own Mag.*

At the other end of the scale were publishers such as Fulcrum Press and Cape Goliard. Fulcrum was founded in 1965 by Stuart and Deirdre Montgomery, and published quality hardbacks and paperbacks of both British and American writers; neither group was then well-known, despite names like Oppen and Dorn among the Americans. Editions of Fisher, Harwood, Raworth, materially assisted their reputations, but Fulcrum was set up to publish Bunting, and his late-flowering of modernism, *Briggflatts,* was their first publication. Goliard, run by Raworth and Barry Hall, received the backing of the major publisher Cape, and published Olson as well as Turnbull and Prynne. Both ceased operations by the mid-1970s, reflecting the end of economic expansion and the withdrawal of vital patronage. But since poetry publishing is as much a passion as the writing of it, small presses have been resilient in surviving, sometimes with Arts Council funding, often without. Much of the activity of the underground, and particularly the small presses, lies outside of the cash nexus. As Ken Edwards wrote in 1985, 'The products of the presses… are not commodities. In fact, insofar as the labour which made them retains its visibility… they may be designated anti-commodities.'[20] The best of the little presses (which may be very little indeed) have often published work that breaks the conventional paradigms of what poetry has been, by publishing work which, to the eyes of commercial poetry editors, appears not be poetry at all.

The Underground

Michael Horovitz's 1969 campaigning anthology, *Children of Albion: Poetry of the 'Underground' in Britain* was the first widely available gathering of the British Poetry Revival and might be seen as a rejoinder to *The New Poetry*.

Essentially this is a collection of writings by persons associated either with Horovitz's long-running little magazine *New Departures*, or with the series of readings/performances called Live New Departures. Both ventures began in 1959, and the latter delivered 1500 'shows' during an eight-year period in the 1960s at various venues, ranging from the Marquee pop club to the Institute of Contemporary Arts.[21] This variety indicates an ability and willingness to mix high and low culture, without having to ironize the difference between them; Adrian Mitchell's dictum that 'Most people ignore most poetry because most poetry ignores most people' was a clear challenge to the exclusiveness of the Movement poets and their book-bound means of distribution (*CA*, pp. 356–57).

In 1960, Horovitz with others (such as Mitchell and Pete Brown, who later wrote song lyrics for Cream) began to write and perform poetry that derived heavily from the American Beat writers, particularly the trinity of Ginsberg, Corso and Ferlinghetti, who were to achieve wide currency when, in 1963, the popular *Penguin Modern Poets* series issued a volume of their work in Britain. At 'Live New Departures' 'gigs' (as poets, like musicians, came to call readings), poetry was read to jazz performed by some of the best British jazz musicians, and, on occasions, Roy Fisher, himself an accomplished pianist, played. In contrast to the Movement, and looking back to the popular performances of Dylan Thomas, these poets believed that the sound of poetry was as important as its sense, performances completing the inert words on the page. Thus a social aim (to broaden the appeal of poetry) coincided with an aesthetic aim: 'voice' in poetry was no longer a metaphor for ironic modulation; the voice was a performance instrument of communal gathering, and (often) the voice of political protest, which broke abruptly with the quietism of the Movement.

Most of the British Beats, however, did not innovate beyond mere imitation of their American models.[22] Rather than the vatic passion of Ginsberg's *Howl* (1955) their followers slipped into easy whimsy. British Beat poetry modulates towards the one-shot (and sexist) joke, possibly as a result of responding too readily to the demands of a live (and, as I shall argue in Chapter 6, male) popular audience.

Many British writers began by reading the American Beats, including Lee Harwood, from 1958–61 a student of English Literature at Queen Mary College. Like others, he discovered their work around 1960, chiefly in Donald M. Allen's influential American anthology, *The New American Poetry 1945–1960*.[23] After the work of the Movement (which Harwood has characterized as 'dull, boring, & smug'),[24] reading the Beats was an imaginative release: 'They said: … "You don't have to have gone to a Public School and Oxford and Cambridge before you can write."'[25] Whereas he found Movement work 'remote', Harwood speaks of

> for the first time picking up a printed book, where people were talking about the world you knew, that you lived in, and were expressing what you felt were your feelings, confused and gauche as they may have been at the time.[26]

A predominantly educated (often art-school and working-class) audience, with interests in CND, drugs, modern jazz and street life, could find affinities with those hipster 'best minds' of Ginsberg's Columbia 'generation destroyed by madness',[27] and authorized Harwood, for example, to write of his own life, environment and involvement with drugs, in 'Cable Street' (1964–65).

> a hundred night cafes. jukeboxes. the whole street vibrating. Algerians twisting in the arab cafe. cafes filled with everybody. what's the difference at night. Mod kids keep calling me Dennis. Why? Do I have some other side that I don't know about? Am I king pusher of Cable Street?[28]

All three American Beats, British writers such as Adrian Mitchell, and the Viennese sound poet Ernst Jandl, read at the most spectacular poetry event of the decade, the Royal Albert Hall Poetry Incarnation of 1965, when over 7000 people listened to four hours of poetry. In Horovitz's polemic this is a central occasion, a success on both aesthetic and social grounds, even if Horovitz's claim that on that day 'poem after poem resonated mind-expanding ripples of empathy' sounds hyperbolic (*CA*, p. 337).

Ginsberg, of course, had by this time become a prophet of the underground, an exemplar of a new, liberated sensibility: at the Albert Hall reading, chanting a mantra to finger cymbals, he was described by Jandl as 'the soul' of the flower-festooned audience (CA, p. 338). 'At poetry readings and teach-ins,' Theodore Roszak wrote, 'he need not even read his verses: he need only appear in order to make his compelling statement of what young dissent is all about.'[29]

But this new-found populism was not congenial to all who had discovered Ginsberg's early work and literary influence. 'There was a whole group of English sub-beat poets', Tom Raworth recalled in 1989. 'It's like tossing the quarter bottle of whiskey out of the mini as you drive down the M16 – it doesn't work at all, there's a whole different way of going about things.'[30] By about 1965 Harwood felt he had learnt all that he could from the Beats, and distrusted the polemical 'ranter' element in their verse, 'telling people how to live'.[31] In an uncollected 'Train Poem' (published in *Great Works* magazine in 1975), entitled 'At the 'New Departures' Reading 1975, Not 65', Harwood looked back to this era to question the sixties' programmatic euphoria; its creativity was ultimately mindlessly destructive:

> Crush the flowers 'underfoot'
> that have been picked,
> and scattered on the floor,
> while talking of 'love & joy'.[32]

Indeed, 'love' – a key word for the underground audience – would become a rhetorical trademark of the poets who were to reap the benefit of the media exposure for accessible popular poetry. These were the Liverpool Poets, Adrian Henri, Roger McGough and Brian Patten, who were to be published in three collections during 1967, including *The Mersey Scene, Penguin Modern Poets 10*, which was (and continued to be, in updated form) an extremely popular volume. They were again able to mix avantgarde and popular culture in an accessible (and saleable) form, and extended their work, not just through a Liverpudlian association with the Beatles, into performance, which lay somewhere between stand-up comedy and the happening. Henri was also a painter and the influence of both neo-Dada and pop art on this work mixes with a certain Scouse sentimentality to produce an entertaining but ultimately fey discourse.

When *Children of Albion* appeared in 1969, some ground had been prepared by *The Mersey Scene*. There are many writers among the 63 included whose work might be thought to be out of place: for example, poems by John Arden, Michael Hastings and Bernard Kops, who are better-known, and more talented, as playwrights. It has been a particular feature of the British Poetry Revival that it has re-discovered radical artists who have been obscured; Horovitz features Paul Potts and Philip O'Connor, the former a remnant of Dylan Thomas' Fitzrovia, the latter a minor, but individualistic, surrealist writer of the 1930s. Some writers, then quite young, published immature work: David Chaloner, Andrew Crozier and John James would be thought of as Cambridge poets, Carlyle Reedy as an intermedia artist, Ian Hamilton Finlay as a leading concrete poet. Some writers were fortunate enough to be represented by mature work: Gael Turnbull, Edwin Morgan, Jim Burns, Tom Raworth, Roy Fisher and Lee Harwood. For example, Roy Fisher's selection includes both late and early work: the favoured anthology pieces from *City* (1961), 'The Entertainment of War' and 'Starting to Make a Tree', the first poem from the major sequence 'Interiors' (1967), and a poem from the late 1950s, 'The Hospital in Winter' which is one of Fisher's least characteristic poems, in that it approaches the realism and rational structure of the Movement Orthodoxy.

Harwood's selection is also uneven, but it also shows a greater immersion in the general concerns of the underground, though with some important reservations. (The reasons for this are partly generational: Fisher was born in 1930, Harwood in 1939.) Two of his finest poems, 'As Your Eyes Are Blue' and 'Plato was Right Though' are included, but so is 'sciencefic', which remained uncollected after the pamphlet *title illegible* (1965), and which, with its surreal edge, shares the whimsicality of the British Beats.

A persistent theme for many writers in the anthology was drugs and drug-taking, in the work of such poets as Anselm Hollo, Alexander Trocchi, Tom McGrath and Mark Hyatt. In *Bomb Culture* (1968), the poet Jeff Nuttall claims that the interest in drugs reflected a desire for the dissolution of an unacceptable self, to effect the 'reasoned derangement of all the senses' that Rimbaud recommended for the 'visionary' poet and which contemporary thinkers, such as Herbert Marcuse, recognized as an attempted utopian gesture.[33]

Various kinds of inconsequential subjective notation of so-called expanded consciousness in the anthology fortunately contrast with poems, such as Mark Hyatt's 'Smoked' and Lee Harwood's 'Love in the Organ Loft'. Hyatt, a heroin addict who committed suicide in 1972, was described by Geoffrey Thurley as 'the strangest and most talented poet' in the anthology; he 'writes like a newcomer to language, to the world it opens up'.[34] In 'Smoked' he balances despair and desire, and describes 'a feeling of dreamy nonchalance, heightened awareness, bursts of introspection, mellowing attitude towards one's fellow man ... and a formidable sense of contempoaraneity' (to quote

Richard Neville, from the hippie Bible *Playpower*, on the effects of mari-
juana):[35]

> It goes through the body like a satellite
>   because one wanted it that way
>   holding back a mouthful of air ...
>   (*CA*, p. 152)

Yet Hyatt combines this with an introspective, self-destructive negativity in
the last line of this first verse: 'trapped in the tears of doom' (*CA*, p. 152).
Self-torture pervades the poem's ecstasy.

> O let time spin around this mind right now
>   & the liquids of these eyes be forever lissom
>   because the substance of the mind feels like lead.
>   (*CA*, p. 152)

The image of love and peace, a cliché of the era, as we have seen, is force-
fully imaged in the controlled and hopeful surrealism of the poem's end,
which no contemporary reader could fail to relate to the continuing war in
Vietnam:

> I hope the war in the apple-orchard ends soon
>   for all the missiles I've are filled with love
>   and they will drop like birds from the sky
>   on the drawings of desire in this heart.
>   (*CA*, p. 152)

This poem may be usefully compared to Lee Harwood's 'Love in the
Organ Loft', which, although it begins in disarming innocence

> It is April – of course. (Why should songs have all
> the good lines? – like 'I love you', too.)
>   (*CA*, p. 97)

deals with the 'morbid masochism' of an involvement with heroin (*CA*, p.
100). The post-Beat Harwood takes over much of the tone of Frank O'Hara
and the New York school he visited, but darkens it considerably. He places
his narrator within the painful context of personal relationships.

> But what can this mean – that I should
> sit here all night watching over my love
> & at the same time I fix
> more than double my usual intake

to feel without compassion my brain wince & flatten
under chemical blows -
cocaine memories now repeated, though on a less brutal scale.

(*CA*, p. 99)

The poem presents a collage of viewpoints, from that of 'cocaine memories' to the 'adoration' for the loved one that 'fills my eyes with happy tears' (*CA*, pp. 99–100); the passage of time is uncertain, as night approaches morning, and everything, except the opposed realities of human life and drug addiction, is 'disturbing and disordered' in a paranoid world of accidental and unrelated occurrences, that counterpoints the narrator's desire for the ordinary (*CA*, pp. 97–100). However, there is a further aspect of the poem that reveals a less savoury trait of the sixties underground. There is a certain self-satisfied (and, given its yearnings, ironical) smugness in its consideration of ordinary people in the 'straight' society, from the point of view of a 'deranged' bohemian.

But everything on this (surface) level is so disjointed
that it can make even this possible act of kindness
appear to 'THEM' as 'foolishness' (if 'they' feel patronizing)
or 'absurdity' (if 'they' feel insecure that day).
(A 'definition' of 'them'/'they': 'They' shampoo their cars on
Sundays, each holding a red plastic bucket.)

(*CA*, p. 98)

When the poem was reprinted, these heavily-laboured final two lines were omitted.[36] In attempting to expose the clichés of the 'straight' society with his scare quotes, Harwood has merely exposed his own.

The generational dichotomy of 'Us' and 'Them' (not to be confused with the class and linguistic distinctions of Tony Harrison's 'Them and [uz]') is often alluded to in the rhetorical gesturing of Horovitz's 'Afterword', whose apparent extemporized structure allows its author to side-step analysis. Its nervous excitement may reflect the time at which it was written – April 1968 – between the Movement of March 22 and the subsequent Paris student and worker riots, and between the two major anti-Vietnam War demonstrations in Grosvenor Square, London, and with apparently concerted unrest breaking out at every educational institution.[37] At times Horovitz writes as if the underground was a formal cultural opposition, waiting for the edifices of 'their' society to tumble so that 'we', the bohemians, can take over. Indeed, as Tom McGrath wrote, 'The revolution has taken place WITHIN THE MINDS of the young.'[38] It was merely a question of turning the subjective and the artistic into the objective and new utilitarian; Horovitz predicted a successful campaign of infiltration: 'Spreading an aesthetic wing for the daily more effectual changes wrought by students – & teachers – all over' (*CA*, p. 372).

But what would this aesthetic wing, this fifth column of underground thinkers and poets be? Ginsberg, Roszak writes, 'is a protest poet. But his protest does not run back to Marx; it reaches out, instead, to the ecstatic radicalism of Blake.'[39] Blake was a pertinent influence during the 1960s (and his work has a presence in the work of many writers treated in this book, particularly Allen Fisher and Iain Sinclair). The Albion who fathered Horovitz's generation of poets was the spirit of a compassionate radical England, who appears principally in Blake's *Jerusalem, Emanation of the Giant Albion* (1804–07). There was a general belief that the revival of poetry and imagination could be an apolitical model for massive societal change. As Horovitz put it, 'The mutual response between people determined to free their spirits can simultaneously give birth to the architecture of that liberation' (*CA*, p. 371). There was a desire to heed the words attributed by Blake to the artist-revolutionary figure Los, in *Jerusalem*: 'I must create a system, or be enslaved by another man's;/ I will not reason or compare; my business is to create.'[40] Creativity, valorized here twice, is elevated over reason; Blake's attack on empiricist philosophy is re-read as an attack upon the instrumentalist reason that, for example, supported the Vietnam War. Blake's teasing ambiguity – that to create a 'system' is actually to replicate one's repression, that one might be enslaved by one's own system – was conveniently ignored. It was read as a libertarian gesture to do 'your own thing' (in the parlance of the day).

Blake's illuminated books may be viewed as some of the earliest small press publications. He was an example to writers who had turned away from the world of the formally published book. More importantly, poetry was a prime weapon in the underground's arsenal, not because it could be used for propaganda purposes, but because it was in aesthetic experience that the very model – what Horovitz calls the 'architecture' – of the change in consciousness and society lay. R.D. Laing, himself an important figure in the underground as an anti-psychiatrist, famous for declaring that insanity was the result of familial and societal repression, and peripherally involved with Live New Departures as a poet and pianist, writes of the oppositional role of the imagination in this battle, as being both psychological self-preservation and radical activity.

> Words in a poem … attempt to recapture personal meaning in personal time and space from out of the sights and sounds of a depersonalized, dehumanized world. They are bridgeheads into alien territory. They are acts of insurrection.[41]

Poetry, it seems, can create an image of another world that is historically irrepressible. Such works 'generate new lines of force whose effects are felt for centuries'.[42]

Lee Harwood, in the conclusion of 'Cable Street', seems to concur with this view. He combines in his multi-faceted narrative the evidence of the senses, drugs, a significant reference to Blake, everyday life (without the supercilious elitism here), and the final plea for a new sensibility, for a political revolution.

> sitting in the dark on this summer night. turned on.
> window open and cars passing. people walking by below.
> the slow rise and fall of my chest. you reading me
> Blake in the half-light. man in house opposite kicks a
> ball round his yard
>
> an ark is moored somewhere in South London.
>
> > O Prince your days are done
> > The Revolution's come.[43]

Horovitz's 'aesthetic wing', he predicted, 'will surely be in the "running" of such countries as last out to, well – 1984?' (*CA*, p. 372). It was a fateful, and bad, guess.

The 1960s were an affluent time for the young, as the 1970s and 1980s proved not to be. Economic well-being, and educational expansion (particularly in the new universities, polytechnics and art colleges) encouraged experimental diversity in the arts, even if the revolution was slower, more ambiguous, than was supposed by Horovitz and others, and found the relationship between utopian politics and its poetry equivocal.

The New Sensibility: Tom Raworth in the 1960s

Behind the pronouncements of Horovitz and others stand not just Blake, but the work of Herbert Marcuse. A non-conformist Marxist philosopher,

Marcuse had described how a capitalist society assimilates working-class protest by making the population define itself only through accelerated participation in consumerism (by advertising and other coercive means). Again, small presses, as Ken Edwards suggests, are part of a rebellion against this. Indeed, it seemed to Marcuse, in *An Essay on Liberation*, written in the United States in 1968, that the wider youth movement and underground was undermining the values of the dominant society, of participating in the 'Refusal' as many others had noted. Moreover, in the words of Fredric Jameson, 'Marcuse sees in the new sensibility and the new sexual politics an application of the artistic impulse to the creation of a new life-style itself, to the concrete acting out of the Utopian impulse.'[44] Marcuse argues that the aesthetic, manifested in the behaviour of the young, is a model for a 'light, pretty, playful' free society, that is nevertheless rational enough to utilize science and technology, not for the reduction of human beings to consumers, but to distribute its scarce resources with equity and compassion.[45]

> Technique would then tend to become art, and art would tend to form reality: the opposition between imagination and reason, higher and lower faculties, poetic and scientific thought, would be invalidated. Emergence of a new Reality Principle: under which a new sensibility and a desublimated scientific intelligence would combine in the creation of an *aesthetic ethos*.[46]

Art, or artistic consciousness – even Horovitz's aesthetic wing – becomes a weapon for establishing that which does not yet exist. 'The new object of art is not yet "given", but the familiar object has become impossible.'[47] The new reality requires a new language, as Blake had realized. Rather than affirming the status quo art must allow the senses 'not to see things any more in the medium of that law and order which formed them'.[48]

Marcuse was adapting the Russian Formalist notion of defamiliarization that my introduction identifies as a fundamental technique of the British Poetry Revival, and putting it to a political use, much as Brecht had. For Marcuse, 'Form is the achievement of the artistic perception which breaks the unconscious and "false" "automatism", the unquestioned familiarity.'[49]

A clear demonstration of the successes and limitations of the New Sensibility may be found in the poems of Tom Raworth, another poet featured in *Children of Albion*. 'Art is making new games', Raworth declares, and his early poems effect a kind of knowing defamiliarization, a motivated derangement, a gesture towards that 'new object' of Marcuse's rhetoric.[50]

Raworth's early poems rework the tenets of Black Mountain poetics. They follow the dictum of Charles Olson's 'Projective Verse' essay: 'ONE PERCEPTION MUST IMMEDIATELY AND DIRECTLY LEAD TO A FURTHER PERCEPTION' without reflection, qualification or discrimination.[51] The poems are improvised, the persistent lower case letters not a cummingsesque affectation, but the trace of an improvisation made swifter by abandoning the shift key on a typewriter (particularly a manual one). 'Intuition I still believed in above reason' (p. 16) he states in *A Serial Biography* of the late 1960s, reaffirming a statement made in an early poem, 'Wedding Day', which had appeared in *Children of Albion*:[52]

i made this pact, intelligence
shall not replace intuition, sitting here
my hand cold on the typewriter
flicking the corner of the paper
(*CA*, p. 268)

The transitions between perceptions are swift and unpredictable, a record of occurrence (the making of this aesthetic pact is not complete without the recording of the flicking of the paper, which itself is the site of the recording). That effect is surrealistic. The spacing of 'i' at the end of the line, and the remark itself

                                         i
inhabit a place just to the left of that phrase
(*CA*, p. 269)

suggests a desire to ironically rid himself of 'the lyrical interference of the individual as ego' as Charles Olson put it,[53] and which Raworth revises as: 'When I started I had all those years of I I I ME ME to wash out';[54] the lower case 'i' would at least be a cleansing.

Olson's essay also quotes Creeley's remark, 'Form is never more than an extension of content',[55] and it would seem that Raworth realigns this remark when he comments less elegantly, but revealingly: 'Form is content stretched to whatever shape best fits against the backcloth given by time.'[56] A time limit structures improvised composition and the limits of the experience related. This is exemplified successfully in 'Morning', which has a traditional narrative structure (a male and a female speaker and a narrator who indicates who is speaking and what actions occur) but the placing of the lines in the improvisation collapses a series of actions into a simultaneous event:

she came in laughing his
shit's blue and red today those
wax crayons he ate last night   you know
he said eating the cake the
first thing nurses learn
is how to get rid of an erection say
you get one whilst they're shaving
you, they give it a knock like
this, he flicked his hand and
waved it down she
screamed, the baby stood in the doorway
carrying the cat
in the cat's mouth a bird fluttered
(CA, p. 271)

The domestic surrealism, which is caused by the running together of fragmentary notations, is heightened by the central 'she/screamed' which we
discover is not a reaction to the demonstration of medically assisted detu-
mescence but to the arrival of the baby-cat-bird as a simultaneous event of
chaotic proportions. Raworth's speedy delivery of such poems in performance is almost dictated by his fidelity to perceptual fluidity. The poem's
form is the trace of the event, an event not circumscribed for moralistic or
social definition as in the domestic verse of the Movement Orthodoxy. It
lengthens both perceptions and the processes of naturalization.

The question of 'success' (and I count this charming and funny poem as
a success) is an important one, yet it seems that Raworth's work in the
1960s, which repeats this defamiliarizing gesture many times, is peculiarly
open to a criticism of inconsequentiality.

'Stag Skull Mounted' of 1970 is a more ambivalent flirtation with the
limits of Raworth's medium, but is arguably a new art seeking a new object.
The text is generated serially, in diary form, without external pattern or
thematic cohesion. Poetic form is the result of poetic activity; content is the
perception of the moment, but this is not unproblematic. There is a note of
pathos and morbidity that underlies many of Raworth's oddest utterances,
as here, in the 'useless pity' for the girl with the twisted spine (TS2000, p.
56).[57] The line-breaks enact constant relocation, a semantic indeterminacy;
the narrator is self-consciously aware as he realizes his complicity in an
emotive transference based on pity:

> i can not love her and her life
> may be filled with warmth   i project my past
> sadness on to all   the weight
> of my thought of her misery may add
> the grain that makes her sad
> (*TS2000* p. 56)

As the narrator 'can not find my way/back to myself', he is increasingly absorbed by literary and conceptual self-consciousness (*TS2000*, p. 60). Instants are recorded as contentless ('*12:10 a.m June 1st 1970*/ the time is now') and the text increasingly but minimally consists of its own meticulous, but pointless, correction: as '12:25' becomes '12:26 a.m. June 1st 1970/ looking at my watch' (*TS2000*, p. 60). The text becomes ever more self-referential; it presents the almost inevitable entry 'word', a silent (blank) entry, and the entries:

> *8:06 p.m. June 10th, 1970*
>
> poem
>
> *9.25 p.m. June 10th, 1970*
>
> poem
> poem
> (*TS2000* p. 62)

These entries ironically satisfy reductive dictionary definitions of a 'poem'; the second supposedly rhymes. The experiment ends dismissively on the brief entry 'this trick doesn't work' (*TS2000*, p. 63). But like other supposed aesthetic dead-ends of the era, Cage's *4'33"* or Beckett's *Breath*, the familiar objects of poetry have been avoided.

Indeed, in a rare introspective remark in the 1971 'Letters from Yaddo', Raworth seems to have his own doubts about his work to date.

> And for ten years all I have done has been an adolescent's game, like the bright feathers some male birds grow during the mating season. I look at the poems and they make a museum of fragments of truth. And they smell of vanity, like the hunter's trophies on the wall ('I shot that poem in '64, in Paris'). I have never reached the true centre, where art is pure politics.[58]

Perhaps the reference to the 'trophy' has less to do with vanity than the fixity of the one shot poem. Raworth's growing interest in attempting sustained process rather than simple improvisation might lie behind the disquiet.

It was Raworth's task, analysed in Chapter 8, to pursue this. This interesting admission, though, embodies the Marcusean notion that art might become not just a 'new game', but politics itself. As Lyotard notes in his 1970 essay 'The Critical Function of the Work of Art', 'I do not believe the function of art is to keep desire aroused in order that it become revolutionary, it is immediately revolutionary.'[59] Perhaps in the solitude of the writers' retreat at Yaddo a grander ambition than repeated defamiliarization was establishing itself. A new game will have to take, or find, politics in the immediacy of poetic form. The characteristic Raworth lyric of the 1960s was in danger of becoming the usual game.

The 1970s: What the Chairman Told Tom

In 1966 the Association of Little Presses was formed as a self-help organization for those involved in non-commercial publication, usually of poetry. Until his retirement as chairman in 1985, Bob Cobbing was a key figure in the organization. Founder members included both large and small presses, for example, Fulcrum and Writers Forum. The AGMs held discussions on practical matters, such as grant aid. At the 1968 AGM there were still only 14 members, but this doubled within a year. Other activities included bookfairs, regular catalogues, for which members printed their own pages, and in 1973 ALP published its guide, *Getting Your Poetry Published*, written by poet Peter Finch, for the assistance of aspiring writers in submitting work to magazines and presses. By 1996 its fifteenth edition had sold 37,500 copies; Finch has expanded it into several handbooks. By 1980 ALP had 122 paid-up members, all of whom were receiving a regular magazine, plus a newsletter containing information, contacts, press profiles and practical advice on everything from sources of cheap ink to bookshop outlets.[60] Underground magazines, known again as little magazines, were more drawn to regular deadlines, standardized formats and quality production standards. A little of the spontaneity of these anti-commodities was lost in the process but the sense of community remained. Allen Fisher has written that part of the desire to run a press is 'to engage with the "communities" of artists similarly involved'; most of the presses were run by practising poets.[61]

The importance of poetry readings – particularly when the poetry demands performance – continued; the smaller venues ran regular readings

above pubs. Yet there was also a move in the 1970s toward large-scale conferences, such as those organized by poet Paul Evans at the Polytechnic of
Central London in 1974 on the British Poetry Revival and followed by the
1977 one on Place; and the biennial Cambridge Poetry Festivals, begun in
1975, and organized by Peter Robinson and others. Funding of poetry readings was assisted by the establishment of the London, and National, Poetry
Secretariats, thus ensuring the poet received a reasonable fee. These schemes
had been one of the principal aims of a short-lived organization convened
in 1970, Poets Conference, a 'trade union' for poets.[62]

Another of Poets Conference's demands, for a radical poetry centre, and
ALP's desire for a permanent base, were both realized, then abruptly for-
feited, in the 1970s. During the late 1960s, the Poetry Society, and its size-
able Victorian property in Earls Court, were in decline. Its general council
consisted largely of non-poets, and Stuart Montgomery was invited to stand
on the council – though as a doctor. He was successful and, after he had
secured a position for Cobbing, one nomination followed another until, by
1975, British Poetry Revival poets were in the majority: Roy Fisher, Lee
Harwood, Jeff Nuttall, Barry MacSweeney, Tom Pickard, as well as emerging writers, such as Bill Griffiths, Allen Fisher and Elaine Randell.[63] There
were plans for reform: to open the building to the public, to establish a
print-room, to run both conventional and experimental poetry workshops,
and to open a viable bookshop. Among the events there were readings,
performances and lectures. Bob Cobbing encouraged younger performers
such as Lawrence Upton, cris cheek and Clive Fencott, who formed their
group jgjgjgjg about this time; and Eric Mottram's Poetry Information eve-
nings, public interviews with Roy Fisher, Harwood, MacSweeney, Pickard,
Cobbing, Ken Smith, and others, some of which were published in Peter
Hodgkiss's critical review magazine, which took *Poetry Information* as its title.
Harwood lectured on 'Surrealist Poetry Today', insisting that Dada and Surrealism offered an energy and an attitude of mind, rather than a set of techniques; he pointed to the work of Raworth and Roy Fisher. Fisher's own
lecture praises the 'sheer closeness of linguistic activity' in the work of Bunting,
and refers generally to the Cambridge poets as having exceeded narrative and
anecdote, and particularly to the work of Andrew Crozier for demonstrating
how 'consciousness is charted' – a concern of his own work at this time.[64]

Between 1971 and 1977 Eric Mottram, then Reader in American Studies
at King's College London, edited the society's journal, *The Poetry Review*,

and in his 17 issues featured over 200 poets, ranging from well-known Americans, such as Oppen and Ashbery, to senior British poets, such as MacDiarmid and Bunting (both of whom had been elected President of the society). The magazine was largely an ongoing anthology of the work of the British Poetry Revival. He generously published long works, such as Tom Pickard's *Dancing Under Fire*, which weaves dream imagery into a texture of post-industrial realism and Northumberland folk tradition.[65]

However, these vital activities were threatened by literary politics. There was tension between the new general council members and some others, 'who can only be called reactionary and narrow', in the words of MacSweeney.[66] These members disliked the work Mottram was publishing and pressured the Arts Council Literature Panel to commission the Witt Report, which recommended more direct Arts Council control over the Society, including the appointment of one Arts Council representative onto the general council. There was the promise of increased funding 'and solid approval of the magazine', *The Poetry Review*, 'so long as Mottram was ousted', according to MacSweeney.[67] Accounts vary, but many members of the council resigned in protest in 1977. Roy Fisher and Lee Harwood, for example, remained on the council for some time, hoping to effect some compromises, but were eventually made to feel uncomfortable by the new regime and resigned.[68] Whether or not mass resignation or negotiation was the correct strategy – and the vilification on both sides lasted decades – the British Poetry Revival lost an essential power-base that has not been re-placed. While the Poetry Society has become an active organization with a popular poetry magazine, it only has occasional links with British Poetry Revival or linguistically innovative writings. Following this incident many poets and publishers boycotted the organization; many of those previously associated with the Poetry Society were frequently and repeatedly refused Arts Council grant-aid, as the now homeless ALP was quick to document conclusively via its newsletter.[69] Meetings would have to switch again to individually organized events, which at least decentred activity from London: Durham and Newcastle were vibrant again, thanks largely to Richard Caddel, as was Cambridge with its Poetry Festivals. Perhaps the British Poetry Revival escaped a stultifying institutionalization, but at the time it demoralized many of the participants, with lasting effects.

Vociferous Sets of Opponents in London and Cambridge

Blake Morrison, in the essay 'Young Poets in the 1970s', offers a view of contemporary poetry which, while it prepared the way for the Penguin anthology he would edit with Andrew Motion in the 1980s, does acknowledge non-mainstream poetries (and the Poetry Society must have at least made these alternatives visible for a while); he documents the so-called London–Cambridge split for the first time and lists, as catalysts, Eric Mottram and J.H. Prynne.

> One vociferous set of opponents has been associated with and promoted by Eric Mottram, who as deposed editor of *Poetry Review* knows to his cost the 'establishment' line.[70]

However, Morrsion's contention that 'there is little sign yet of an important new poet emerging from under' Mottram's 'wing' can be refuted by examining the work of two young writers, Allen Fisher and Bill Griffiths, who shared the Poetry Society's Alice Hunt Bartlett Award for 1974.[71] Morrison, with his sense of the poem as a small-scale crafted artefact, could not be expected to value their extensive intermedial and avant-garde practices. In 1975, Fisher listed involvement in 34 such projects, including collages, found texts, mail art, experiments in process music and conceptual art, as well as performances.[72] Such works were often generated by fixed procedures and evolving processes, and interactions between the two, as well as often humorous interventions in his systems with personal 'impositions and invitations'.[73]

Bill Griffiths' exemplary use of disruptive technique, which re-shapes his particular concerns with prison as a representative repressive institution and with urban deprivation, as well as his interests and expertise in Anglo-Saxon and Romany literatures, were demonstrated in *Cycles*, Griffiths' first sustained sequence, published in 1976. It opens, appropriately, with 'Dover Borstal'. As Nuttall points out: 'Syntax and experience are so manifested as to compel the poem to be read as poetry (as art) – not as a news report'.[74] Its heteroglossic nature is unsettling and unstable. The juxtaposition of the Latin and the demotic with which it opens is a characteristic procedure to avoid transparency, to break through limitations of discourse which are implicitly as real as the prison which is the poem's apparent focus.

> Ictus!
> as I ain't like ever to be still but
> kalieidoscope,
> lock and knock my sleeping[75]

The poet's measure of time – the beat of 'Ictus!' – complements the prisoner's rhymed rhythm of incarceration, as he 'does time'. The commitment to kaleidoscopic experience pitches dream against reality.

> Do you know it's the sea?
> the speaking sound
> and I woke like a dragon's dream
> taut-limb around and my teeth were avid
> in wonder[76]

This almost heroic self prefers alertness and action to meditation as the dream dissolves a social reality that is pervasively sadistic and repressive:

> The ships, turquoise,
> cutting open the sea
> smiling killing
> OK[77]

It is a landscape and seascape of cuts. Dover, 'kinging the blue', is replete with imperial war-histories and the modern ironies of the borstal: 'the barbwire is German/it is made with razorblades'; the modern prisoners are defined, like their lives, by repetition and inescapably by the 'screws': 'thief you're a thief you/ hey you thief come on'.[78]

Redemption is figured in a discontinuous statement that suggests, at least that financial or verbal exchanges can be altered by re-stamping, by violence: 'I think on the pattern of an action/till the gold of the answer I can beat anyway'.[79] This meditation on theft in a violent poetry – a 'beat' – of stolen discourses is neither 'news' nor revolutionary tract. Its open syntax re-forms the world as text; it both refers to, and evades, social reality.

Blake Morrison, dismisses the *Poetry Review* poets by noting, 'alongside Mottram's polemical theorizing – poetry as revolution and poetry as research – the poems themselves look wan';[80] and conjectures:

> A more feasible alternative may come from the work and teaching of J.H. Prynne, who in Cambridge at any rate has a considerable reputation; but again there is no clear sign of what his following amounts to.[81]

That the editors of the Ferry Press and Grosseteste Press, Andrew Crozier and Tim Longville, later edited the Carcanet anthology *A Various Art* to document this period, confirms the existence, and strength, of this group, although one of its members, Peter Riley, emphasizes that Prynne and Crozier were merely the originators of an 'impulse', and that 'certain people worked together to a greater or lesser extent from about 1966 to 1970'.[82] Perhaps the most typical work belongs to the 1970s, when the influence of American projectivist verse, largely derived from Charles Olson, fused with the resources of the English lyric.

The work of Andrew Crozier in the 1970s is a clear example of this mixture. *The Veil Poem*, published in 1974, opens with a deliberately unfinished fragment; it is the record of perception *in* language, not a description, and is indebted to the commitment to process found in Olson's work:

> and the storm I hear wind and rain
> raging is an effect of bathwater
> emptying into the drain.[83]

The philosophic ease, which owes equally to Wordsworth, is trenchantly domestic, even when determining 'What hides in darkness and what truths/it veils'.[84] The world reveals itself, not as a given, but through acts of slow perception; a garden tree is 'flowing smoothly through its changes' and the shadowy narrator realizes, 'I cannot dominate it', an attitude of reverence towards the autonomy of the world, unlike the Movement Orthodoxy's use of empirical details (and Crozier was one of the first to criticize them as such).[85] One of the sections quotes, without irony, Wordsworth's invocation to the 'Wisdom and Spirit of the Universe' which 'giv'st to forms and images a breath/and everlasting motion', and this traditional Romantic theme is elsewhere restated in terms derived from A.N. Whitehead, the twentieth-century philosopher who rescued and redefined a holistic cosmology that Wordsworth might have applauded.[86] Whitehead's critique of the bifurcation of mind and nature – which Olson had drawn on before – is elaborated in perceptual and phenomenological terms, not too distant, as one might expect from Roy Fisher's Poetry Society lecture, from the terms of Fisher around this time:

> This is
> the ordinary world, naturally incomplete and
> is no wise to be verbally separated
> from your picture of it.[87]

The punning on 'wise' and 'naturally' introduces the question of language as a mode of thinking, hence the echo of Wittgenstein in the passage. A household fireplace provides a domestic image of process; stasis engenders collapse, as coals

> settle slowly
> into themselves and something slips …
> You should never stop.[88]

The poem ends with a description of the careful building of this fire to preserve it; this action is emblematic of the wisdom that nurtures process and which returns the narrator to human relationships:

> The dust beneath my
> fingernails is all the wisdom I have
> to take with me upstairs to my wife.[89]

Both Griffiths and Crozier offer inclusive discourses and ambitiously emphasize the role of language in mediating, and acting upon, the world. While Crozier absorbs literary tradition, Griffiths is a writer who takes an anarchist stance towards a received past, including literature itself. In a later text he rhetorically overstates the case: 'What better disguise for evil/ than sonnets?'[90] Yet Griffiths' involvement with Anglo-Saxon sources – his translations and dictionaries, often self-published, away from the world of academic scholarship – suggests an openness to the past, not mediated by the repressive mechanisms of a selective history; he possesses an ability to juxtapose a remarkable range of materials. I agree with Clive Bush: 'Griffiths's greatest ability is to combine the severest of ethical judgements without losing a sense of open intellectual, social and historical curiosity.'[91]

Naming the Rocks in a Larger than National Way; The Poetry of Place

Charles Olson provided a theory and practice that was influential upon a wide range of British Poetry Revival poets. His theories of projective verse emphasized a kinetics and improvisatory way of writing that appealed to Raworth and others. Treating the page as a compositional open field has been widely practised. However, writers as different as J.H. Prynne, Allen Fisher and Iain Sinclair seemed drawn to Olson's *Maximus Poems* for the way they articulate rich information and documentary sources concerning geography and history. The poem is focused upon Gloucester, Massachusetts, a site important in early North American settlement history, but which, by the 1940s, was a run-down fishing port. Olson's historical span is wide and when he notes, 'Descartes, age 34, date Boston's/settling', he is identifying an originating moment of American civilization with his sense of a dissociation of sensibility within Western thought.[92] The 1959 essay 'Human Universe' goes further and presents all post-Socratic philosophy as a false discourse of logic, classification and idealism, as opposed to a genuine discourse that takes language as an action upon the real.[93] (In this first aspect but not the second Olson prefigured post-structuralist thought; he also used that shifting term 'postmodern' to characterize such thinking.) Olson took the pre-Socratic Heraclitus' maxim, 'Man is estranged from that with which he is most familiar' as axiomatic and Whitehead's process philosophy as his guide.[94]

Such work appealed to poets during the withdrawal from the oppositional politics of the 1960s, in that it could be used as a model for a re-articulation of Britain from less immediately political perspectives. The poetry of place, after the particularities of Roy Fisher's *City* and Harwood's 'Cable St', seemed to offer a local universalism. Olson's fellow Black Mountain poet, Edward Dorn, resident in England, advised young British poets in 'Oxford' in *The North Atlantic Turbine*, published by Fulcrum in 1967, to define themselves against geographical structures 'naming themselves and the rocks' as a way both larger and intimate than concerns with nationality, and this was taken up by J.H. Prynne in *The White Stones*, published by Cape Goliard in 1969, in various attempts to avoid humanistic and accepted socio-historical representations of Britain.[95] In 'The Glacial Question, Unsolved', he uses a variety of cited geological and archeological sources to ask, to open, the question whether the Pleistocene Epoch is over. On such an enormous timescale, Prynne works through his persistent verbs of knowing and being, to hyphothecize about the effect of the Epoch's process upon 'us', how 'we' are its sentient residues:

> We know where the north
> is, the ice is an evening whiteness.
> We know this, we are what it leaves:
> the Pleistocene is our current sense, and
> what in sentiment we are, we
> are, the coast, a line or sequence, the
> cut back down, to the shore.[96]

This mode of address, intimate but expansive, is far from the open measures and notations of Olson, and might be thought to court the Movement embrace of the third person plural, were it not for the fact the embrace is a generous one historically, and not at all confined to the immediate demands of empiricism. As Reeve and Kerridge point out of his lyrical moments:

> they are not established in Prynne's poems as self-sufficient or privileged moments, around which the world could be concentrically organized. The lyricism they give rise to does not transfigure its environs into a stable display of support for the feeling subject.[97]

It is emphatically literary; indeed, the 'battle' may be the Anglo-Saxon poem rather than the landscape from which it takes its name in the following lines:

> It is
> the battle of Maldon binds
> our feet: we tread
> only with that weight & the empire
> of love, in the mist.[98]

Reliance upon an imperial love seems dangerous in a restricted nation whose history can bind. Whereas Olson could more individualistically and intimately address the 'islands/of men and girls' as 'Isolated person in Gloucester, Massachusetts, I, Maximus', Prynne, employing a traditional English rhetorical practice, and using the third person plural, evoking an unlocatable community, sounds no less isolated.[99]

Allen Fisher's *Place*, a project undertaken between 1971 and 1979, was published in four volumes of approximately 100 pages each. They are the Olsonesque and notational *Place* (1974), the more polemical and analytical *Stane* (1977), the lyrical *Becoming* (1978) and *Unpolished Mirrors*, a series of Blakean monologues, published in 1985. Early on in *Place*, Fisher identifies with, and dissociates himself from, Olson's persona: 'I, not Maximus, but a citizen of Lambeth'.[100] Fisher's commitment to procedure and system distinguishes his work from Olson's theory of kinetic process, and draws him nearer to the chance procedures of Jackson MacLow, although the writing in *Place* often shares Olson's notational urgency and his use of juxtaposition. The project's central concern is Fisher's own reading about, experience of, locality and history, particularly focusing upon London. Its considerable resources – it has been called a 'content-specific' work by Peter Barry

– are not offered as evidence of a single argument, a thesis on place, but are parts of the work's 'shading', Fisher's term to describe correspondences *and* contradictions that can be traced between the intricately numbered sections of its open system'.[101] The work constitutes not a totality but an expansive presentation of various meanings and perspectives.

The work's overall structure is complex, but this can seem curiously inessential, given Fisher's hope that a reader might join the text at any point as if – in his persistent metaphor for the work, and for London itself – joining the surface of a moving sphere.[102]

```
the centre moves          continues to
move
us              many centres
ecumenopolis
and
or the loci of a point on a moving sphere

I who am where I am
feel the surges of
of the pulses that are
not my heart's[103]
```

Fisher presents the many Londons of the ecumenopolis as a kind of multiple archaeology, of 'place of living, locality, house borough city country planet', which is yet intimately involved in the socially constructed, psychosomatic self, 'the place of being, body, breath, brain'.[104] As the poet notes sardonically, connecting the two senses of place; 'my father's blood condition/conditioned'.[105]

Fisher acknowledges the influence of Raoul Vaneigem's *The Revolution of Everyday Life* upon his thinking, and of the Situationists, who were influential both upon the underground movements of 1968 and, more lastingly, upon the European avant-garde. They suggested a politics or a relocation of politics, within everyday experience, one again suited to a post-1968 failure.[106] The Situationists engaged in work 'where the exploration of the city reveals the *psycho-geography* created by the physical and mental conditions of twentieth-century society'.[107]

In 'Place 48', from *Stane*, Fisher goes further than the Situationists and presents interconnected instances of cosmic, ecological, biological and political forces to acknowledge the complexity of 'everyday life'. It shares an impulse, in its borrowings from Olson and Whitehead, but not a language, with Crozier's *The Veil Poem*. Fisher's language is more akin to Bill Griffiths', in that its linguistic re-orderings of experience work through juxtaposition and collage: 'The fly on its food route', for example, displays its 'thrust & parry of energy' while the self intervenes in the food chain, by small-scale gestures, suitably notated in an utterance as incomplete as the apprehension of this process.[108]

> I break the web silks
>   the fly escapes
> lands on food in kitchen
>   its legs coated with[109]

The 'correct place' for action will be defined by 'context': 'I have no wish to close the opening petals/that lead the bee', yet the narrator can 'see the context in which I ward off pigeons'.[110] These microcosmic interventions are presented as more pertinent than those permitted through the rituals of social democracy. They look forward to postmodernism's rejection of such metanarratives in favour of *petite histoires*. This 'citizen of Lambeth' asks 'do I think my vote/counts in the neck pulse of the local councillor'.[111] In this expansive 'Dynamegopolis', where 'the place of living' and the 'place of being' interact, political power is registered as much on the human organism as at the ballot box.[112]

Iain Sinclair's *Lud Heat* (1975) is another book which charts a palimpsest London, one which Fisher goes so far as to acknowledge within his own project as part of its reading, in *Stane*, in a note entitled 'To Iain Sinclair, on the publication of his book *Lud Heat* in 1975'.[113] Fisher registers both *Lud Heat*'s similarities to, and differences from, *Place*, but points to an essential shared recognition that 'there are subtle mechanisms at work subjugating our psyches, trying to keep … our senses, awareness at a lower level than they need be'.[114]

Lud Heat mixes open form poetry and tightly written prose that combines scholarly discourse with the style of the New Journalism (along with line drawings and Sinclair's own photographs). Its initial premise is that Hawksmoor's London churches emanate psychic energies which affect the population's actions. (This thesis is used in Peter Ackroyd's novel *Hawksmoor*, for which he has been satirized in later books by Sinclair!) Fisher is quick to sense the subjective element of this pattern-making: '*Lud Heat* assumed the kind of symbolic value particular architectural forms possess: what associations they are capable of evoking in individuals …. It is from these buildings that the energies of the area are – I was going to say "generated"'.[115] Fisher baulks at the very term that Sinclair uses, and in which he believes, and this marks the difference between them. However sceptical Sinclair can sound – like Yeats with his strategic mysticism – one takes Sinclair's work less than seriously if one rejects outright the structures and meanings of his pattern-making. As in *Place*, theory is grounded in the everyday; Sinclair charts his own life as a council grass cutter, working between the talismanic churches, in journals and poems. He also bears witness to the autopic films of Stan Brakage and the sculpture of his friend the poet (and later performance artist) Brian Catling as artists making similar patternings, and superimposing them upon his own concerns. Whereas Fisher uses theory and his reading to create a divergent, contradictory patterning of self and place, Sinclair is drawn to converging combinations of esoteric wisdom and mysticism, which makes his text more monologic than Fisher's, and more certain of its allegiance to materials: '*the scientific approach* a bitter farce/unless it is shot through with high occulting'.[116] The danger is that the totalizing fiction that develops will amount to a paranoiac sense of interconnectedness, something Sinclair recognizes:

> it is so connected we share all
> symptoms & meaning,
> bicycle wheel spins
> a wobbly mandala.[117]

Although the conspiracy theory seems cosmological, Sinclair does share with Fisher an apprehension of the psychosomatic resonances of place. In Sinclair's case, this is particular and oracular, as he presents hay-fever and sunstroke as solar viruses in prose which is as startling in its comparisons as the poetry is in its spare juxtapositions:

> As the ego breaks I am host to another being, who pushes through and not with the pink tenderness of new skin – but with old flesh, hard as wood'.[118]

This abandonment of the human perspective might seem open to charges of fascist mysticism, but this is refuted by noting not only that Sinclair often weaves his pattern-making into the fabric of everyday life but, like Fisher, he can recognize the darkest possible contemporary attachments to place beneath the social democratic surface:

> here: Hackney South & Shoreditch where
> Mr Robin May polled the National Front's
> best result   2,544 votes.[119]

As in Fisher, the ballot box is both dangerous and a diversion from real, complex energies.

The presence of Blake as a guiding spirit in both Fisher's and Sinclair's work is not just a fashionable hangover from the sixties' children of Albion. Blake, another 'citizen of Lambeth', developed, in his similarly self-published 'Prophetic Books', a mythology to articulate his ambivalence towards an earlier radicalism, in a way not dissimilar to the 1970s withdrawal from social radicalism. The employment of a mythic method is the later choice of Sinclair's *Suicide Bridge* (which, along with *Lud Heat* and the novel *White Chapell, Scarlet Tracings* (1987), form a trilogy.) In this, Blake's Sons of Albion from *Jerusalem*, are embodiments of contemporary evil, taking on such contemporary personae as the Kray Twins. By contrast, Fisher's *Unpolished Mirrors* – the final part of *Place*, one character, operating not unlike one of Blake's spectres or emanations, speaks generally but prophetically of 'a coming English Revolution'.[120]

Prynne, Fisher and Sinclair were not alone in developing what has become known as a poetry of place. A whole issue of *Joe Dimaggio* magazine in 1975 was dedicated to the theme.[121] The Polytechnic of Central London British Poetry Conference 1977 featured 21 poets constellated around the notions of 'Inheritance Landscape Location', the title of the accompanying essay by Eric Mottram, who clearly marshals theories of place as delineators of a special knowledge and perception, 'both local and international', operating in opposition to 'official British culture' which Mottram represents as having shrunk 'in response to the pressures of British economic and political decline from the raving days of Empire and Influence'.[122] Far from simply withdrawing from politics, after the collapse of the underground, the poetry of place enabled poets to expand the notion of politics beyond both parliamentary and purely personal articulations of it.

The Uses of Autonomy

J.H. Prynne's work of the 1970s, published in eight books or pamphlets and collected in 1982 in *Poems* (and again in an expanded edition of 1999), is a by-word for difficulty and enigma. Prynne had abandoned the Olsonian human universe for a writing that encouraged the invasion of the poetic text by non-poetic discourses – usually identifiable ones – and a textual compactness that is all the more complex for the survival of traditional lyric and rhetorical effects. Reeve and Kerridge in their 1996 study of the work of Prynne, *Nearly Too Much*, write:

> The technical material is not there to be understood by some superbly informed reader, but neither is it completely opaque. Although there may be local accuracy, and the line of specialist description is perhaps always there to be followed by the reader expert in a particular field, this is not the sole purpose. The uses can also be figurative, in a way that begins to convert these specialized vocabularies into something more open to readers who may, in postmodernist fashion, have renounced their aspirations to totality.[123]

It is clearly a poetry where what is said is unclear, and our focus must attend to its mode of saying. My examples are drawn from the most intransigent of these texts, *High Pink on Chrome* (1975), in which the language of subjectivity seems to be penned in by the specialist lexis of agricultural biochemistry.

> The distance (2) from a self
>   protein is not by nature
> either just or rational but
>   the mirror image of both.[124]

This passage – it could be a gentle cut-up – hinges syntactically upon the unlike collocation 'self/protein', teasingly separated by enjambement, while grammar binds it; justice and rationality do not reside in that little distance. Reeve and Kerridge see a Bakhtinian doubly oriented speech in this work, and note the double discourses in Prynne: 'When a pun is on the cusp between different discourses, each of its two possible senses carried with it the other a "hidden polemic"'.[125] Here the double discourse explicitly points to a mirroring, as though the doubling, troubling distance between justice, rationality and self were reflected by the biological energy element of a protein, which 'not by nature' but by culture, can be seen as its inverted other. Reeve and Kerridge offer us a contemporary way of reading Prynne's concerns (one in line with the general theory of this study) but I want to examine Prynne's work of the 1970s via the perspective of that decade, provided by the poetics of two younger Cambridge poets – Peter Ackroyd and Veronica Forrest-Thomson – to show how textual autonomy was valued at the time.[126]

Peter Ackroyd – better known as a novelist and biographer – published a provocative cultural history, *Notes for a New Culture*, in 1976. Ackroyd attempts to demonstrate that language has become the only content of literature. The resultant formal autonomy of the text, a kind of windowless monad, marks its final victory over the attempted annexations by aesthetics, the self and humanism. For Ackroyd, Prynne's work is important both for having admitted non-poetic discourses and for having expunged the poetic voice, leaving only 'written surface'.[127]

Prynne uses technical discourses and changes their function by inserting them into a poem, and, as Ackroyd points out, the utterances seem coldly anonymous, rather than double. The readers are 'not asked to participate in the lucidity and harmony of the poetry, we can only recognize its exterior signs'.[128] Yet such signs as the stanzaic shape tease the reader with what, literally at first sight, appears a traditional poem.

> In feare and trembling they descend
>   into threatened shock. Faire and
> softly, too far from the dry arbour.
>   The chisel plough meets tough going,
> we spray off with paraquat 2½ pints
>   per acre. And the ^{51}Cr label shews
> them and us in your same little boat,
>   pulling away from the vacant foreshore.[129]

In parts, meaning can be constructed, but as a whole a reader might suspect the stanza only dimly refers outside itself, as it draws attention to its language: the archaic but opposing 'feare' and 'faire', the specialist bio-chemical lexis. The text is perhaps more readable in the ecologically-aware twenty-first century than 1976, the agricultural 'chisel plough' more obviously an image of harm: however much we pretend we are Wordsworth on the lake, the shoreline is vacant, and we are, demotically speaking, all in the same boat, an 'all' that makes the division between 'them and us' (Harwood's or Tony Harrison's) irrelevant as the dry arbour is threatened with contamination. The first line carries overtones (and spelling) that suggest Miltonic expulsion from Eden.

Yet Ackroyd, reading according to his restrictive theory, prefers to read such clues as part of the historical dimension of the poem's triumphant autonomy. 'Ambiguity is caused by a language coming into itself against the power of that aesthetic context which had given it meaning and strength for so long.'[130] Ackroyd senses a tension between the poem as an historically determined entity and its invasion by language in its rich varieties; so that pastoral and chemistry assist the text's linguistic complexity, amounting not to a thematic resolution but to the affirmation of its very autonomy, its ultimate non-utility.

This absolutist argument is supported by a precocious use of post-structuralist theory – applications of the work of Lacan and Derrida, for example – which is peculiarly out of step with its later uses in Britain as an element of a radical critique. Neither does autonomy operate as a critique as it does in the thinking of Adorno (and Marcuse, to whom I shall return at the end of the next chapter). However much his argument may be felt to draw close to my own distinctions between a poetry of the said and a poetry of the saying, ultimately Ackroyd seems to be asking for a poetry of non-saying. He claims Prynne's poetry in the name of an essentially conservative formulation of autonomy which sees this difficult work as a deliberate and necessary withdrawal from the 'dispirited nation' to which Ackroyd refers, and from the 'call for personal "liberation" which became fashionable in the sixties' as well as the 'humanistic kitsch' of its popular poetry.[131] History and politics are thus denied a role, reduced simply to serving autonomy as pure discourses on a poem's surface: an aestheticism without aesthetics.

Veronica Forrest-Thomson's *Poetic Artifice* has been vital to the theoretical argument of this study; her notion of suspended naturalization, her concept of artifice, and the relation between the two, have been crucial to my thinking.[132] However, it also possible to historicize this attempt to develop an ambitious theory of twentieth-century poetry, one which would account for the poetic devices which create the autonomy that Ackroyd values. Like Ackroyd, she had absorbed French theory, yet so thoroughly that it does not surface in her text, for which the guiding spirit is William Empson. Published in 1978, her theory was arguably influenced by, and had some influence upon, the Cambridge poets; her work is published alongside theirs in *A Various Art*. Her theory elevates artifice over poetry's referential function but offers a model of reading that presents naturalization – the reading of a text as a statement about the external world – as a process that is best suspended to encourage concentration upon the poem's artifice, which she itemizes as levels of conventional, phonological/visual, syntactic and semantic devices. Most readers of poetry ignore this exacting route, preferring to move rapidly from text to paraphrase.[133] She is scathing of 'the general dreariness of English verse' in the Movement mode, which works in complicity with bad naturalization, which does not dwell upon the levels of artifice.[134] Prynne's work may not be read via this short cut. Its 'tendentious obscurity' makes this necessarily impossible; for Forrest-Thomson, Prynne's work represents the supreme exemplar of the theory: it recaptures 'the levels of Artifice, of restoring language to its primary beauty as craft by refusing to allow its social comprehension'.[135]

At the conventional and visual levels, my example from *High Pink on Chrome* is shaped as a poem, with regular stanzaic form (I have often the sense of Prynne taking Renaissance texts as visual patterns, such as the empty stanza shapes in Puttenham's *Art of English Poesy*). At the level of sound organization there is tension between its rhythm – the third line can arguably be scanned as a regular dactylic line with subtle alliterative moments – and the semantic components, such as ^{51}Cr, which resists traditional scansion. The almost subliminal internal eye rhyme of 'plough' and 'tough' resists its comprehension as statement. The verse is syntactically unclear, with several broken back sentences, cut-up; it leaves a coherent grammatical unit that still seems to have said very little.

Forrest-Thomson rejects the absolutism of Ackroyd. 'It is only through artifice that poetry can challenge our ordinary linguistic orderings of the world, make us question the way in which we make sense of things, and induce us to consider its alternative linguistic orders as a new way of seeing the world.'[136] Naturalization may be *suspended* to enable this challenge, but eventually the poem must have sense made of it by an active reader. Good naturalization is a reading that accounts for poetic devices, that reads the discourse through them, much as Reeve and Kerridge do in their readings of Prynne's doubleness. It could be said of Prynne's poems that the semantics of science '^{51}Cr', possibly the chrome of the title, with its own peculiar self-reference, 'shews' that the 'them and us' are indeed in the same boat. The poem's final line, whether Wordsworthian or not, teases with a voice or presence that pitches selfhood against ecological disaster, but has to be read *through* the thick layering of historical linguistic resources that suggests the historical dimension to this harm. Almost as though Prynne were responding to Forrest-Thomson's theories, his later verse, particularly in the 1990s, opens the discourses it carries in many directions, a multiple saying that evades the said for as long as possible.

Barry MacSweeney's *Odes* offer a tough view of politics in the late 1970s. Having made a precocious beginning in the late 1960s, even being picked up by a major publisher as a possible Geordie complement to the Liverpool Poets, and having mixed with a broad range of poets, from Bunting and

Pickard, to Prynne and Mottram, who steered him away from such celebrity, MacSweeney developed a range and authority that remained in his writing until his death in 2000.[137]

Pound had approvingly quoted Bunting's bilingual equation 'Dichten = condensare' in his *ABC of Reading* (1951), to demonstrate that condensation is the essence of writing,[138] but in *Odes*, whose title might suggest a debt to Bunting's own two books of *Odes*, MacSweeney's 'style is compressed, paratactic'.[139] This is not the economy that comes of careful revision but is an economy built into the compositional process. Condensation is so acute, its resultant autonomy frustrates the processes of naturalization. Perhaps learning from the increased impaction found in the work of Prynne at this time, as he too moved from the Olsonian inheritance, MacSweeney has said, 'I've worked towards this condensing of language, this cutting across meaning, not having words next to each other which are supposed to be there … I think they are shocking.'[140]

By squeezing metaphoric language into this indeterminacy MacSweeney, like Griffiths, has ensured that the poems *stay poetic*. Celerity is a guerilla tactic against a language that belongs increasingly to the controllers of our society. In 'Far Cliff Babylon' MacSweeney can adopt a persona that declares with frightening simplicity (in lines that are parodied throughout the piece):

> I am 16.
> I am a Tory. My
>
> vision of the future represents
> no people.[141]

The Babylonian exile of the reggae of the era ('I have no people/They represent me') merges with the sinister tones of Iggy Pop's lyric, 'No Fun', that operates as a resistant echo of the other NF, the National Front, which, as we have seen from *Lud Heat*, was a small but potent force throughout the 1970s.[142] More positively, 'No Fun' counterpoints another slogan: 'No more apartheid'.[143]

The poem is a state of the nation address, to adapt a term that MacSweeney would ironically use for a number of his angry poems of the 1980s. The sceptre of unemployment hovers in the surreal image of

> your natty dread future is a dole card
> stamped with asteroids exploding

> across the city of my
> birth.[144]

The reader is forced to join in the processes of the language, cannot rest in too many of the familiar notions of space/time, social detail, idea, or traditional image, most of the comforting impedimenta of 'poetry'. In 'Far Cliff Babylon' there comes the stark realization that 'I have died every day since I gave up poetry./Dangerous condescending humans lapped it up.'[145] Despite this, the real triumph of these poems is that they 'move' the reader – in both senses of the word. Yet the 'movement' of the poems, the celerity of the text, resists that static aestheticization of the feeling, that comforting, introspective notion, of having been 'moved'. It recalls what Forrest-Thomson said of the alternative linguistic orderings evoked by poetic artifice. That the lines 'I am 16/I am a Tory' quote the young William Hague, leader of the Conservative Party from 1997 until 2001, makes the poem seem prophetic, a bridge to the poetry of the 1980s and 1990s, and beyond.

Notes

1 Ken Edwards, 'Reviews' (of Mottram, Pryor, Halsey and Reed), *Reality Studios*, vol 2. no. 1 (1979), p. 9. See his 'The Two Poetries', *Angelaki*, vol 5, no 1 (April 2000). This chapter uses only a small proportion of the data collected in Chapter Two, 'Counter-Movements' in my PhD thesis, 'Some Aspects of Contemporary British Poetry', University of East Anglia, 1988, pp. 79–181.

2 *The Penguin Book of Contemporary British Poetry*, eds. Blake Morrison and Andrew Motion (Harmondsworth: Penguin, 1982), p. 11.

3 Gavin Selerie, 'Introduction', *North Dakota Quarterly*, vol. 51, no. 4 (Fall 1983), pp. 5–18, at p. 6.

4 See Eric Mottram, 'The British Poetry Revival 1960–1974', *Modern Poetry Conference, 1974* (London: Polytechnic of Central London, 1974), pp. 86–117. See Edwards, 'Reviews', p. 9. See Barry MacSweeney, 'The British Poetry Revival 1965–79', *South East Arts Review* (Spring 1979), pp. 33–46.

5 The revised form appears as 'The British Poetry Revival, 1960–75', in *New British Poetries*, eds. Robert Hampson and Peter Barry (Manchester: Manchester University Press, 1993), pp. 15–50.

6 Roy Fisher, *Three Early Poems* (London: Trangravity Press, 1971), p. i.

7 Roy Fisher, speaking on the *Poetry Now* radio programme, BBC Radio 3, 20 November 1981. James Keery's '"Menacing Works in my Isolation": Early Pieces', in *The Thing About Roy Fisher*, eds., John Kerrigan and Peter Robinson (Liverpool: Liverpool University Press, 2000), pp. 47–85, traces and analyses a number of other early pieces and shows that Fisher

strayed not only close to the New Apocalypse, but to the Movement Orthodoxy.

8 Roy Fisher, *Poetry Now*, 20 November 1981.

9 *Ibid.*

10 *Migrant* 1, July 1959, flier inserted loosely in issue.

11 See Gael Turnbull, 'Charlotte Chapel, The Pittsburgh Draft Board and *Some Americans*', *PN Review*, 28 (1982), p. 10; and 'Little Magazine Index: Migrant', *Poetry Information*, 17 (1977), pp. 95–98.

12 The text of the Fisher poem (*Cambridge Opinion*, 41 (October 1965), p. 24) has a different lineation from that published in *Poems 1955–1987* (Oxford: Oxford University Press, 1988), pp. 50–51, one much closer to the practice of Williams' triple measure.

13 In addition to Gael Turnbull's 'A Gesture to be Clean', *Cambridge Opinion*, 41 (October 1965), pp. 18–20, this edition carried Williams' own notes 'Measure ... a loosely assembled essay on poetic measure', pp. 4–14. The poets included were Turnbull, Bunting, Jim Burns, Tom Clark, Andrew Crozier, Anselm Hollo, Fisher, Tim Longville, Tom Pickard, Jeremy (sic) Prynne, Michael Shayer, John Temple.

14 Simon Perril, 'Trappings of the Hart: *Reader* and the Ballad of *The English Intelligencer*', *The Gig*, 4/5, November 1999/March 2000 ('The Poetry of Peter Riley'), pp. 196–218, at p. 197. The phrase 'community of risk' is Drew Milne's, and it is one that will return with respect to Cambridge Poetry in the 1990s.

15 Crozier's magazine had various titles: *The Wivenhoe Park Revue, The Park: The Wivenhoe Park Review*, for example. See Mottram, 'The British Poetry Revival 1960–1974', pp. 102–03.

16 See *Ibid.*, pp. 102–03. John Riley was murdered in 1978. See *For John Riley*, ed. Tim Longville (Wirksworth and Leeds: Grosseteste, 1979), and John Riley, *Selected Poems* (Manchester: Carcanet, 1995).

17 Jeff Nuttall, *Bomb Culture* (London: Paladin, 1970), p. 159.

18 For the early history of Writers Forum, see Eric Mottram, 'Writers Forum: A Successful Campaign' in *Bob Cobbing and Writers Forum*, ed. P. Mayer (Sunderland: Ceolfrith, 1974) pp. 15–24, and Eric Mottram, 'Beware of Imitations: Writers Forum in the '60s', *Poetry Student*, 1 (1975), pp 6–7, 32–35. My 'Bob Cobbing: Sightings and Soundings', in Robert Sheppard, *Far Language: Poetics and Innovative Linguistic Poetry 1978–1997* (Exeter: Stride Research Documents, 1999), pp. 61–67, describes the workshop during the 1990s, at pp. 64–66.

19 These were collected in *Tristan Tzara, Selected Poems* (London: Trigram Press, 1975) and reprinted, with additions, in *Chanson Dada, Tristan Tzara, Selected Poems* (Toronto: Coach House Press/Underwhich Editions, 1987)

20 Ken Edwards, 'Writing and Commodities', *Association of Little Presses Catalogue 1985* (London: ALP, 1985), n.p. Indeed this visibility often involved the giving away of little press publications, despite the existence of such catalogues.

21 *Children of Albion: Poetry of the 'Underground' in Britain* (Harmondsworth: Penguin, 1969), p. 320–26. Subsequent citations in the text are marked as *CA.*

22 See Geoffrey Thurley, *The Ironic Harvest* (London: Arnold, 1974), pp. 197–207. For example he noted that the anthology contained 'much that is ephemeral, slack and modish ... and ... much less palatably, the obligatory stock of Protest' (p. 205).

23 A number of British Poetry Revival writers noted *The New American Poetry 1945–1960*, ed. Donald Allen (New York: Grove Press, 1960) as having been their first introduction to contemporary poetry, in answer to a questionnaire I conducted in 1982.

24 Lee Harwood, answer to questionnaire, 1982.

25 'Interview with Lee Harwood', by Helen Dennis at Leamington Spa, 29 November 1980, unpublished, p. 6.

26 *Ibid.*, p. 6.

27 Allen Ginsberg, *Howl* (San Francisco: City Lights, 1956), p. 9.

28 Lee Harwood, *The White Room* (London: Fulcrum Press, 1968), p. 22. 'Cable Street' may also be found in *Conductors of Chaos*, ed. Iain Sinclair (London: Picador, 1996), pp. 141–48.

29 Theodore Roszak, *The Making of the Counter Culture* (London: Faber, 1970), p. 129. See also Iain Sinclair *The Kodak Mantra Diaries* (London: Albion Village Press, 1971) for an account of Ginsberg and the underground from an important British Poetry Revival writer.

30 'The Big Green Day: Tom Raworth talks to Don Watson about British poetry's tottering state', *City Limits*, 16–23 February 1989, p. 57.

31 'Interview with Lee Harwood', p. 3.

32 'At the 'New Departures' Reading 1975, Not 65', *Great Works*, 5 (1975), p. 15.

33 Quoted in Edmund Wilson, *Axel's Castle* (London: Fontana, 1961), p. 215.

34 Geoffrey Thurley, *The Ironic Harvest* (London: Arnold, 1974), p. 206.

35 Richard Neville, *Playpower* (Frogmore: Paladin, 1971), p.101.

36 See Lee Harwood, *HMS Little Fox* (London: Oasis Books, 1975), p. 86.

37 See *Student Power* eds. Alexander Cockburn and Robin Blackburn (Harmondsworth: Penguin, 1969).

38 Quoted in Nuttall, *Bomb Culture*, p. 204.

39 Roszak, *The Making of the Counter Culture*, p. 126.

40 William Blake, *The Complete Poems*, ed. W.H. Stevenson (London: Longman, 1972), p. 644.

41 R.D. Laing, *The Politics of Experience and the Bird of Paradise* (Harmondsworth: Penguin, 1967), p. 37.

42 *Ibid.*, p. 37.

43 Harwood, *The White Room*, p. 28.

44 Fredric Jameson, *Marxism and Form* (London: Oxford University Press, 1971), p. 111.

45 Herbert Marcuse, *An Essay on Liberation* (Harmondsworth: Penguin, 1969), p. 33.

46 *Ibid.*, p. 32.

47 *Ibid.*, p. 45

48 *Ibid.*, p. 45.

49 *Ibid.*, p. 46.

50 Tom Raworth, *Visible Shivers* (Oakland: O Books, 1987), in 'Dear Ed' from the 1971 'Letters from Yaddo', n.p.

51 Charles Olson, 'Projective Verse' quoted in Donald Allen and Warren Tallman, *The Poetics of the New American Poetry*, (New York: Grove Press, 1973) pp. 147–58, at p. 149.

52 Tom Raworth, *A Serial Biography* (second edition) (Berkeley: Turtle Island, 1977), p. 16.

53 Olson, 'Projective Verse', p. 156.

54 Raworth, *A Serial Biography*, p. 28.

55 Olson, 'Projective Verse', p. 148.

56 Tom Raworth, *Visible Shivers*, n.p.

57 Tom Raworth, *Tottering State* (third edition): *Selected Early Poems 1963–1983* (Oakland: O Books, 2000), p. 57. Subsequent citations in the text are marked as *TS2000*. The poems from Horovitz, *Children of Albion* quoted in the text are also to be found in *TS2000*.

58 Raworth, *Visible Shivers*, n.p.

59 Jean-François Lyotard, 'Notes on the Critical Function of the Work of Art' in *Driftworks* (New York: Semiotext, 1984), pp. 69–83, at p. 73.

60 Most of the information about ALP is drawn from Bob Cobbing, 'ALP – The First Fifteen Years', *Poetry and Little Press Information* 5 (1981), pp. 3–32. See also Bill Griffiths and Bob Cobbing, *ALP The First 22½ Years* (London: The Association of Little Presses, 1988).

61 Allen Fisher, quoted in Selerie, 'Introduction', p. 15.

62 Another aim of the organization was for 'a change in the role of the Poet Laureateship, from an "out to grass" pension to paid ombudsman, spokesman and ambassador for the national interest of all poets' (MacSweeney, 'The British Poetry Revival', p. 42). They attempted to persuade the Heath government following the death of C. Day Lewis, proposing Adrian Mitchell as candidate. John Betjeman was appointed.

63 Cobbing, 'ALP', pp. 13–15.

64 Mottram, 'The British Poetry Revival', p. 114.

65 See 'Poetry Review', *Poetry Information* 20/21 (1979–1980), pp. 142–54, for a full index and for Mottram's note "Editing Poetry Review', p. 154–55.

66 MacSweeney, 'The British Poetry Revival', p. 44.

67 *Ibid.*

68 At a reading given on 24 January 1980 in Norwich, Roy Fisher introduced the poem 'Sets' (*Poems 1955–1987*, p. 106) by saying it was a response to the 'paranoia and lack of restraint' on the part of the Council before the resignations.

69 The July 1977 *ALP Newsletter*, quoted in Cobbing, 'ALP', p. 19, states, '1977/78 looks like being a very bad year for little presses publishing anything other than fairly orthodox material.'

70 Blake Morrison, 'Young Poets in the 1970s', in *British Poetry Since 1970: a critical survey*, eds. Peter Jones and Michael Schmidt (Manchester: Carcanet, 1980), pp. 141–56, at p. 145.

71 *Ibid.*, p. 145.

72 See Allen Fisher, *Prosyncel* (New York: Strange Faeces Press, 1975), p. 5.

73 *Ibid.*, p. 38.

74 Jeff Nuttall, 'Bill Griffiths', *Poetry Information* 15 (1976), pp. 13–17.

75 Bill Griffiths, *Cycles* (London: Pirate Press and Writers Forum, 1976), n.p.

76 *Ibid.*, n.p.

77 *Ibid.*, n.p.

78 *Ibid.*, n.p.

79 *Ibid.*, n.p.

80 Morrison, 'Young Poets in the 1970s', p. 145.

81 *Ibid.*, p. 146.

82 Peter Riley and Kelvin Corcoran, 'Spitewinter Provocations: An interview on the condition

of poetry', *Reality Studios*, 8 (1986), pp. 1–17, at p. 3.

83 Andrew Crozier, 'The Veil Poem', in *A Various Art*, eds. Andrew Crozier and Tim Longville (Manchester: Carcanet, 1987), pp. 71–76 at p. 71. The text had been separately published as *The Veil Poem* (Providence, RI: Burning Deck, 1974).

84 Crozier, 'The Veil Poem', p. 72.

85 *Ibid.*, p. 72.

86 *Ibid.*, p. 74.

87 *Ibid.*, p. 75.

88 *Ibid.*, p. 73.

89 *Ibid.*, p. 76.

90 Bill Griffiths, *Rousseau and the Wicked* (London: Invisible Books, 1996), p. 31.

91 Clive Bush, 'Dance Hymns on a Semi-Stable Planet: Bill Griffiths', in his *Out of Dissent* (London: Talus Editions, 1997), pp. 211–303, at p. 303. See also Eric Mottram, '"Every new book hacking on Barz": The Poetry of Bill Griffiths', *Reality Studios* V, 1–4, 1983.

92 Charles Olson, *The Maximus Poems* (New York: Jargon/Corinth Books, 1960), p. 128.

93 Charles Olson, 'The Human Universe', in *The Poetics of the New American Poetry*, eds. Donald Allen and Warren Tallman (New York: Grove Press, 1973), pp.161–74.

94 Charles Olson, *The Special View of History* (Berkeley: Oyez, 1970), p. 14.

95 Edward Dorn, *The Collected Poems 1956–1974* (Bolinas: Four Seasons Fountain, 1975), p. 210.

96 J.H. Prynne, *Poems* (Edinburgh and London: Agneau 2, 1982), pp. 65–66.

97 N.H. Reeve and Richard Kerridge, *Nearly Too Much: The Poetry of J.H. Prynne* (Liverpool: Liverpool University Press, 1996), p. 37.

98 Prynne, *Poems*, p. 75.

99 Olson, *The Maximus Poems*, p. 12.

100 Allen Fisher, *Place* (Carrrboro: Truck Press, 1976), n.p.

101 Peter Barry, 'Allen Fisher and "content-specific" poetry in *New British Poetries*, eds., Robert Hampson and Peter Barry (Manchester: Manchester University Press, 1993), pp. 198–215, at 201.

102 See Fisher, *Prosyncel*, p. 9.

103 Allen Fisher, *Becoming* (London: Aloes Books, 1978), p. 23.

104 Fisher, *Prosyncel*, p. 9.

105 Allen Fisher, *Stane* (London: Aloes Books, 1977), p. 52.

106 Fisher, *Prosyncel*, p. 9.

107 Robert Hewison, *Future Tense: A New Art for the Nineties* (London: Methuen, 1990), p. 26.

108 Fisher, *Stane*, p. 11.

109 *Ibid.*, p. 11.

110 *Ibid.*, p. 11.

111 *Ibid.*, p. 11.

112 Fisher, *Becoming*, p. 84.

113 Fisher, *Stane*, pp. 30–31. See *Poetry Information* 15 (1976), for the original of this 'review', 'A Confluence of Energies', pp. 3–6; it also contains 'Iain Sinclair/Lud Heat/ *The Albion Village Press*: a tracking and an interview by Chris Torrance and Phil Maillard, pp. 7–12. See also my *Iain Sinclair* (Tavistock: Northcote House, forthcoming) for a more detailed read-

ing of Sinclair's poetry, fiction and documentary.

114   Fisher, *Stane*, p. 30.

115   *Ibid.*, p. 30.

116   Iain Sinclair, *Lud Heat* (London: Albion Village Press, 1975), p. 89.

117   *Ibid.*, p. 34.

118   *Ibid.*, p. 86.

119   *Ibid.*, p. 102.

120   Allen Fisher, *Unpolished Mirrors* (London: Reality Studios, 1985), p. 1. See also Peter Middleton, '(Subject) essay on Allen Fisher's *Unpolished Mirrors* & current English Poetry. (Title) *The Poetic Project*', *Reality Studios*, 4 (1982), pp. 31–36.

121   *Joe Dimaggio* 11, ed. Jeremy Hilton, (1974)

122   Eric Mottram, 'Inheritance Landscape Location: Data for British Poetry 1977', in *PCL British Poetry Conference – June 1977* ed. Paul Evans (London: Polytechnic of Central London, 1977), pp. 85–101, at p. 87.

123   Reeve and Kerridge, *Nearly Too Much*, p. 18.

124   Prynne, *Poems*, p. 258.

125   Reeve and Kerridge, *Nearly Too Much*, p. 112.

126   For collections of their poetry see Peter Ackroyd, *The Diversions of Purley* (London: Abacus, 1987), Veronica Forrest-Thomson, *Collected Poems and Translations* (Lewes: Allardyce, Barnett, 1990). Forrest-Thomson died in 1975.

127   Peter Ackroyd, *Notes for a New Culture* (London: Vision Press, 1976), p. 130.

128   *Ibid.*, p. 130.

129   Prynne, *Poems*, p. 257.

130   Ackroyd, *Notes for a New Culture*, p. 131.

131   *Ibid.*, p. 136.

132   The impact of both Ackroyd and Forrest-Thomson may be seen in a piece written during the 1970s, in my *Far Language: Poetics and Innovative Linguistic Poetry 1978–1997*, (Exeter: Stride Research Documents, 1999). 'Reading Prynne and Others', pp. 9–12. Alison Mark has published *Veronica Forrest-Thomson and Language Poetry* (Tavistock: Northcote House, 2001) and is preparing a new edition of *Poetic Artifice*.

133   See Forrest-Thomson, *Poetic Artifice*, (Manchester: Manchester University Press, 1978).p. xi, and Jonathan Culler, *Structuralist Poetics* (London: Routledge, 1975), pp. 131–88.

134   Forrest-Thomson, *Poetic Artifice*, p. x.

135   *Ibid.*, p. 142.

136   *Ibid.*, p. xi.

137   The early book was *The Boy from the Green Cabaret Tells of his Mother* (London: New Authors, Hutchinson, 1968). MacSweeney had published in *Vogue* as well as *The English Intelligencer* so one can imagine that he was confused enough when, at the age of 20, he was nominated for the Oxford Professorship of Poetry. MacSweeney turned to the small presses for the next 25 years until he was anthologized by Iain Sinclair in *The Tempers of Hazard* (with Thomas A. Clark and Chris Torrance) (London: Paladin, 1993), pp. 133–285 and in *The Book of Demons* (Newcastle upon Tyne: Bloodaxe, 1997), and in the posthumous *Wolf Tongue* (Tarset: Bloodaxe Books, 2003). He is well served by Clive Bush, 'Parts in the weal of kynde, Barry MacSweeney', *Out of Dissent*, pp. 304–416.

138 Ezra Pound, *ABC of Reading* (London: Faber, 1951), p. 152.
139 'MacSweeney' (interviewed by Eric Mottram), *Poetry Information*, 18 (Winter/Spring 1977–78), pp. 21–39, p. 36.
140 *Ibid.*, p. 37.
141 Barry MacSweeney, *Odes* (London: Trigram Press, 1978), p. 57.
142 *Ibid.*, p. 58.
143 *Ibid.*, p. 58.
144 *Ibid.*, p. 57.
145 *Ibid.*, p. 60.

3

Starting to Make the World: The Poetry of Roy Fisher in the 1960s and 1970s

Thinking with Birmingham as it exists

In Roy Fisher's first sustained success, the poetry and prose sequence *City*, there is constant interplay between an elaborate fictiveness and a denotative realism, but whenever that realism seems the easiest course, he often opts for those techniques of defamiliarization, which I have already established as a basic strategy of the British Poetry Revival. Indeed, *City*, published in 1961 by Migrant Press, though considerably revised in 1963, is one of its first flowerings.[1]

City consists of 10 poems and 16 prose passages ranging from a paragraph to a page. If Fisher had yet to perfect his means – some of the poems owe to a lush lyricism not too distant from his own early New Apocalypse poems; others stray close to Movement paradigms – he had found his obsessive material: the city of Birmingham, a theme on which he continued to play variations well into the 1990s, a non-programmatic poetry of place. A sequence from *Birmingham River* (1994) opens, 'Birmingham's what I think with'.[2]

In the late 1950s Fisher returned to the city to find that it was being redeveloped partly because of wartime bomb damage, partly for purposes of social engineering; his own childhood memories made him realize 'how much the place was dependent upon very evanescent, temporal, subjective renderings of it, which might never *be* rendered'.[3] Poems related by theme are grouped together, though not in a logical sequence. The text is actually an assemblage of varieties of writing about the city, including fragments of abandoned novels. Towards the beginning there are many prose passages describing, from a bird's eye view, the physical contours of the city and its gradual demolition. Texts which refer to the city's short century of industrial development are placed together, while passages which are autobiographical and exhibit a pessimistic sensibility are generally found in what Fisher described as 'a sort of well-written yearning towards the end'.[4]

One sees resistance in 'the impacted lives of the inhabitants', since 'the meaningless of news ... all wedge together to keep destruction out,' (*DLD*, p. 17) though the old architecture 'dwarfed and terrified' the people 'by its sheer size and functional brutality' (*DLD*, p. 20). On the other hand, the redeveloped city is also 'bred out of a hard will, but as it appears, it shows itself a little ingratiating ... speciously democratic', a fact to which Fisher's work has often returned with a suspicion and resistance of its own (*DLD*, pp. 22–21).

Despite the American connections afforded through Gael Turnbull, *City*, though a revisiting of modernism, shows no specific influence of the Americans he was in contact with, other than a certain looseness of diction and metrics. Indeed, although *City* focuses upon place, it cannot, like work by writers already examined, be thought of as influenced by the contemporary American concern with topography, as in Olson's *Maximus Poems* or William Carlos Williams' *Paterson*. A. Kingsley Weatherhead expresses the difference succinctly: '*Paterson* is bland and frank; it lacks imaginative intensity and a sense of distress.'[5] Fisher writes of wanting 'to believe I live in a single world', of 'keeping my eyes at home while I can', but admits, 'The imaginary comes to me with as much force as the real, the remembered with as much force as the immediate', which in *City* is sometimes overwhelming for its 'unwilling hero', but occasionally liberating (*DLD*, p. 29). This is highlighted by Weatherhead's comparisons: '*Paterson* lacks the occasional quality of dream, the obliquity, and the surrealism of *City*'.[6]

Fisher often presents the city as an hallucination: 'It could be broken like asphalt, and the men and women rolled out like sleeping maggots' (*DLD*, p. 27). In Fisher's work we recognize, not the contemporary social realist perspectives of Larkin, but the unknowable City of modernism: the fog-shrouded capital of T.S. Eliot, the musical geography of Bely's *Petersburg*, or the haunted Paris of Breton's *Nadja*. Malcolm Bradbury writes that 'realism humanizes, naturalism scientizes, but modernism pluralizes, and surrealizes'.[7] No wonder the unwilling hero comments of Birmingham: 'Most of it has never been seen' (*DLD*, p. 23). The hero is the centre of this revitalized perception. Yet as Bradbury also reminds us, 'In much modernism [the city] is the environment of personal consciousness, flickering impressions.'[8] The alienation of 'looking through another's eyes' gives way to an aesthetic

and detached enjoyment of plural perspectives and eventually to the discovery of a distinct use for these unique visions, one which informs most of
Fisher's subsequent work (*DLD*, p. 29). Fisher explains his working method:

> I would say to myself: I am on a number fifteen bus in Birmingham. I am familiar
> with the sensibility of Paul Klee or Kokoschka but I'm not familiar with the places
> they were at, but I'll play some perceptual games and I will de-Anglicize England –
> which seems to me absolutely essential.[9]

Most writing about England that Fisher had read at that time, he assumed,
'was produced by people who were products of the public school system. I
was always feeling for alternative gestures or angles in'.[10] If most of it had
never been seen – particularly through working-class eyes – it was necessary
to take the imaginative permission from outside England 'to write about
city-matters': he instances 'the milieu of a passage of text from a Kafka
Diary'.[11] The fragments of narrative in *City* – an intense account of a mysterious cat-burglar clinging to a roof, for example – resemble the remote
precision of the fragments of narrative or description Kafka jotted between
passages of anguished self-analysis. But the effect is more general. Fisher's
city is perceptually akin to the evanescent Paris of Breton's *Nadja*, a book
which describes (rather than enacts) the effect of the surrealist method of
associative mental release upon observations. This can be seen in simple
trompe l'oeil; what at first appears, to the narrator, to be an embracing
couple on a station platform metamorphoses into 'a stout engine-driver',
the lovers' arms turning into 'a small brown paper parcel' under his arm
(*DLD*, p. 22). Taken as a whole, the city is most characteristically seen as 'a
composite monster, its unfeeling surfaces matted with dust' (*DLD*, p. 23).
Before this sensation becomes oppressive, an imaginative transformation is
effected, as

> the creature began to divide and multiply. At crossings I could see people made of
> straws, rags, cartons, the stuffing of burst cushions, kitchen refuse. Outside the Grand
> Hotel, a long-boned carrot-haired girl with glasses, loping along, and with strips of
> bright colour, rich, silky green and blue, in her soft clothes. For a person made of
> such scraps she was beautiful. (*DLD*, p. 23)

Fisher has said, 'I have to make the city strange in order to move my mind in
it at all.'[12] This de-Anglicizing is related directly here, by Fisher, to the Russian
formalist technique of defamilarization. 'Art is a way of experiencing the artfulness of an object,' writes Shklovsky; 'the object itself is not important'.[13]

Fisher's delight in the vision of the girl made of scraps remains faithful to the prolonging of perception: she is made artful. However, as an object she, and the city out of which she is conjured, *is* important to Fisher, a facet of his technique to which I shall return.

A poem from the 1970s, 'Paraphrases', contains a spoof letter from a schoolteacher, whose desire for immediately naturalizable poetry that may be taught to GCE pupils with ease, is gently mocked. She accuses Fisher of '*holding something back*' in what she calls the 'interestingly titled/ "Starting to Make a Tree"' from *City* (*DLD*, p. 114).

'Starting to Make a Tree' carries a title like the lyrics, but it is presented as blocked prose. The grammatical unit, at one point, does not coincide with the lineation of the 'paragraphs'. It may owe something to similar poems in prose written by Turnbull about this time, although it may be usefully described as an example of what more recently has been called 'poet's prose'.[14] This text, by its assertive hybridity, draws attention to itself formally, and to its thematic re-negotiations of the whole of *City*'s impulse to discover a 'single world', to turn the artfulness of defamiliarization to a social purpose. The text describes in fastidious stages, a group of people apparently manufacturing a tree from 'a great flock mattress; two carved chairs; cement; chicken-wire; tarpaulin; a smashed barrel; lead piping; leather of all kinds; and many small things'; the same detritus of the city that constitutes the carrot-haired girl (*DLD*, p. 25). The poem is partly a riddle, the most ancient form of defamiliarization, or 'holding something back'. How the city achieved its devastated condition is hinted at by two 'clues': the 'chemical blue of the soil' suggests toxic contamination; the 'flatness of the horizon on all sides except the north' suggests the demolition described elsewhere, but behind both is the possibility of post-apocalyptic survivalism (*DLD*, p. 25). Whatever the case, building the tree would be a genuine human act as against the inhuman austerity of the city described elsewhere in both realist and defamiliarized terms. Instead of being made from new materials, like the new buildings, it is a kind of tribal fetish, a communal junk sculpture. Ian Gregson argues that this junk sculpting 'works self-referentially to show what Fisher was attempting in composing *City*'.[15] Certainly *City* is an assemblage: 'Like each material gathered ... each bit of subject-matter that makes up *City* is a stubbornly diffuse and singular material derived originally from the local environment.'[16] This is only partly true, since Gregson ignores the aspect of community in these preparations for making. The

narrator is for once a meticulous observer, who is also part of the population of this primitive-futuristic Birmingham; the tribe is preparing to radically transform its environment, and the first person plural becomes the
dominant pronoun. The tree significantly is to be made in the image of the
human being: 'We were, nonetheless, a little excited, and hindered the women
at their cooking in our anxiety to know whose armpit and whose groin
would help us most in the modelling of the bole, and the thrust of the
boughs' (*DLD*, p. 25). This making, as Silkin has noted, is charged with 'sly
sexuality'.[17] An erotico-aesthetic pleasure principle suggests that this monument might represent, however problematically, human beauty, to amelio-
rate the composite monstrosity of the city. The text ends as the hope is
expressed – they never actually make the tree – as the tribe plans, and dis-
cusses 'how we could best use' the parts to assemble the non-functional
fetish (*DLD*, p. 26). 'Our tree was to be very beautiful' (*DLD*, p. 26). The
eventual ordering, like the narrator's earlier rag-bag defamiliarizations of
the 'beautiful', is going to be aesthetic. Yet it offers a utopian but un-real-
ized vision of the single world. Defamiliarization, far from merely distanc-
ing and aestheticizing, makes the city more civic, by de-Anglicizing the
signs of its specious democracy, which are presented in its prose sections.

As the earliest extended work of the British Poetry Revival, *City* stands as
an impressive attempt to chart urban realities of the late 1950s when post-
war austerity was breaking down, in a far from realistic style. Even though
it occasionally fails, its use of poetry, prose and poet's prose points to formal
innovations to come, both in Fisher's own work and in others'.

Interiors: Unscheduled Things

Fisher's subsequent works involving prose are generally hybrid forms or
poet's prose; he has seldom turned to a formalized genre, such as prose
fiction, nor to a fluid one such as prose poetry. They are nearly always the
result of schemata or systems of writing developed solely for the purposes of
generating themselves. The results of adopting these experimental processes
and procedures are Fisher's most formally daring texts, which often with-
draw from the topological and social concerns that are sometimes privileged in readings of his poetry. Fisher's partial renunciation of lyric from
the mid-1950s onwards was a way of accommodating his own lack of faith

in the prestige forms of the empirical lyricism of the Movement Orthodoxy, and to engage with formal means.

Interiors with Various Figures, composed in the early 1960s, is mostly
lineated prose, with indented second and subsequent lines. They look at
first like the long cadences of Whitman or Ginsberg but are, in fact,
'antimetrical', according to Fisher.[18] Like 'Starting to Make a Tree', they
project what Fisher usefully calls a 'head voice ... they are not articulated at
all, although they are dramatic'.[19] Both of these examples contributed to the
subsequent development of Fisher's verse, as metrical contours are loosened
in response to the growing demands of this voice. Most surprisingly, the
conceptual movement of the prose of *Interiors* is derived from 'reading the
English translation and just getting the crack of' Wittgenstein's *Tractatus
Logico-Philosophicus*.[20] Fisher adapted 'the idea of a proposition which is
about to hold firm and to be expanded or qualified quite formally', in his
reading of that work. 'I was just making forms with remarks' – Wittgenstein's
own term for his later propositions[21] – 'which, if written tightly, were my
units'.[22]

> Of all the rooms, this is a very small room.
>
> I cannot tell if it was he who painted the doors this colour; himself
> who lit the fire just before I arrived.
>
> (*DLD*, p. 33)

Given the concerns of the pieces – the relationship between various figures
in various interiors, as here in 'The Small Room' – it seems that Fisher was
simply deriving a form, but, as we shall see, he shares some concerns with
the remarkable book that permitted the poem. Although he is not one of
those discussed in Marjorie Perloff's *Wittgenstein's Ladder*, he joins that large
company of twentieth-century writers who have turned to that philosopher
either for a poetics or for 'lyric paradigms', as Perloff puts it; [23] it is interesting
to compare Fisher's adaptation of propositional form with the parodic and
poetic uses Rosmarie Waldrop makes of it in her 1987 book *The Reproduction of Profiles*, which 'writes back', to Wittgenstein's propositions.[24]

Although Fisher sees a strict logic and linearity in Wittgenstein's work,
one which agrees with the philosopher's contention that his 'remarks' move
'in a natural order and without breaks', Wittgenstein warns the reader of
occasions of 'sudden change, jumping from one topic to another',[25] yet privately his urge to order was more desperate, as he confided: 'Forcing my

thoughts into an ordered sequence is a torment for me.'[26] Perloff's investigation of the famous numbering of the *Tractatus* (which *Interiors* does not emulate) shows that its progress is not as austerely logical, nor as 'firm', as Fisher supposed. She concludes that its inconsistencies operate as a 'clinamen, a bend or swerve where logic gives way to mystery'.[27] Fisher's propositions, although not formally logical, have a similar temporary 'firmness', a provisionality, so that the 'expansion' is not always linear and we experience a Wittgensteinian 'jump' or a Perloffian 'swerve' into mystery and defamiliarization. Indeed, Fisher has a practical but radical sense of his formalism: 'The only point of using any form is to create freedom forms and not to do things about the imposition of order on chaos and this sort of rubbish.'[28] The necessity to escape deadening conformism suggests the attractions of a non-literary model.

The title, *Interiors with Various Figures*, stresses a painterly analogy, the emphasis upon the visual found here, and the procedures of painters in creating sequences from the same objects, particularly their ways of organizing visual elements systematically or in sequences or even by superimposition, as variations. Indeed, Fisher's collection of pictorial images was used as stimulus. The 'figures' – usually pairs – are in relationships, and it is important to remember the wilfulness of the word 'various', for I am not convinced by Mottram's argument that the poems are 're-estimating married life',[29] nor as certain as Needham, in considering 'The Small Room', that 'one is invited to identify this woman trapped in a small room, with the woman in "Experimenting" who had wanted more walls'.[30] The identities of speakers are often indeterminate, though the sense of claustrophobia or what Mottram calls 'the possible insanity of allowing hallucinatory vision of ordinary things and daily relationships to happen at all' is pervasive.[31]

The function of each interior is to effect a transformation of these 'various' persons. In 'The Small Room' the occupant has sovereignty over the room and thus over the person in it:

> He is allowed to buy the same sort of electricity as everybody else, but his shirt, his milk bottle, his electricity resemble one another more than they resemble others of their kind. A transformation at his door, at his voice, under his eye.
>
> (*DLD*, p. 34)

There is the suspicion that 'he' has willed the person there for the room's unspeakable event; the poem possibly defamiliarizes the experience of a hair-cut though it could be something more sinister: 'Shave the hairs from my body. Which of us thought of this thing?' (*DLD*, p. 34). The room seems a closed system of correspondences, threatening the person's integrity. In the poem to which Needham compares this, 'Experimenting', the most dramatized of the texts, there is much play upon the role of the walls in protecting the stabilizing interior from the 'void' beyond. The woman, certainly nervous, but perhaps neurotic, claustrophobic, even agoraphobic, asks "'At least – why can't you have more walls?"/Really scared. I see she means it.' (*DLD*, p. 32.)

The narrator can offer small comfort ('there's one wall each, they can't outnumber us'), can only remind her of the formlessness in the exterior: 'our situation's better than beyond the backyard, where indeed the earth seems to stop pretty abruptly and not restart'(*DLD*, p. 33). This is a terrifying vision of Wittgenstein's observation that 'A spatial object must be situated in infinite space'.[32] There are interiors within interiors, claustrophobia within claustrophobia. In 'Experimenting', for example, the speech of the woman is an enclosed space, a trap:

> So I have to put my face into her voice, a shiny baize-lined
>   canister that says all round me, staring in:
> 'I've tried tonight. This place!'
>
>   (*DLD*, p. 32)

This relationship is conducted not so much by interpersonal reactions but through the objects of intersubjective space, 'Trying it on, though, going on about the milk bottle, tableleg,/The little things.' (*DLD*, p. 32.) But this affects the man's perceptions: 'Only a little twilight is left washing around outside, her unease interfering with it as I watch.' (*DLD*, p. 32.) Yet the indeterminacy of tone allows one to read this poem (and others) differently. It could be a description of a staged drama, or it could be a deliberate melodrama, given the woman's ejaculations. The possibility of humour and parody is signalled by the male's question to the female: 'What have you been reading then?' The answer might include Harold Pinter, an intimate text by Charles Bukowski, 'A Game of Chess' from Eliot's *The Waste Land*, or even the neo-Romanticism that Fisher had rejected earlier in his career; how else to explain the hilarious litany: 'And when the moon with horror ... Comes blundering blind up the side tonight ... we hear it bump and scrape'? (*DLD*, p. 33).

The motifs recur, repeated deliberately as part of the work's procedure, on the model of a painter using the same studio objects in several paintings.

Each interior contains some of the oppressive elements, a fact which binds the texts together: alcoholic drinks, milk bottles, haircuts, as well as reappearing baize, and various cupboards, carpets, doors, walls and windows.

For example, the lampshade and the light switch – even electricity itself in 'The Small Room' – are aspects of one recurrence: the light bulb. In 'The Small Room', the paranoiac narrator remarks, 'That bulb again. It has travelled even here.' (*DLD*, p. 33.) Transferred between locations, it becomes a universal, not simply the usual permissible recurrences of simile and metaphor. The woman's fingers in 'Experimenting' are 'white like unlit electric bulbs', (*DLD*, p. 32) and such repetition, painterly in procedure, also rehearses the ultimately threatening existential reality behind Wittgenstein's cool proposition: 'If I know an object I also know all its possible occurrences in space.'[33] But what is theorized as plenitude is experienced as a world of limited, conspiring elements or 'unscheduled things' as one poem puts it (*DLD*, p. 40). *Interiors* suggests finally that 'Objects are what is unalterable and subsistent; their configuration is what is changing and unstable',[34] something which disturbs the integrity of an observing self.

Improvising on the Cut Page

The Cut Pages was composed on a set number of sheets sliced from a 'diary of demoralization'[35] which contained personal matters and from which Fisher, now rejecting the stance of unwilling hero, wished to be free. It was, significantly, this work of 1970 which broke a four-year writer's block, and Fisher's habit of pessimistic introspection.

Whereas the bleak diaries had been the composed record of actions that had already happened, an improvisation is the act of what happens, during composition, a cutting loose. The programme of having 'no programme … produced rapid changes of direction', as Fisher said (*CP86*, p. 8). Fisher writes of having 'no programme beyond the principle that it should not know where its next meal was coming from' (*CP86*, p. 8). There are frequent discontinuities between paragraphs. The free improvised jazz practised by Evan Parker, Derek Bailey and others progresses by complete changes of musical dynamic, the deliberate avoidance of pre-established patterns. When Fisher remarks, in what appears to be an embedded statement of intent, 'This discontinuity is my discontinuity', (*CP86*, p. 30) he is not far from Parker, who is quoted in Bailey's book *Improvisation*, as saying, 'I change, the music changes'.[36] This is neither an admission of self-centredness, nor of formlessness. Another passage from the text reads: 'Laws for the empty. Patterns for the free.' (*CP86*, p. 34.) *The Cut Pages* necessitates the abandonment of concepts of form based upon fixed structures in favour of a fulfilling (the opposite of 'empty') pattern making activity, in favour of an improvisation coterminous with the print of the paragraph, or the space of the page.

Page-space is as crucial in *The Cut Pages* as it is for concrete poetry. Not only is the cut page the performance space, the paragraphs, varying in length from one word to several conventionally-formed sentences, lack the solidity of the blocks of earlier works. The paragraphs end without full stops and seem to hang on the page. The drop to the capital letter of the subsequent paragraph often connects with redirected energies. Implications for the book presentation of the texts are not lost on Fisher, comparing it to his other works.

> It is out of scale to the rest of the writing ... it occupies an enormous amount of space for what is transacted in it ... I could see it better as a free-standing thing, preferably artistically done and certainly not a small print text.[37]

This question of the 'ratio of didactic event to space'[38] suggests that the 14 'pages' are lightly textured, but, in fact, they are dense. Fisher's unfulfilled desire for an 'artistically done' quality art edition with large print would realize the isolation of the paragraphs, make them available for bracketed contemplation, break the flow of the reading eye.[39] When Fisher remarks, 'Occasionally artists take images out of it, I would like to have it so it would work for artists', he seems to imply a process of freeze-framing and extraction, the opposite of the improvisation that produced it.[40] This is possible with improvised writing since its reception can never be as durational as music.

The Cut Pages is, as Needham points out, 'an attack on those who would impose rigid structures upon their experience', the emptiness of 'Law'.[41] The opening lines of the work are more obviously patterned than most. If there is a thematic focus it is upon notions of patterning and transformation, structure its object of attack. Its parallel phrases offer verbal emphases lacking elsewhere, its visual arrangement the most unconventional of the book:

Coil	If you see the coil hidden in this pattern, you're colour-blind
	Pale patterns, faded card, coral card, faded card, screen card, window fade
Whorl	If you can see this word and say it without hesitation you're deaf
	Then we can get on with frame
Frameless	Meat-rose, dog-defending, trail-ruffling

(CP86, p. 13)

The reader might recognize here a reference to the cards used for testing colour-blindness, a quadruple coil, present only in a pattern, as later in the section: 'If you can see the numeral 88 in the pattern' (*CP86*, p. 14). This also suggests the 88 keys of a piano which demand to be patterned in performance, and a pattern in a wallpaper: 'The Old 88; the wallpaper piano' (*CP86*, p. 14). The mind moves in this way, when freed to follow its conceptualizations, not as a stream of consciousness, but as a *conscious* set of jumps, even as articulatory acts of language rather than of reference. The effect is to preserve that performative saying, to resist the naturalizable statement. As the text comments elsewhere, perhaps ironically: 'He will not refer, but will act.' (*CP86*, p. 22.)

A series of associative patterns or leaps, along with the sonic echoes of cs, fs, and ds, the 'patterns' and 'cards' of the second paragraph, for example, show not the results (whatever that could be), but the working, of such thinking, ending with the filmic 'window fade' which seems to close visuality. 'Whorl', an almost synonym and almost rhyme for 'coil' (as well as 'word'), is foregrounded in its audial materiality; it is difficult to aspirate its 'h' sound.

The generative principle for such prose is not only improvisation, but repetition and parallelism, such as in the opening lines (and in certain of the *Interiors*). There are frequent passages of lists with repeated nouns, as well as patterns of repetition which are similar to the incremental, intonational flow found in speech: 'On the march. March a path to march on.' (*CP86*, p. 15) Yet the text is not dramatic, and this apparent speech patterning reflects its improvisatory origin. Such marking, particularly noun repetition rather than the deployment of pronouns, exists in speech as a way of keeping the object of attention clear if the context is not. Conversely,

pronouns are used just as often without nouns, a feature of speech when the
context is obvious, or shared. The text evokes these structures of self-evi-
dence, although the discourse is far from clear. Additionally, there are concepts that repeat throughout the book, perhaps deliberately fed back into
the improvisation, to do with patterning, and transformation, part of its
metaphorical skein: cracks, growth, frames, breath, and corrosion.

The remark, 'Then we can get on with frame' teases at the edge of the
idiomatic, but the lack of plural on the word 'frame', and the absence of an
article for the noun, work against some skeletal plot paraphrase concerning
an eye test for new glasses. 'If you can see' does suggest the voice of an
optician, but on its second occurrence, it is transformed parodically. A frame
will also fix (another repeated word), and the rejection of frame as concept
introduces the reader to a series of alarming possibilities, even of perceptual
and referential anarchy, 'frameless' and therefore unbounded. The reader
may sense the 'dog-rose' and the dog's tail in the word 'trail', in the last line
above; the 'defending' suggests a guard dog, but this dog is more defended
than defending, a characteristic reversal. Its significance here lies in the sense
of its own process, the search for pattern. The entire project of *The Cut
Pages* is to invite a reader to improvise, to see patterns where normally there
are none; it issues a challenging 'if you can see' that remains conditional,
that refuses the fixity of conclusion and lengthens the process of naturalization, keeps the text in the realm of the Levinasian saying while offering the
fixity, indeed materiality, of the page, its mute and inevitable saidness.

The Cut Pages is Fisher's most formally audacious work, which puts him
in the company of some of the American language poets with their poet's
prose or new sentence work, as Marjorie Perloff has realized: 'Fisher's "cutting" of the page, with its removal of words from their "planned situations",
anticipated a mode that became prominent in the US, ... at least a decade
after Fisher had written the (evidently unknown to them) *Cut Pages*.'[42] It
can also be seen in the context of' The British Poetry Revival as close to the
hybrid and improvised prose in Gael Turnbull's *Trampoline* (1968), which
may have suggested a model, and to the improvisations of Tom Raworth,
particularly 'Stag Skull Mounted', composed within months of Fisher's 1970
pieces; it may also be seen as generally predictive of the use of page space in
poets writing after Fisher.[43]

It is Writing

Roy Fisher writes a poetry that foregrounds its own artificiality, and this itself is foregrounded in the poems of the 1970s, published in *The Thing About Joe Sullivan* in 1978. Indeed, foregrounding, in the technical sense, involves 'all salient linguistic phenomena which in some way cause the reader's attention to shift from the paraphrasable content of a message ... to a focus on the message itself.'[44] It resists naturalization, in a way of holding a text in suspension, so that its qualities of saying are extended, its fixity in the meaning of the said, delayed.

'The Only Image' consists of a series of simple propositions concerning its opening observation, and is as fundamental to Fisher's poetics as Williams' similar framing of the red wheelbarrow, or even Stevens' of his snowman, are to theirs:

> Salts work their way
> to the outside of a plant pot
> and dry white.
> (*DLD*, p. 106)

This becomes 'the only image' of the title, the only counter in its metaphoric change. 'The rest,' the poem states, 'comes as a variable that shifts/in any part, or vanishes' (*DLD*, p. 106). Linguistic relations, particularly those of metaphor and simile, are as arbitrary and free as they had been in *The Cut Pages*, although here Fisher is remarking upon the process. The only image can be related, through comparison, to any other. (The 'salts' are also, paradoxically, a metaphor for the possibilities of metaphor.)

> I can
> compare what I like to the salts,
> to the pot, if there's a pot ...
>
> The salts I can compare
> to anything there is.
> Anything.
> (*DLD*, p. 106)

Metaphor has a clearly subversive, rather than decorative, rhetorical role. In Ricoeur's formulation, it

> brings together things that do not go together and by means of the apparent

misunderstanding it causes a new, hitherto unnoticed, relation of meaning to spring
up between the terms that previous systems of classification had ignored or not allowed.[45]

Fisher has called the poem a 'formal "work-out"', adding, 'For me it's a
work of delight in making the picture of the salts on the plant-pot and
using them for that great void' of linguistic relation which lies open to the
poet, the general economy of language's surplus; since it can be compared
to anything, no metaphor or simile need be proffered.[46] It is this facility of
language that allows for the saying to remain elusive before the power of the
said that must inevitably embody it, a game of hide and seek between the
metaphor's fixed vehicle and its indeterminate tenors.

'It is Writing' defiantly asserts its textuality; it argues for a poetry that
frustrates moral interpretation, that implicitly supports the argument of
'The Only Image'. Poetry becomes foregrounded as the subject of its own
discourse, even while the temptations of artifice (in being able to transform
suffering) are being ostensibly disavowed.

> I mistrust the poem in its hour of success,
> a thing capable of being
> tempted by ethics into the wonderful.
>   (*DLD*, p. 108)

Similar scepticism about the function of poetry is evident in the conditional
opening lines of 'If I Didn't', which denies the possibility of foregrounding its
artifice, in one sense, in the very act of undertaking it in another.

> If I didn't dislike
> mentioning works of art
>
> I could say
> the poem has always
> already started, the parapet
> snaking away, its grey line guarding
> the football field and the sea
>
> – the parapet
> has always already started
> snaking away, its grey line
> guarding the football field and the sea.
>   (*DLD*, p. 112)

It is almost as though it were not possible to deal with the epiphany of involuntary memory ('the looking down/ between the moving frames') without 'mentioning works of art'. (*DLD*, p. 112) The re-lineation of the repeated report of the perception of the parapet foregrounds the fact of its necessary mediation by a 'work of art'. The 'poem' here contrasts with its anterior memory which, as memory, is also an event. The enjambement of the first occurrence of this phrase attempts to disguise the continuous presence of a particular moment of recollection.

Part of Fisher's impulse to de-Anglicize England is realized through foregrounding the aestheticism of the gaze; years after *City* he is still on the number 15 bus, thinking with Birmingham and the Midlands. 'In the Black Country' uses the simple declarative style Fisher developed during the 1970s, and even opens with a simile, metaphor's weak cousin.

> Dudley from the Castle keep
> looks like a town by Kokoschka,
>
> one town excited
> by plural perspectives
>
> into four of five
> landscapes of opportunity
>
> each one on offer
> under a selection of skies.
>   (*P55–87*, p. 106)

Fisher distances the empirical Dudley by prolonging the reader's apprehension of the town, a classic act of defamiliarization. The last line, 'Art's marvellous', is sardonic about the use of art to achieve this, even while the reader is made aware of the possibilities of the actual Midlands town through the incongruous art of Kokoschka; the temptation of the wonderful is suspended. Dudley achieves 'clarity' through the very 'confusion' of its confrontation with the expressionist style of Kokoschka's landscapes; the reader's perception of both has been revitalized and altered; an alternative ethic to that of the wonderful and the marvellous is asserted.

There is a certain instability in the textual voice that 'mistrusts' the poem. It is most often a disembodied voice, a position, that the reader reads. As Barthes writes, 'Linguistically, the author is never more than the instance saying *I*; language knows a "subject", not a "person".'[47] Fisher dramatizes this lightly, in a poem which, complete with title and dedication, opens:

Of the Empirical Self and for Me
for M.E.

In my poems there's seldom
any *I* or *you* –

  you know me, Mary.
      (*DLD*, p. 109)

Thus the poetic discourse opens self-consciously with a series of puns on its title and the name of the dedicatee, a playfulness at the level of the signifier unusual in Fisher's work that represents the unstable nature of the self that is barely represented in the text. The empirical self is cut off from its own 'me'. 'Me' is also the 'M.E.', the addressed Mary of the text, who is also, 'linguistically' as Barthes would say, the position 'you'. Pronominal usage of 'I' and 'you' is rejected, but only by their very assertion; 'the "I" is always located unlocatably', as Bell and Lland assert.[48] Each becomes a possible position for the other and the first person plural is fastidiously avoided to preclude intersubjective agreement. However, despite this playful beginning, rhetorical austerity returns; attention shifts from the instability of the self to the nature of that self's self-confirming apparatus of sense data and perceptual instabilities. Merleau Ponty claimed that the blending of intersubjective perceptions confirmed the world; Fisher seems to argue the opposite. The poem is concerned, moreover, with that area of tension between the fictive and the real already examined, though now from the point of view of the discrepancies between the self and its perceptual construction in making the world. The night, innocently presented at first, nevertheless limits perception until the empirical selves are once more unstable: 'two invisible ghosts' (*DLD*, p. 109). The senses have defeated their own claims to clarity and replaced it with comic confusion.

  A tall man passes
  with what looks like a black dog.
  He stares at the milk, and says
      It's nice to be able
      to drink a cup of
      coffee outside at night ...
          (*DLD*, p. 109)

Once the man has vanished, this confusion prompts the question, ' So – / What kind of a world?' (*DLD*, p. 109). The world is constructed by agents of perception with all their phenomenological indeterminacies; reality is a spectral trace, a mark (those frequent Fisher lexes), something almost artificial, photographically printed: 'lightning-strokes repeatedly/bang out their reality-prints' (*DLD*, p. 109).

'The Poet's Message' continues this enquiry by opening with two parallel questions about the function of subjectivity and text, what kind of 'message' and what kind of 'man/comes in a message?' (*DLD*, p. 108). The second of the questions seems more engaging and elicits not so much a clear response as a teasing confession. Its tone is assertive, while its own 'message' – the first unanswered question – is curiously oblique and conditional.

> I would
> get into a message if I could
> and come complete
> to where I can see
> what's across the park:
> and leave my own position
> empty for you in its frame.
> (*DLD*, p. 108)

The self is only the validating principle of the poem insofar as it is an absence, or a 'position' in Barthes' sense. It stands behind the point where the scene focuses on the artificial retina of a camera, and its 'message' would ideally be the unmediated view of a park, which it knows to be an impossibility. The view is blocked by the absent self's paradoxical self-consciousness. Not much of a man comes in a message, but enough, in this case, to frustrate realistic description.

City had, of course, used memories of a vanishing Birmingham, but the role of memory and its loss, its correlative shadow, become problematic in Fisher's work of the 1970s. Most of these poems are quite slender with little evidence of metrical contour, and consist of brief, almost gnomic, propositions upon their subjects. In the case of 'On the Open Side', Fisher attempts 'getting Proust down to matchbox proportions', as he jokingly put it.[49] Not only is the memory fleeting and involuntary, it seems eternal, prelinguistic, and – more importantly – autonomous:

> – the other life,
> the endless other life,
> endless beyond the beginning

... holds and suddenly presents

a particular, but totally insignificant scene to the mind (*P55–87*, p. 111). 'That was all,' the poem concludes, 'Something the other life wanted – / I hadn't kept it.' (*P55–87*, p. 111.) The self is disrupted by this autonomous image, strangely significant with its haunting insignificance, its doubtful value. Elsewhere, in surprise, the narrator says,

> So I start
> at the single recurrence of a counter
> I expect never to need.
>   (*P55–87*, p. 135)

Unlike Proust, the recurrence does not involve the recovery of the past. Fisher is 'fascinated with memory,' because of its non utilitarian nature; 'I'm impressed by its disregard for time and narrative sense. Or even for the simplest categories of thought'.[50] The 'counter' can't be used or exchanged in anything like the market this economic metaphor suggests. Its patterns of association offer not the old, but the new; they do not so much recover the past, as flood the present with the blank screen of nostalgia.

In many ways the obsessive concern with Birmingham (the narrator's need to think with it as yet another counter) has dictated that later poems, such as the more discursive 'Wonders of Obligation', 'Introit: 12 November 1958' from *A Furnace*, his most ambitious long work of 1986, and 'Six Texts for a Film' (1994), are re-memberings of the body of the city, and constitute what Peter Barry calls Fisher's '"composite-epic" of urban material'.[51]

'Handsworth Liberties' is yet another such attempt, in *The Thing About Joe Sullivan*, and is one of Fisher's most impressive sequences. Like all such sequences, the 16 parts do not develop narratively, as they negotiate adolescent memories of particular locations in Birmingham that Fisher associated with particular pieces of music. Indeed it is the street that dominates the sequence, not the people, who appear only as traces upon it: 'The place is full of people./ It is thin. They are moving' (*P55–87*, p. 118). Even when

> A mild blight, sterility,
> the comfort of others'
> homecoming

is invoked, it is still the incomplete yet immobile environment that claims the poem's attention:

> apart from the pavement
> asphalt and grit are spread
> for floors; there are railings,
> tarred. It is all
> unfinished and still.
>   (*P55–87*, p. 121)

Other poems from the sequence consciously de-Anglicize memories of the 1940s, as had parts of *City*. The procedure to refuse to name objects which then appear indeterminate, a form of semantic indeterminacy developed from *The Cut Pages,* is introduced to deal with the characteristic material. Thus the presentation of the city horizon, which certainly resembles the northern prospect of one of the 'clues' of 'Starting to Make a Tree', 'pale new towers in the north/right on the line', operates here through non-descriptiveness, as it were (*P55–87*, p. 117). One of Fisher's favourite descriptive adjectives is 'non-descript'.

> It all
> radiates outwards
> in a lightheaded air
> without image.
>   (*P55–87*, p. 118)

Realism is forced, not just into the strategies of foregrounded artifice, but into a register of 'waves', since there is no presentable 'image', just this version of the 'traces' and 'marks' presented in other poems. Occasionally a 'flicker' might reveal a partial, but insignificant, image.

> There is a world.
> It has been made
> out of the tracks of waves
> broken against the rim
> and coming back awry; at the final
> flicker they are old grass and fences.
>   (*P55–87*, p. 117)

Sometimes, 'At the end of the familiar', there is stark realist enumeration but with the barest of elaboration:

> brick, laurels, a cokeheap

across from the cemetery gate –
a printing works and a small
cycle factory; hard tennis courts.
        (*P55–87*, p. 121)

But this exists in a state of tension with formalist abstraction: 'With not even a whiff of peace/tranquilities ride the dusk' (*P55–87*, p. 119).

Shklovsky's formalism is easily mistaken for pure aestheticism, especially when he declares that the 'object' that undergoes defamiliarization is not important.[52] As has been seen the object – usually Birmingham – for Fisher *is* very important; there are social and political reasons for his de-Angliciz-ing. The Russian formalists themselves were rigorously criticized, both by Trotsky and the Bakhtin Circle before the Stalinist years enveloped them all. Shklovsky's 1940 volume *Mayakovsky and His Circle* was a rejoinder to that criticism, in which he reformulates his concept of defamiliarization. He repeats part of his 1917 essay, particularly Tolstoy's claims that 'if the entire life of many people is lived unconsciously, then that life, in effect, did not exist'.[53] This has an obvious existential and moral dimension often missed in readings of the original essay. Shklovsky developed this (opportunely) with an examination of some statements of Lenin. His conclusion is that Lenin took an interest in 'eccentricism in art, a skeptical attitude toward the conventional, and the illogic of the unusual'.[54] Although Shklovsky is trying to prove that 'eccentric' art can be 'realistic', he is also showing its political potential, that 'the absurdity of the capitalist world could be shown through methods of eccentric art'.[55] One avenue for this radical art would lead to the dramatic alienation techniques of Brecht's poetics of the theatre; the other would concentrate upon destroying habitual associations within thought and language. In 'Handsworth Liberties' – the pun on the second word is intentional – moments of eccentric illumination occur during

a trip between two locations
ill-conceived, raw, surreal
outgrowths of common sense, almost
merging one into the other.
        (*P55–87*, p. 118)

Such a meeting of the extraordinary within the quotidian produces

on an ordinary day a brief
lightness, charm between realities;

on a good day, a break
life can flood in and fill.
>   (*P55–87*, p. 119)

As Shklovsky argued, the most radical art works are not those that thematize revolution or class war. Indeed thematizing itself imposes a limit upon the possibilities of expression.

Memories and things in Fisher's poetry of this time are often invested with an additional autonomy from reference; things achieve a necessary freedom as the recognisable world is phenomenologically reduced:

Travesties of the world
come out of the fog
and rest at the boundary.
>   (*P55–87*, p. 122)

These 'travesties' are not quite visual or tactile, but synaesthetic, evanescent; they are only

strange vehicles,
forms of outlandish factories
carried by sound through the air,
they stop at the border,
which is no sort of place;
then they go back.
>   (*P55–87*, p. 122)

Although 'they come/out of a lesser world', they offer an approach to perceptual freedom: 'I shall go with them sometimes/till the journey dissolves under me' (*P55–87*, p. 122).

Fisher has stated that the 'political content' of his work consists of 'descriptions of consciousness, reminders of the complexity of the perceptual mechanisms which show us the world.'[56] 'For me,' he adds, 'it is the private memories and private fantasies of individuals which actually create the public, social world.'[57] An art that consciously defamiliarizes breaks the false perceptual automatism which habitualizes readers to a particular version of social reality. In the fourth poem of the sequence there is yet another trip unnamed between locations, one in which all that is solid melts into a world of exchange which is not primarily economic:

Something has to happen here.
There must be change.

It's the place
from which the old world fell away
leaning in its dark hollow.

We can go there
into the seepage,
the cottage garden with hostas
in a chimneypot

or somewhere here
in the crowd of exchanges
we can change.
                    (*P55–87*, p. 118)

As I have shown in the previous chapter, Marcuse's *Essay on Liberation* had faithfully described, and contributed to, the utopian aspirations of the underground of the 1960s, and was partly inspired by a reading of Shklovsky. *The Aesthetic Dimension*, published in English in 1978, the same year as *The Thing About Joe Sullivan*, belongs to the years of the failure of the ideals of the New Sensibility (and to the years of the British Poetry Revival's retreat). Marcuse's earlier work hoped for the establishment of an *aesthetic ethos* in social reality; the later work concentrates upon aesthetics *per se*, upon the new object for art that others, such as Tom Raworth, were attempting to approximate, but Marcuse admits the 'element of despair' in the 'retreat into a world of fiction' from the realm of radical praxis.[58] Yet he says, 'The encounter with the *truth of art* happens in the estranging language and images which make perceptible, visible, and audible that which is no longer, or not yet, perceived, said, and heard in everyday life.'[59] In contradistinction to the essentially conservative use of autonomy by Peter Ackroyd in *Notes for a New Culture*, Marcuse believes, 'The autonomy of art contains the categorical imperative: "things must change".'[60] Fisher offers the correlative: 'we can change' amid his aestheticized perceptual data.

Although both Fisher and Marcuse are in agreement upon this point, the nature of the desired change is debatable. Marcuse writes as a Marxist, although from an unorthodox position; not only is he utopian, but he has stood much previous crude Marxist aesthetics, which Marcuse characterizes as simplistically regarding text as the direct evidence of a dominant ideology, on its head.[61] The problem with this view of the autonomy in contradiction of *The Aesthetic Dimension* is that he cannot tie it to a specific Marxist futurology any more than could Shklovsky. And it is precisely

Shklovsky's insistence upon 'skepticism' that prevents this. Fisher has de-scribed his poems as 'sceptical formulations of life ... an anarchic response to ... the whole mass of tiny interlaced circumstances that carry you along, make the present in which you exist'.[62] During a reading Fisher once re-marked that while the messages of his co-reader – former Child of Albion and socialist Adrian Mitchell – 'were very clear ... whatever political ele-ment was in my poems was apparently too obscure to see'.[63] 'That's non-sense,' Mitchell interjected: 'Your politics are absolutely apparent ...One or another form of anarchism.'[64] But Fisher has warned, 'Not that you'll find me a Marxist ... or an anarchist in any formal sense;' [65] the scepticism of a writer who declares, 'No system describes the world' necessarily runs deep (*DLD*, p. 90).[66]

By the end of the 1970s, defamiliarization in Fisher's work is no longer a technique only to de-Anglicize England, but is part of a general poetics of readerly engagement to resist naturalization. What Fisher's poems of this time are enacting is precisely Marcuse's utopian permission to say that which has yet to be said in everyday life, though Fisher characteristically formal-izes that in individual terms:

> As far as I see it, a poem has business to exist, really, if there's a reasonable chance that somebody may have his perceptions rearranged by having read it or having used it. The poem is always capable of being a subversive agent, psychologically, sensuously, however you like.'[67]

Notes

1   Roy Fisher, 'City', pp. 14–30, *City* (Worcester: Migrant Press, 1961) is a significantly differ-ent text to that published in Roy Fisher, *Poems 1955–1987* (Oxford: Oxford University Press, 1988), pp. 14–30, and reprinted in *The Dow Low Drop: New and Selected Poems* (Newcastle upon Tyne, 1996), pp. 13–30. Subsequent citations to this text, and others from this edition, in this chapter will be marked *DLD*. Citations to *Poems 1955–1987* will be marked *P55–87*. *City* started life as the residua of a prose work called 'The Citizen'. The arrangement of the 1961 edition was made by fellow-poet Michael Shayer. Fisher then re-arranged this assemblage to constitute the text now known under that title. My discussion of *City* here is more narrowly focused than my 'De-Anglicizing the Midlands: The Euro-pean Context of Roy Fisher's *City*', *English*, vol. 41, no. 169 (Spring 1992), pp. 49–70. In this article I analyse the realist prose passages more thoroughly, though my argument is essentially the same.

2   Roy Fisher, *Birmingham River* (Oxford: Oxford University Press, 1994), p. 11.

3   Roy Fisher, *Nineteen Poems and an Interview* (Pensnett: Grosseteste Press, 1975), p. 19. Parts
     of this interview are reprinted in *Interviews Through Time, and Selected Prose*, ed. Tony
     Frazer (Kentisbeare: Shearsman Books, 2000).
4   Eric Mottram, 'Conversation with Roy Fisher, *Saturday Morning*, 1 (1976), n.p. [p. 16] Parts
     of this interview are reprinted in *Interviews Through Time, and Selected Prose*.
5   A. Kingsley Weatherhead, *The British Dissonance* (Columbia and London: University of
     Missouri Press, 1983), p. 38.
6   *Ibid.*, p. 33.
7   Malcolm Bradbury, 'The Cities of Modernism' in *Modernism*, eds. Malcolm Bradbury and
     J. McFarlane (Harmondsworth: Penguin, 1976), pp. 96–104, at p. 99.
8   *Ibid.*, p. 100.
9   Roy Fisher, *Turning the Prism: An Interview with Roy Fisher by Robert Sheppard* (London:
     Toads Damp Press, 1986), p. 25. Parts of this interview are reprinted in *Interviews Through
     Time, and Selected Prose*.
10   *Ibid.*, p. 25.
11   *Ibid.*, p. 24.
12   *Ibid.*, pp. 9–10.
13   Viktor Shklovsky, 'Technique as Device', in *Russian Formalist Criticism*, ed. Lee T. Lemon
     and Marion J. Reis (Nebraska: University of Nebraska Press, 1965), p. 12.
14   Gael Turnbull's poems such as 'Six Fancies' in his *A Trampoline: Poems 1952–1964* (London:
     Cape Goliard, 1968), n.p. suggest this. See also David Miller, 'Heart of saying; the poetry of
     Gael Turnbull' in *New British Poetries*, eds. Robert Hampson and Peter Barry (Manchester:
     Manchester University Press, 1993), pp. 183–97. For 'poet's prose' see Stephen Fredman,
     Poet's Prose: The Crisis in American Verse (Cambridge: Cambridge University Press, 1983).
15   Ian Gregson, *Contemporary Poetry and Postmodernism: Dialogue and Estrangement*
     (Basingstoke: Macmillan, 1996), p. 176.
16   *Ibid.*, p. 176.
17   Jon Silkin, *The Life of Metrical and Free Verse in Twentieth-Century Poetry* (Basingstoke:
     Macmillan, 1997), p. 305.
18   Mottram, 'Conversation with Roy Fisher', [p.14].
19   *Ibid.*, [p. 15].
20   Fisher, *Turning the Prism*, p. 18.
21   Ludwig Wittgenstein, *Philosophical Investigations* (Oxford: Basil Blackwell, 1968), p. vi.
22   Fisher, *Turning the Prism*, p. 18.
23   Marjorie Perloff, *Wittgenstein's Ladder* (Chicago; University of Chicago Press, 1996), p. 200.
24   Rosmarie Waldrop, *The Reproduction of Profiles* (New York: New Directions, 1987)
25   Wittgenstein, *Philosophical Investigations*, p. vi.
26   Perloff, *Wittgenstein's Ladder*, p. 8.
27   *Ibid.*, p. 42.
28   Mottram, 'Conversation with Roy Fisher', [p. 11].
29   Eric Mottram, 'Roy Fisher's Work', *Stand*, 11:1 (1969–70) pp. 9–18, at p. 17.
30   J.D. Needham, 'Some Aspects of the Poetry of Roy Fisher', *Poetry Nation* 5 (1975), pp. 74–
     87, at p. 79.
31   Mottram, 'Roy Fisher's Work', p. 17.

32 Ludwig Wittgenstein, *Tractatus Logico-Philosophicus* (London: Routledge & Kegan Paul, 1961), p. 9.

33 *Ibid.*, p. 9.

34 *Ibid.*, p. 13.

35 Roy Fisher, *The Cut Pages* (London: Oasis Books/Shearsman Books, 1986), p. 9. This second edition is the one referred to in the text, and future citations will be marked *CP86*. The text was originally published in *The Cut Pages* (London: Fulcrum Press, 1971).

36 Quoted in Derek Bailey, *Improvisation* (Derbyshire: Moorland Publishing, 1980), p. 151.

37 Fisher, *Turning the Prism*, p. 20.

38 *Ibid.*, p. 20.

39 *Ibid.*, p 20.

40 *Ibid.*, p. 20.

41 Needham, 'Some Aspects of the Poetry of Roy Fisher', p. 84.

42 Marjorie Perloff, 'Cutting-Edge Poetics: Roy Fisher's "Language Book", in *The Thing about Roy Fisher* eds. John Kerrigan and Peter Robinson (Liverpool: Liverpool University Press, 2000), pp. 149–72, at p. 169.

43 See the improvisations 'Twenty Words, Twenty Days' in Turnbull, *A Trampoline*, n.p.

44 G.N. Leech, 'Foregrounding' in *A Dictionary of Modern Critical Terms* ed. Roger Fowler, (London and Boston: Routledge and Kegan Paul, 1973), p. 75.

45 Paul Ricoeur, *Interpretation Theory: Discourse and the Surplus of Meaning* (Texas: Christian University of Texas Press, 1976), p. 51.

46 Fisher, *Turning the Prism*, p. 15.

47 Roland Barthes, 'The Death of the Author', in *Image – Music – Text*, ed. Stephen Heath (London: Fontana, 1977), p. 145.

48 Ian F.A. Bell and Meriel Lland, 'Osmotic Investigations and Mutant Poems: An Americanist Poetic' in *The Thing About Roy Fisher*, eds., Kerrigan and Robinson, pp. 106–127, at p. 108.

49 Roy Fisher, speaking on the *Poetry Now* radio programme, BBC Radio 3, 20 November 1981.

50 *Ibid.*

51 Peter Barry, '"Birmingham's what I think with," Roy Fisher's Composite-Epic', *The Yale Review of Criticism*, vol. 13, no. 1 (2000), pp. 234–68, at p. 88.

52 Shklovsky, 'Technique as Device', p. 12.

53 Viktor Shklovsky, *Mayakovsky and his Circle* (London: Pluto Press, 1974), p. 114. See Trotsky's attack, 'The Limitations of Formalism' in *The Modern Tradition*, eds. Richard Ellmann and Charles Feidelson, Jr (New York: Oxford University Press, 1965), pp. 340–49. Bakhtin's attack may be found in 'From M.M. Bakhtin and P.N. Medvedev, "The Formal Method in Literary Scholarship", 1928' in *The Bahktin Reader*, ed. Pam Morris (London, New York, Sydney, Auckland: Arnold, 1994), pp. 136–60.

54 *Ibid.*, p. 117.

55 *Ibid.*, p. 117–18.

56 Roy Fisher, 'Poetry Now', broadcast on BBC Radio 3 on 10th November 1981.

57 *Ibid.*

58 Herbert Marcuse, *The Aesthetic Dimension* (London and Basingstoke: Macmillan, 1978), p. 1.

59 *Ibid.*, p. 72.
60 *Ibid.*, p. 13.
61 See *Ibid.*, pp. 1–6.
62 Fisher, *Nineteen Poems and an Interview*, p. 17.
63 Fisher, *Turning the Prism*, p. 14.
64 *Ibid.* p. 14.
65 *Ibid.*, p. 12.
66 This attitude is curiously close to Proudhon ('My system? I have no system!'), or to the epistemological anarchism of Paul Feyerabend's *Against Method* (London: Verso, 1978): 'No theory ever agrees with all the *facts* in its domain', p. 11.
67 Roy Fisher, *Interviews Through Time, and Selected Prose*, p. 64.

4
Keeping the Doors Open: the Poetry of Lee Harwood in the 1960s and 1970s

Meetings Disintegrating

Lee Harwood's first book-length publication in Britain was *The White Room* (1968), published by Fulcrum Press. The first section, 'Early Poems 1964–1965' contains 'Cable Street' and some poems reprinted from the 1965 Writers Forum pamphlet, *title illegible*. The section collecting the poems from *The Man with Blue Eyes*, his award-winning New York publication, opens with Harwood's first mature poem, 'As Your Eyes are Blue', dating from 1965; while it is influenced by the New York school of Ashbery and O'Hara, a good many of the salient features of Harwood's subsequent work are also displayed here. In a recent short piece Harwood recalls the US volume from which the poem came, and seamlessly moves from outlining influence to outlining his own poetics:

> Meeting John [Ashbery] turned me round. Being in his company, reading his poems with more care than before, seeing his approaches to writing and his personal tastes was a wonderful lesson and release. I finally realized one could make poems that worked like Borges' fictions. Poems that created a world and invited the reader to enter, to wander round, to put in their own two cents, to use. The personal was interwoven in this work, but there was much more involved than the personal … An awareness of co-existing worlds or realities. Of playfulness and seriousness spliced together.[1]

'As Your Eyes are Blue' is a love lyric, addressed from a shadowy 'I' to an insistently addressed 'you'; gender is unspecified, but certain clues suggest the poem is a covert homoerotic lyric. Homosexuality was illegal when the poem was penned, so perhaps it is not purely literary considerations that leave a reader unable to identify a coherent author-subject behind the various discourses. Hesitancy and textual discontinuity are both evident in broken utterance and syntactic rupture from the start.

As your eyes are blue
you move me – and the thought of you –
I imitate you.

(*CFR*, p. 15)

The feeling of loss and obsession is unmistakeable, and is contained within a loose syntax; the parenthetical 'and the thought of you' indicates that this is not a poetry of definitive statement, but attempts to keep the saying open in immediate response and moment by moment revision. The early Harwood found structural homologies in French, *nouvelle vague* cinema: 'If you look at people like Truffaut, Godard, and Resnais, you find this continual cross-cut collage effect – no plot, no beginning-middle-end routine. It's like a big circle instead.'[2] This could easily serve as a description of this poem; it immediately cuts to another scene.

yet a roof grey with slates
or lead. The difference is little
and even you could say as much
through a foxtail of pain   even you

(*CFR*, p. 15)

Punctuation is erratic and is not used for syntactic closure, but for the articulation of occurring and recurring thoughts. The 'foxtail of pain' is a semi-surrealistic metaphor that teases with possible semantic resolution amid its dream-like indeterminacy. The foxtail quivers out of sight the moment it is seen, and yet its indefinable pain remains. Spatial lineation aids the cross-cut effect in providing a non-stanzaic, non-metrical means of delineating conflicting discourses, selves, and voices, so that it is both polyphonic and hetereoglossic, in Bakhtin's terms. By avoiding the rhetorical restraint of the iambic base, the poem can rapidly change voice or register. Incidents are arranged without recourse to the logic of argument or the verities of realism. Aspects of conventional realist enumeration that do enter, (for example, 'a roof grey with slates/or lead') are curiously inessential; in the textual presence or literal absence of the obsessive loved one, 'the difference is little' (*CFR*, p. 15). However, as the unlikely commentator, J.H. Prynne, wrote of *The White Room*, it displays 'an intensely affective life floated out onto language through an almost indefinitely transferable allegory of "feeling"'[3] on a sliding scale that can allegorize the poem's objects, or not, as it wishes. For example, interior details are imbued with a value that balances the indifference.

> when the river beneath your window
> was as much as I dream of. loose change and
> your shirt on the top of a chest-of-drawers
> a mirror facing the ceiling and the light in a cupboard
> left to burn all day   a dull yellow
> probing the shadowy room   'what was it?'
>
> (*CFR*, p. 15)

This suddenly intrusive speaking voice is ascribed to neither the 'you' nor the 'I'. Its connection with the next few lines is uncertain. The loss is married to an unspecified threat:

> 'cancel the tickets' – a sleep talk
> whose horrors razor a truth that can
> walk with equal calm through palace rooms
> chandeliers tinkling in the silence as winds batter the gardens
> outside   formal lakes shuddering at the sight
> of two lone walkers
>
> (*CFR*, p. 15)

The sense of unease underlies every section like a dream, whether it is the razored truth that could haunt the idyllic scene, or the yellow light of the domestic interior. The elaborate fictiveness shamelessly foregrounds the pathetic fallacy as an elegant element of its own artifice. The tension between what Harwood calls his 'puritan' self-disclosure and 'cavalier' fiction-making is a distinguishing feature of all his writing; when they co-exist in a poem, as here, they polyphonize the text, produce complexity, hold open a condition of saying in that tension. Indeed, the fiction corrects itself, as if aware of its incredible nature, relocating the absorbed walkers, who threaten to become romanticized against their sympathetic background, in a more quotidian human landscape.

> of course this exaggerates
> small groups of tourists appear and disappear
> in an irregular rhythm of flowerbeds.
>
> (*CFR*, p. 15)

The continual breaks in the text – jump-cuts – demonstrate how Harwood uses 'the cinematic technique of co-existing realities'.[4] Yet this co-existence occurs within the context of human consciousness and a fragile, possibly duplicitous, relationship:

you know even in the stillness of my kiss
that doors are opening in another apartment
on the other side of town   a shepherd grazing
his sheep through a village we know
high in the mountains the ski slopes thick with summer flowers
and the water-meadows below with narcissi
the back of your hand and –

(CFR, pp. 15–16)

From this excursion into memory the poem is brought back to the lover, who is represented only as parts of the body: eyes, hands, shoulders operating as indices of homoerotic obsession, without directly specifying gender. The open conjunction suggests the possibility of extension: an inventory of the lover or of some intimate secret, perhaps even of homosexuality itself. It appears to offer the reader a chance to complete the utterance him or herself (a feature of Harwood's later verse) or it can be read as cautiously self-censoring. The poem switches to a London scene of aporia and confusion:

a newly designed red bus drives quietly down Gower Street
a brilliant red   'how could I tell you …'
with such confusion
                          meetings disintegrating
and a general lack of purpose only too obvious
in the affairs of state.

(CFR, p. 16)

The poem retreats from the confusions of the public world, but fails to avoid the subject of loss. A new story begins, affirmatively, in another capital city; its quotation mark is left unclosed, to ambivalently suggest either infinite continuation or abrupt abandonment, and its lower case letters accentuate its separation from the rest of the poem.

                yes, it was on a hot july day
with taxis gunning their motors on the throughway
a listless silence in the backrooms of paris bookshops

(CFR, p. 16)

The story fades into resignation: 'why bother one thing equal to another' (CFR, p 16). Throughout the poem there is this growing feeling of hopelessness and longing: events are self-defeating; 'dinner parties whose grandeur stops all conversation'; and 'even the radio still playing the same/records

I heard earlier today' (*CFR*, p. 16). Stasis is matched by repetition. The way this poem mediates its empirical and imaginary experiences is more important than what is said about them. There exists the constant pull towards the fictive or the memorized, while erotic obsession still draws the 'I' towards 'you' and its personal and private domestic interior. Evasion only leads to the threat of loss and removal, which brings the tickets, the bus and the taxis in the poem to some thematic point as the male lover leaves. The movement is circular

> but
>   the afternoon sunlight which shone in
> your eyes as you lay beside me watching for ... –
> we can neither remember – still shines as you
> wait nervously by the window for the ordered taxi
> to arrive   if only I could touch your naked shoulder
> now   'but then ...'
>
>   (*CFR*, p. 16)

There can be no buts, the poem implies. Now is irrevocably cut off from then, and memory is already imperfect. But desire is irrepressible in its anxious repetitions:

>   – and still you move me
> and the distance is nothing
> 'even you –
>
>   (*CFR*, p. 16)

The poem ends with these repetitions, giving it an enigmatic anti-narrative circularity that Harwood admired around this time in his favoured French film makers. His running together of discontinuous elements avoids comparison and symbolism: the reader is placed at what feels like the temporary pausing of sequences of perceptions and reflections that are indeterminate (each defamiliarizing the content and register of the others) but capable of possible extension. While the reader has to enter into dialogue with these perceptions and fictions in order to begin to complete them, the selves presented in the text are 'positions' (as in Fisher's work), though here partly absorbed by the complex of discourses. Harwood seems to have the details of this poem in mind, when he says that his general aim is to create a poem where there is

> some sort of perspective where the man was outside himself as well as inside himself. So that if you are describing a scene in a room and then mention that cars backfire

in the street outside, the scene becomes much more credible ... [It] makes the moment seem the more valid because it's in perspective. It's not just suspended in some egocentric vision, and it becomes like a world.[5]

What Could Have Been

The heroes of Harwood's modern 'mythology' in the bulk of his long ever-shifting narrative poems of the 1960s – mostly to be found in *The White Room* but others in *Landscapes* (1969) – are gunslingers, gauchos or insecure consul officials in forgotten colonies, all of them questors without a grail, hopelessly haunted by images of love. Meaningless isolated men populate artificially ornate narratives. In those with a colonial setting, the characters' meaning has been removed as much by history as by the sudden breaks in narrative continuity. Philip Larkin, in 1969, could satirize post-imperial withdrawal in his ironical 'Homage to a Government' (the technocratic and mildly reformist Wilson administration), but Harwood's 'The Doomed Fleet' activates the affective mythic imagery of vanishing Imperial adventure.[6]

> the entire palace was deserted, just as was
> the city, and all the villages along the 50 mile
> route from the seaport to the capital.
> It was not caused by famine or war –
> 'It was all my fault.'
> (*CFR*, p. 58)

This childlike plea is the storyteller's, who repentantly intrudes into the fiction. He is the single 'commander-in-chief' of the operation and he is responsible for the narrative deteriorating into cliché.

> Maybe they never did get there and, instead,
> the whole expedition lay at the bottom.
> This already begins to sound like a very bad boy's story.
> (*CFR*, p. 60)

Self-consciousness is not simply a literary technique, but is a way of emphasizing how experience is inevitably distorted by discourse; boy's stories were often the instrument of instilling a sense of Englishness in young readers during the years of Empire. From beneath the civilities of the story, the totalitarian impulse rises: 'Nothing that would disturb the carefully planned/ vanity was tolerated. That was the new order.'(*CFR,* p. 58) The admission here of vanity (mediated by the surprise of a line-break), suggests a tragic rigidity among those for whom the narrative attempts to speak. The expedition and the narrative are both self-consciously manipulated, both doomed, as options narrow, towards a staged inevitability. The final section of the poem begins:

Age began to show ... and the divisions widen
and become even more resolute and rigid.
'What could have been' became altogether another story
like the family photos in the captain's wallet
– there was no room for sentimentality now.

(*CFR,* p. 60)

'Power' and 'menace' operate not merely in the purpose and armoury of the battleships, but in the area of linguistic control. The sailors

didn't understand 'pity'. The very word
had been deliberately deleted from all the books
scattered among the fleet.

(*CFR,* p. 59)

Following this Borgesian incident, the now inflexible characters are in the power of the fictions that have written them; they operate not just like boy's stories, but are even more carefully controlled to exclude the possibility of flexible emotional response. The characters are lost in static posturing, beyond 'what could have been': 'The heavy service revolver seemed somehow too/melodramatic to be real enough for its purpose' (*CFR,* p. 60). The helplessness that 'a feeling of finality' brings about is absurdly artificial and operates both at the level of storytelling and in the story; this dual aspect, and the sense the reader has of moving from one level to the other, stops the story presenting such Bergsonian *rigeur* in the characters as comic.

'Finality' is a key term in a number of Harwood's fictions at this time: it is the undefined goal of the quest, but, as it approaches, unreality engulfs everything. However much this mode is borrowed from the New York School, with its narrative harnessing of the effects of surrealism, the alluring promise of the fiction hangs suspended in a final realist image of corrosion and purposeless movement: 'Salt waves broke over the rusted iron decks' (*CFR,* p. 61).

A Catalyst not a Cameo: The Poetics of the Open Work

A third Fulcrum volume, *The Sinking Colony*, was published in 1970. The texts formally display semantic and syntactic indeterminacy and discontinuity; in this they hark back to 'As Your Eyes are Blue', while the subject matter continues the focus of the fictions. Harwood theorized these poems in a new way:

> Ideally, I want the poem to be like a beautiful object, a box that's all slotted together; and then I leave it on the table and leave the room, and you come in and handle it and pass it on ... When [the poem] is read it becomes bigger and has more power.[7]

This implies that the poem is not primarily self-expressive but, more importantly, its objectivity, its materiality, involves the realization that a poem 'is an object made by the writer, that he gives to the reader'.[8] But the reader is not the ideal reader of reception aesthetics, one 'constituted' or 'implied' by the text, but the multiplicity of readers who actually do read and use these texts. While Roy Fisher argues for the poem to be considered a subversive agent, Harwood sees a poem as a catalytic object that causes various changes within its readers, without itself changing. But to do so the poem must be part of the reader's responses, dialogic in Vološinov's sense. Umberto Eco writes, 'As he reacts to the play of stimuli and his own response to their patterning, the individual addressee is bound to supply his own existential credentials'.[9] Poems such as Harwood's will operate as what Eco calls 'open works', in collusion with the fact by being 'quite literally "unfinished": the author seems to hand them on to the performer more or less like the components of a construction kit'.[10]

Although this could define Harwood's work adequately enough, he additionally has the dialogic aim of using textual lacunae and fragmentation to get 'the audience involved in the poem'.[11] As Harwood explained in a interview, quoting the end of his poem 'Linen' from *The Sinking Colony*:

> I don't believe any work of art is really good unless it involves some kind of audience participation ...
>
> touching you   like the
> and soft as
> like the scent of flowers and
> like an approaching festival
> whose promise is failed through carelessness.[12]

The poet is not afraid to supply his own concluding similes, but, as Harwood said, 'Each of us has got a different concept of what touching flesh is like ... I should respect your view'.[13] Active readers can become the co-producers of this poem, a strategy that, although not always successful, avoids the rhetorical manipulations of Movement discourse. If there is to be a 'we', it is not one tyrannized into supposed consensus but one formed through this textual dialogue.

The open work is not simply what anybody reads into it. Harwood argues that the poems of *The Sinking Colony* have 'ideally ... infinite possibilities and alternatives'.[14] But Eco makes a finer distinction when he says: 'The *possibilities* which the work's openness makes available always work through a given *field of relations*', in the case of 'Linen' through a focusing upon the intimate notion of touching skin; we are literally given a couple of options which balance Harwood's own pair of Ashberyesque and baroque similes.[15] There is no single view but neither is the poem 'an amorphous invitation to indiscriminate participation'.[16] Indeed, it can be argued that the textual openness towards the reader, the textual equivalent of Levinas' sense of the asymmetricality of all relationships, consists more in its invitation, in its willingness to abandon the said in favour of a gesture of the continual performance of the saying in a dialogue with readers, than in its expectation of actual completion. The gaps are not actually for filling (I have been reading this poem for a quarter of a century and have never felt implored to utter an extemporized response or scribble on the text). What the reader actually acknowledges is a textual act of respect, as Harwood indicates above, on the part of the author, a passage from the authority of the author to the inevitable authoring of the reader. It foregrounds the channel of communication; it is the act of welcoming responsibility that waits for the response of the other. As Jill Robbins states: 'Ethical language is described ... in terms of the operative distinction between the saying and the said, which corresponds roughly to the difference between the kind of speech that foregrounds the relation to the addressee, and a denotative speaking that that absorbs alterity into thematization'.[17] Harwood signals the saying even while he carefully, fragmentarily, fictively or minimally uses, of necessity, the language of the said. He also imposes a reciprocal responsibility on the reader, to maintain an openness of reading to match his gesture of hospitality.

If Harwood's portrait of Englishness in 'The Doomed Fleet' shows it at its most tenuous, when its self-confirmatory rituals are transplanted to the colonial situation, where threat on both sides may completely destroy such displays of civilized nationhood, then 'Animal Days', in *The Sinking Colony*, is a poem which offers up those certainties to a textual disruption so great that they begin to turn into their opposites, into pastoral or romance, while yet the terror still pervades the text, the worse for being undefined. It is almost as though the words are punctuating silence, or scissored page space; it was influenced specifically by Ashbery's collage 'Europe', and perhaps more generally by Burroughs' technique of cut-up.[18]

The apparent assertiveness of the opening (a quotation from an English cavalry officer, A.D. Wintle), 'The polo season would start early in April/so there was no time to be wasted', euphemistically evades a definition of the actions to be committed, which contrasts with '"the endurance"/ surviving the fear' (*CFR*, p. 119). The title suggests a lack of respect for the natives (they are little more than beasts) but also connects with an image of care: 'holding a young rabbit in my hands ... setting it free in a hawthorn thicket/ safe from the dogs' (*CFR*, p.120). In such a context – are we meant to think of animals, the colonized, the colonizers? – the isolate quotation, 'They have no tradition of keeping their colonies neat' reverberates with multiple ironies (*CFR*, p. 120). The poem ends by fragmenting and juxtaposing the fairytale ('"knights on horses"? "gentle ladies"?' the poem asks earlier) with a further refusal to relate unbearable details (*CFR*, p. 118).

> Like oppressors   striking fear into people
> with threats of pillage and 'no quarter'
>
> Inside the walls where
> 'No!'
> too heavy   on evenings like this
>
> in the courtyard
> 'the battlements'
>
> (*CFR*, p. 121)

Now Put It Together

In the poem 'One, Two, Three', from the 1971–72 section 'Qasida Island' in the 1975 book *HMS Little Fox*, the reader is oriented towards the completion of the poem by the insistent final line: 'Now put it together.' (*CFR*, p. 171.) This line has a distinct function within the third section, but it is clearly an invitation to construct a new entity from the three separate parts of the title's instructions for assembly. Its fragments are no longer gestures of openness, but are motivated by their delicate contexts which enact its theme of resistance to separation. Parables of Mughal and colonial power are juxtaposed with notations of the personal in quite new ways.

'One' begins, 'An emperor gives a gift, stylishly,/and a Mughal miniature records it.' (*CFR*, p. 169.) There is an immediate admission that, to be affected by this art, the viewer has to engage with its otherness, that it too is a gift that may not simply reduced to 'colour & gold on paper, height 7³⁄₁₆ inches': (*CFR*, p. 169), however much the minutiae are obsessive.

> we're dazzled – all this art
> and surprises   'Keeping the doors open'
> Right?
>   (*CFR*, p. 169)

'Keep your doors open,' Harwood says in a 1970 interview, quoting the phrase from a Hopi rite of passage, 'is what real learning is doing.'[19] As the text itself is open, then the reader's faculties should remain open in the face of being 'fascinated by the delicacy' of art objects (*CFR*, p. 169). But such delicacy is

>   real enough
> aesthetic coat-trailing aside.
> The delight beyond the technicalities
> – not pursuing, but there
> to be recognised
>   (*CFR*, p. 169)

Our existential condition unavoidably enters this process of artistic reception and recognition; the realm of 'private separations', a recurrent theme for Harwood, is here managed positively (*CFR*, p. 169).

> When 'we' moves from the general
> to the particular?
>
> To talk of *you* now ...?
> amongst all this 'delight'
> – moving into that other level –
> the poverty of this, one without the other,
> the delight more a refuge than any whole thing

when you're away

(CFR, p.169)

There can be no real aesthetic appreciation without the necessary interaction between 'levels' and in the interplay between a 'you' that represents a particular addressee as well as a general reader, that one kind of otherness may enrich our knowledge of, and responsiveness to, some apparently unconnected other. The work of art is inert until actively absorbed into the life-world of each particular respondent. Each reader of Harwood's text is required to bring in 'that other level', to at least consider it, to create the 'whole thing' for him or herself. The section concludes with a fait accompli.

Up in the hills the court is assembled,
the gifts exchanged
From the balcony I see you cross a courtyard,
could almost touch you –
but the distance.
            Be well.
the moonlight on your face
as you sleep now

(CFR, p. 170)

The narrator 'enters' the art-work (a rhetorical feature of many of Harwood's poems); the division between art and life-world is transgressed to emphasize their interdependence. When this happens, appropriately enough, the emperor is no longer merely giving, but is involved in an act of 'exchange', an image of the reciprocation evoked throughout the section. Yet even this perspective is not totally satisfying because the 'distance', the 'private separations', still remain. The section ends on a note of private intimacy, perhaps a reminder that such intimacy is only meaningful in the world of actual, and not vicarious, situations.

It is towards this originary world that the second section is oriented. Its almost slight notations of heterosexual love-making move exclusively onto 'that other level' on which the other is a lover. There is little of the damaged romance of earlier poems, no allegory of feeling, or pathetic fallacy. The artful landscape is not suddenly forested with beautiful flowers but is an irritating intrusion: 'away the hills/ (Fuck "the hills")' (CFR, p. 170). Why this should be so is apparent in the parallel pronominal structure, and in the complete absorption by, and obsession with, 'my mouth on your throat/ my body smells of your body' (CFR, p. 170). The balanced 'hold me' and 'I

hold you' both pleads for, and suggests, sexual exchange and reciprocal responsibility; the poem rejects the one-way communication of either a writer
or a lover.

The baroque of Ashbery – what Harwood calls the 'cavalier' – has been
exchanged for the 'puritan' discourse derived from a reading of Robert Creeley
in the late 1960s; Harwood has spoken of wanting to 'write directly, in a
personal way, but … that it must be straight … and it must be set in contexts', such as those of the hills, or of the details of the two surrounding
sections.[20]

The third and final section returns us to the colonial ambience – perhaps
India – of 'Animal Days':

> There are many fields
> and the fortresses are so far apart.
> The troops stand in line on the parade ground
> while the sun beats down on them
> and their bored officers.
>   (*CFR*, p. 171)

'There are many settings', (CFR, p. 171) the poem continues, emphasizing
the question of choice and the multi-facetedness of both the ordinary and
the extraordinary events of the past, yet the inadequate Britishness is asserted by reference to what is ultimately a record of deceit:

> A group of men can sit stiffly
> for a regimental photo of the survivors of the disaster,
> and then try to look neat and alert.
>   (*CFR*, p. 171)

Whereas the first section had dealt with aesthetics, linking with the sexual
exchanges of the second section, the third deals largely with historical knowledge (both public and private) and the lack of 'recognition' and the lack of
exchange with history, which parallels a similar lack of exchange in 'One',
and contrasts with the personal responsibility of responsiveness of 'Two'.
Against the inert posturing that attempts to halt this exchange the reader is
asked to imagine the children of 'the survivors' of the undescribed 'disaster'

> living in a calm beyond this knowledge?
> It is not so much a question of guilt
> on either side, but maybe some form of recognition

which rarely happens.

(CFR, p. 171)

And it is this knowledge, a knowledge of the otherness of people through history, that is allowed to die, to pass from recognition,

> leaving behind only feelings of confused longing
> that quietly spread beyond any conscious resentment.

Now put it together.

(CFR, p. 171)

This longing is the cause of an unfocused nostalgia, yet another separation, that refuses to keep the doors of real learning – real knowledge – open. It is the duty of those of the present to put the knowledge together in a way so as to recover what lies 'beyond the technicalities', to exchange the human realities behind the stiff 'regimental photo' and integrate that into a world that does include the aesthetic and erotic and even, as here, a knowledge of unspeakable catastrophe that cannot be recovered by the 'confused longing' of subsequent *post*-colonial generations (*CFR*, p. 171). Reading history we suddenly become aware that it is reading us. The poem enacts three varieties of response and lack of response to otherness: other cultures, other people, other times, and suggests the connections between them that can only be made by an imaginative embrace of the others.

Yes and No; The Comprehension of Process

'Harwood knows the uses of discontinuity, of partial description, of tangents whose vector energies can be gripped by the imagination, working to cohere information and feeling out of an interior coherence of the poetic action', writes Eric Mottram, of the work of the 1970s, and this description is particularly apt to the 12-part 'notebook' written between 1970 and 1972, *The Long Black Veil*, [21] which Harwood described as 'the end-product, the "flower" of my work to date'.[22] With its Olsonian notation, its open field procedures, and its appropriation of the ideogrammic method of juxtaposition, it is Harwood's longest meditation upon erotic obsession, yet it is also a quest for the 'comprehension of process', (*CFR*, p. 129) to quote the poem's epigraph from Ezra Pound. Such process is another Olsonian inheritance (reaching back to the philosophy of Whitehead). It is a quest enacted through memory ('What have we *left*/ from all *this*?' (*CFR*, p. 130)); Harwood explains the temporal organization of his poem: 'One actuality in time set by (beside) another, causing waves to go between the two'.²³ Yet the image he proffers of memory, in this most self-contradictory of his poems – he describes it as both process and product – contradicts the possibility of that comforting simultaneity. The image, borrowed from Borges, of a pile of coins, each representing a memory of the preceding memory, shows 'how our memory distorts and simplifies events the further we move from them' (*CFR*, p. 131).

> two years passed 'Oh Jung'
> the cycle not repeated
> only the insistence
>   (*CFR*, p. 130)

This distinction between vital insistence and dead repetition exists in a tense relationship with actual memory. The questor figure from earlier texts has learnt that memory is not just a series of surprising recollections but is both contained and refracted through process and mutability. Memory is paradoxical, cannot be resolved into the singularity of narrative. There is a strong desire to feel 'totally in one place', (*CFR*, p. 157) though this is undercut: 'the dream echoed again and again … in many places' (*CFR*, p. 160).

The 'Oh Jung' above is itself a reiterated insistence carried over from a quotation in the immediately preceding passage.

> 'Concepts promise protection
> from experience.
>   The spirit does
> not dwell in concepts. Oh Jung.'
> (*Joanne Kyger – DESECHEO NOTEBOOK*) (*CFR*, p. 130)

There can be no sheltering from experience in conceptualisations, in intellectual systems of knowledge, even in this, the most allusive and literary of Harwood's works.²⁴ The 'Preface' ends:

> But what of the essence of this? 'Oh Jung's' insistences. The Sufi story of the famous River that tried to cross the desert, but only crossed the sands as water 'in the arms of the wind', nameless but
>
>   (*CFR*, p. 131)

The Sufi parable, truncated so abruptly, demonstrates that movement or process always involves surprising metamorphoses. Repetitions also undergo metamorphosis at their reappearances; this involves a continual defamiliarization. The theme turns rather than re-turns. The repetitions are both structuring the text and yet decentring it thematically as it progresses, in a dialectic of repetition and surprise.

Book One plays with the distance between word and thing, unhappy nominalism a reflector of existential distance. 'How I ache now' is equivalent to the 'endless skies/ that ache too much' that appear several lines later (*CFR*, p. 132). Despite the alienation, nature is suffused with longing. The text is hesitant, constantly revising itself. 'It's light/ I mean your body.' (-*CFR*, p. 132) But the body also is the constant referent of Book One amid the general failure of reference ('the words? how can they ...') and the 'distance' between lover and lover, and the 'unbearable distance' of the 'endless skies' (*CFR*, p. 132). 'Your body, yes I'm talking about it/ at last I mean this *is* the discovery.' (*CFR*, p. 132.) Yet there can be no purposeful inventory of bodily elements. The book ends:

> dawn – light – body – words – raven – skies – ache- distance – valley – sun – silos – farms – ridges – creek – each other – birds – wind
> The Flight – BA 591

(CFR, p. 133)

These are the nouns of the first half of the section – an alienating inventory of what is irrecoverably lost. The flight number is an objective sign of the reality of distance. What survives this distance, as always in Harwood's poetry, is an enigmatic impression, a moment from a love-affair that has been frustrated: a cinematic sequence, frozen in the frame.

> you stop and half turn
> to tell me ...
> that doesn't matter
> but your look
> and this picture I have
> and at this distance
>   (*CFR*, p. 132)

This is one version of what Harwood calls 'the dream': 'anything that goes on in my head, whether it be thoughts or imaginings, day-dreams or sleep dreams. They all give pictures of "the possible", and that is exactly their value.' (*CFR*, p. 135.) The 'dream', though, is only articulated in this poem through

the mediation of the transcriptions of real events, most importantly the recording of the events of a precarious love affair and its aftermath and memories. 'I hold you to me in a small room – the night air so heavy. Inside "the
dream"…' (*CFR*, p. 134). And, as we have seen, the 'dream' recurs again and
again in different locations, linking them by paradigmatic connection.

One possible version of 'the dream' harks back to, is nostalgic for, the
fictions of *The White Room*, yet they are now unnecessary evasions of the
real that is emphatically celebrated in the notebook (mostly in journal-like
passages which depict travels with the lover around North America) and in
its new-found 'straight-talking' diction.

> There's no steamer bringing you to me
> up-river at the hill-station
> No long white dress on the verandah
>
> It is …
> I hold you.   Isn't this enough?
>   (*CFR*, p. 137)

The landscape becomes prey to the pathetic fallacy, as in 'As Your Eyes Are
Blue', is 'only a description of my love for you' (*CFR*, p. 137). The reiterated
depictions of the lover's body turn upon both her presence and her absence,
affected by the complexities of the situation: the poem's title, a haunting
country and western song by Lefty Frizzell, hints that the relationship is
adulterous, and as covert in its way as earlier homosexual encounters.

In Book Six – mid-way through the text – 'the questions of complexity'
are dealt with most fully (*CFR*, p. 142). Harwood quotes E.M. Forster's
obituary for André Gide which praises Gide for transmitting much of 'life's
complexity, and the delight, the duty of registering that complexity and of
conveying it' (*CFR*, p. 142). Complexity is the twentieth-century existential
condition. It is in his use of Jung's essay 'Marriage as a Psychological Relationship' that Harwood develops both a theory for a constantly decentring
process in his work which suggests a structural homology for the 'comprehension of process', and a model for human relationships.

> The distinctions
>
> 'Oh, Jung' (1875–1961) on 'Marriage …' (1925)
>
> The container *and* the contained
> not *or*

one within the other
a continual shifting and that both ways
– more a flow – from the simplicity to the complexity,
'unconscious' to conscious,
                         and then back again?
and the move always with difficulty, and pain   a pleasure
                                (*CFR*, p. 142)

 In Jung's theory of marriage, the container is a complex character, the contained simple and psychologically dependent upon the other. There are
pleasurable but also painful resolutions between them as the container looks
in vain for his or her level of complexity in the partner, whose simplicity is
also disrupted by the search. The contained, however, comes to accept his
or her position and becomes acutely aware of the necessity for self-fulfilment.
Harwood subverts the underlying submissive-dominant polarity of Jung's
essay, with his emphatic '*and*' which suggests that the roles are interchangeable, dynamic and discontinuous (by implication, disturbing sexuality and
gender). The relationship in the poem, it must be recalled, is far from a
'marriage' in conventional terms.[25]
 With such mutability, process is both a mode of consciousness and a
mode of communication:

not so much a repetition
but a moving around a point, a line
– like a backbone – and that too moving
(on)
                    (*CFR*, p. 142)

Part of the function of the 'backbone' moving around a (moving) point is
that there should be no single point of view, that it should be 'complex'.
The 'straight-talking' of certain parts of the poem do not contradict the
elaborate artifice of others. They are, to have recourse to the concepts of
quantum physics, complementarities: mutually exclusive positions that support one another, echoed later in the text: 'Yes and No' (*CFR*, p. 154). Yet
the most explicit model of this 'moving/ (on)' in the poem is

yang and yin
light and dark
 (*CFR*, p. 143)

which is accompanied by a drawing of the 'yang and yin' Taoist emblem.[26]

At one level this is a re-statement of the passage above on marriage where the two partners are in a dialectical but equitable harmony. Yet the earnest unities of Taoism are undercut – complemented – by an all too worldly, weary, quotation from Stendhal in which Julien Sorel's love, and by implication, our narrator's, is described ironically as 'still another name for ambition' (*CFR*, p. 143).

The poem offers multiple models of experience, many ways of approaching complexity; the instability of the lover and the erotic becomes the paradoxical centre of the poem as he is balanced between love and ambition, and marriage and adultery.

Jung furnished the introduction to Wilhelm's translation of the *I Ching*, from which Harwood quotes, incompletely, in Book Six.

> BEFORE COMPLETION   Wei Chi/64
> But if the little fox, after nearly completing the crossing,
> Gets his tail in the water,
> There is nothing that would further.
>
> (*CFR*, p. 143)

'This hexagram,' the commentary to the *I Ching* explains, predicts a 'hopeful outlook'; it 'indicates a time when the transition from disorder to order is not yet completed'.[27]

The poem continues with a not entirely convincing image of the transformation of the lover. 'Complexity' includes a transformative, as well as merely linear, process, catalysis, to use Harwood's earlier metaphor.

>   in the half light …
> A minotaur? a cat? tiger?   Her face
> a metamorphosis   seen   at once   many times.
> Our powers generating …
>
> (*CFR*, p. 143)

'Book Twelve: California Journal' brings about a full ravelling of the complexities of earlier books, yet focuses upon the lover. It is ironic to centre oneself in decentring, abandoned to the openness of the 'dream' that evokes possibility, but constantly returns to the lover, to pitch one time against another, only to find the farthest memories metamorphosed in the vagaries of recollection. When the continual shifting of place and movement, of change and exchange, and of dream and the here and now, come to poetic fulfilment in an extraordinarily powerful piece of prose, it is not a resolution.

Making love, the final blocks clear. My body taken into her body completely, and then her body into my body ...

She anoints my wrists

the anointment a ritual like the sweetening of the body before burial, before our parting. My not realising the completeness of this until now ...

The ritual of – repeated again – No. We make love – to each other – in turn. The body glowing, dizzy, ... walking through clouds. The faces transformed again.

She puts the bead bracelet around my wrist

(*CFR*, pp. 160–61)

The ritual is a necessary insistence, not a casual repetition, which involves characteristic transformation and metamorphosis. As in 'One, Two, Three' there is a ritual exchange. 'She accepts the objects – the stone, the orange blossom./She gives the objects – the whittled twig, the dried seed pod.' (*CFR*, p. 161.) The love-making is complete in both the sense that it has reached a certain stage of intensity; but it may also be a final act with its funereal equation of 'before burial' and 'before our parting': so the 'completeness' of the anointing is not comprehended at the time. The poem ends with what might be a simple imperative or the fragment of a larger utterance, 'lie naked upon the bed', which returns to the unstable, dynamic insistence of human sexual relationships (*CFR*, p. 161). But the pervasive 'dream' and its echoes ensure that the story will never be a simple one, that the text's end will never be definitively conclusive.

In the face of 'a multiplicity of approaches', as Harwood puts it, there can only be a relativistic discourse, the polyphonizing of a lyric impulse and the dispersal of narrative energies.[28] 'The narrative function', notes Lyotard,

is losing its functors, the great hero, its great dangers, its great voyages, its great goal. It is being dispersed in clouds of narrative language elements – narrative, but also denotative, prescriptive, descriptive, and so on.[29]

'The Long Black Veil' is an act of such dispersal, a recognition that 'each of us lives at the intersection of many of these ... language elements.'[30] The 12 books are, with their Poundian precision and erotic uncertainty, Harwood's mutability cantos. Out of these elements, like postmodern science, it is 'producing not the known, but the unknown', but like a lover, it always returns to the known, to find it changed, even in memory or language.[31]

Harwood's poetry signals the saying even while he carefully, fragmentarily, fictively or minimally uses, of necessity, the language of the said. All of his poetry, before and since 'The Long Black Veil', has maintained a level of restlessness that refuses to settle on one satisfactory image, saying or ending. It will always move levels, whether by fragmentation (as in 'Animal Days'), juxtaposition (as in the ideogrammic method in 'The Long Black Veil' or 'Dreams of Armenia'), fictive transition (as in *Dream Quilt*) or seriality as in 'Days and Nights: Accidental Sightings'.[32] Relocated in different discourses, the poems are heteroglossic, enacting dialogues in which both the author and active reader have a word, that will resist the finality of the said of the last word, but attempt to offer an unresolved saying. Yet as Eric Mottram realized, this process can only *delay* naturalization, just long enough for contemplation and use. The reader must 'take up the poem, not to solve it quickly but to discover its design without the thrust of vulgar consumer immediacy'.[33]

Notes

1   Unpublished Note. The poem 'As Your Eyes are Blue' is published, as are other Harwood texts cited in this chapter, in *Crossing the Frozen River: Selected Poems* (London: Paladin, 1988); future citations to this volume will be marked *CFR* in the text.

2   'Lee Harwood', in 'A Conversation' with Eric Mottram, *Poetry Information* 14 (1975/1976), p. 12.

3   J.H. Prynne, 'Harwood – Love and "Cold Fear"', *Varsity* 24/v/69, p. 6.

4   Lee Harwood, 'Surrealist Poetry Today', *Alembic* 3 (1975), p. 50.

5   'Extracts from a Conversation with Lee Harwood', Victor Bockris, *Pennsylvania Review*, 1971, pp. 7–14, at p. 9–10.

6   This poem may be found in Philip Larkin, *High Windows* (London: Faber, 1974), p. 29.

7   'Extracts from a Conversation with Lee Harwood', p. 8.

8   *Ibid.*, p. 11.

9   Umberto Eco, 'The Poetics of the Open Work', in *The Role of the Reader* (London: Hutchinson, 1981), pp. 47–66, at p. 49.

10   'Extracts from a Conversation with Lee Harwood', p. 19.

11   *Ibid.*, p. 9.

12   *Ibid.*, p. 9. The poem is found in *CFR*, p. 113.

13   *Ibid.*, p.9.

14   *Ibid.*, p. 9.

15   Eco, 'The Poetics of the Open Work', p. 62.

16   *Ibid.*, p. 62.

17   Jill Robbins, *Altered Reading: Levinas and Literature* (Chicago and London: The University

of Chicago Press, 1999), p. xiv.

18   Ashbery's poem 'Europe' may be found in the volume *The Tennis Court Oath*, reprinted in
      Ashbery, *The Mooring of Starting Out: The First Five Books of Poetry* (Manchester: Carcanet,
      1997), pp. 59–159, at pp. 124–50. Burroughs' account of cut-up may be found in *The Job*
      (London: John Calder, 1984), pp. 27–31.

19   'Extracts from a Conversation with Lee Harwood', p. 11.

20   'Lee Harwood', 'A Conversation', p. 14. Robert Creeley's work of this era may be found in
      The Finger (London: Marion Boyars, 1970.)

21   Eric Mottram, 'Beware of Imitations: Writers Forum Poets and British Poetry in the '60s',
      Poetry Student 1 (1975), p. 33.

22   Quoted on the dust jacket of *HMS Little Fox* (London: Oasis Books, 1975), in which the
      poem first appeared, pp. 5–34. It is reprinted in *CFR*, pp. 127–161.

23   Quoted in Mottram, 'Beware of Imitations', p. 33.

24   As well as the epigraphs and the 'Preface' there is a certain significance in the poem's sub-
      title. Like Kyger's poem it is 'a notebook'. The notebook format allows for the necessary
      notational openness that admits the vast range of material used. See my previous account of
      this work, 'Lee Harwood and the Poetics of the Open Work' in Robert Hampson and Peter
      Barry, *The New British Poetries* (Manchester: Manchester University Press, 1993, pp. 216–33.
      My PhD, 'Some Aspects of Contemporary British Poetry' (University of East Anglia, 1988)
      contains an exhaustive reading of the text.

25   Carl Gustav Jung, 'Marriage as a Psychological Relationship', in *The Portable Jung*, ed.
      Joseph Campbell (New York: Viking/Penguin, 1971), particularly pp. 171–72, which I have
      summarized here.

26   The linking of Bohr's complementarities and indeterminacy with Jung's psychology and
      then with Taoism may seem esoteric as a way of directing attention towards 'process' as a
      twentieth-century register of complexity, Jung himself wrote that 'Oriental texts ten centu-
      ries old introduce us to philosophical relativity.' (*The Portable Jung*, p. 475.)

27   *The I Ching*, the Richard Wilhelm Translation, (London and Henley: Routledge and Kegan
      Paul, 1951), p. 248–49. Harwood quotes from the 'Judgement', but omits the word 'success'
      which appears after 'BEFORE COMPLETION'.

28   Quoted in Mottram, 'Beware of Imitations', p. 33.

29   Jean-François Lyotard, *The Postmodern Condition: A Report on Knowledge* (Manchester:
      Manchester University Press, 1984), p. xxiv.

30   *Ibid.*, p. xxiv.

31   *Ibid.*, p. 60.

32   Both 'Dreams of Armenia' (pp. 36–41) and 'Days and Nights: Accidental Sightings' (pp 12–
      15) are to be found in *Morning Light* (London: Slow Dancer Press, 1998).

33   Mottram, 'Beware of Imitations', p. 33.

5

The Persistence of the Movement Orthodoxy in the 1980s and 1990s

The Penguin Book of Contemporary British Poetry

The anthology which claimed to succeed Alvarez's *The New Poetry* was *The Penguin Book of Contemporary British Poetry* of 1982, edited by the critic-poets Blake Morrison and Andrew Motion. Despite the bland inclusiveness of the title, it admits to being self-consciously 'didactic', and claims to exemplify the work and literary taste of a particular 'poetic generation'.[1] Older writers, and those included in Alvarez's collection, have been excluded. Its introduction several times draws comparisons with *The New Poetry*, which is characterized as 'the last serious anthology of British poetry' (*CBP*, p. 11). Taking over Alvarez's notion, but not his metaphor, of literary reactions and feedbacks, they comment that the 20-year hiatus had been a long one, 'if the cycles of literary history in this century are anything to go by' (*CBP*, p. 11). In the opinion of the editors, the intervening period had been barren; during 'much of the 1960s and 1970s,' they declare, 'very little … seemed to be happening' (*CBP*, p. 11). The summary history of Chapter 2 may be read as a contestation of this extraordinary statement. In much the same way as Conquest had suppressed the poetry of the 1940s, Morrison and Motion, both knowledgeable and knowing commentators, chose to disregard the poetry of the British Poetry Revival.

The anthology's didacticism consists in its claim to illustrate a 'decisive shift of sensibility', a fresh 'cycle', yet another 'reaction' (*CBP*, p. 11). One condition of such a revolution is that 'young poets of very different backgrounds and temperaments may feel themselves, or be felt by critics, to be working along similar lines' (*CBP*, p. 11). Perhaps the critics rather than the poets will write the manifestos of what 'a number of close observers' – and who could they mean but themselves? – 'have come to think of as the new British poetry' (*CBP*, p. 12).

In contrast to Alvarez's 'personal anthology' theirs is often breathtakingly strident, but is just as often contentedly modest.[2] Like Conquest before them and others after, they seem both to want to lay claim to the new while remaining within a recognizable orthodoxy or tradition. They represent the early 1980s as a period of transition, and they predict nothing short of a 'reformation of poetic taste' in the light of the work of their chosen poets who have 'developed a degree of ludic and literary self-consciousness reminiscent of the modernists ... as a way of making the familiar strange again' (*CBP*, p.12). Far from concurring that any of these aspects is genuinely novel, I wish to argue that the introduction and anthology represent a development of the Movement Orthodoxy. Far from being a 'reformation', its poetry operates within the original faith of the 1950s, while allowing for development and assimilation. As Morrison had written in 'Young Poets in the 1970s', an article to which I have already referred, 'The fathers of the 70s generation of poets have not been the modernists, but the dominant figures in British poetry since 1945... Many ... do sound distinctly like Philip Larkin and Ted Hughes.'[3] They have assimilated modernism to the point where it has simply become a 'lesson': 'it no longer has anything of urgency to say'.[4]

In fact, some of the emergent writers of *The Penguin Book* have assimilated the surface features of modernism, are distantly 'reminiscent' of the shock of the new. In the work of Craig Raine there are a number of references to Joyce, Picasso and Dali, but as John Ash points out, 'Nowadays surrealism is used as a kind of "permitted colouring"'.[5] This is the case when Raine compares a jellyfish to one of Dali's famous melting watches. The witty reflection upon time is mediated through a potentially anarchic comparison, but, in the final analysis, modernism has provided little more than a repertoire of analogies.

In their introduction Morrison and Motion use such a trait to declare rather cautiously that their poets 'may be said to exhibit something of the spirit of post-modernism' (*CBP*, p. 20). 'The Martian Writes a Postcard Home' not only named the short-lived 'Martian' movement of which Raine was the only significant member, but is a popular classroom exemplar (in my experience from Year 7 to MA level) to teach the effectiveness of figurative language, especially the simile: an open book is like a bird, a TV screen is like a windy day seen through a window, dialling a telephone is like tickling an animal (*CBP*, pp. 169–70). This is the poem's attraction and its danger. The solved riddle offers small reward for the pleasures of recognition.

In Raine's poetry 'the familiar is at its most strange', as James Fenton puts it.[6] The familiar (usually the trenchantly domestic) is made just strange enough to keep its familiarity a temporary novelty. Unlike Roy Fisher's 'Interiors' which refuse to yield up all their mystery, in Raine's work there is an immediate re-familiarization, what Forrest-Thomson calls bad naturalization, once the simile or metaphor has been resolved: a bar of soap is the answering paraphrase to the expression, 'cubist fish/ with perfumed eggs' (*CBP*, p. 170). The result of this social naturalization is ultimately to reduce the wonder of the world it claims to glorify.

From a vantage point beyond 2000 it can be seen that it is not Raine, but Seamus Heaney and Tony Harrison who have been the spirits of the age. A generous and thoughtful selection of the work of Seamus Heaney is 'deliberately put first in our anthology', since he is regarded by the editors as 'the most important new poet of the last fifteen years' (*CBP*, p. 13). Both his 'emergence and example' are appraised. However, the editors' persuasive rhetoric concerning modernism and post-modernism cannot disguise the fact that Heaney is an anti-modernist writer. As Morrison himself states in his *Seamus Heaney*, also published in 1982,

> Heaney's place in twentieth-century poetic tradition is ... full of ambivalence and contradiction. Quaintly inhabiting a world in which Ezra Pound and 'making it new' might never have happened, he has embraced the role of Romantic poet.[7]

It is not surprising to discover that Heaney began writing within the Movement ethos. In Belfast he 'served his apprenticeship under Philip Hobsbaum', whose widely-favoured format for creative writing workshops was adapted by the Ulster group: it emphasized the notion of 'craft', but also civility and rationality (*CBP*, p. 16). And yet, it was clearly the chance discovery of the early, canonical work of Ted Hughes that persuaded Heaney that his own non-cosmopolitan background could furnish suitable material for contemporary poems. Although he could have arguably found these in the work of John Montague or Patrick Kavanagh, Hobsbaum (a contemporary of Hughes at Cambridge) 'encouraged Heaney to strive for Hughes' muscularity and energy'.[8] Heaney himself praises 'Hughes's voice' for being 'in rebellion against a certain kind of demeaned mannerly voice. It's a voice that has no truck with irony', and Heaney censures the 'Larkin voice ... the Movement voice ... of literate middle-class culture'.[9] This is a standard reading of the difference between *New Lines* and *The New Poetry* writing, but Heaney's

sense of his Irishness also separates him from Movement rhetoric and irony.
However, as Morrison points out, Hobsbaum, 'favoured a poetry that combined the wit and metrical tightness of the Movement with the power and
physicality of Ted Hughes, a combination his young Derry protegé achieved
only too well'.[10] Indeed, Heaney's early verse seems to work in the British
context rather than the Irish (it was published in London by Faber rather
than in Dublin, by the Dolmen Press, for example) and it fulfilled Alvarez's
demand for a covenant between the skill and control of Larkin and the
urgent energy of Hughes (or of Plath for that matter). Morrison refers to
Heaney's shaping by '1950s "rationalism"' and by '1960s "extremism"', and
to his 'taking something from both camps while going forward into a new
domain'.[11]

'The Death of a Naturalist' – not in Morrison and Motion's volume, but
widely anthologized, particularly for schools – plots progress from the
narrator's sexual innocence

> the mammy frog
> Laid hundreds of little eggs and this was
> Frogspawn,[12]

to experience, when the spawn evolves from 'dots' into threateningly sexu-
alized frogs:

> The great slime kings
> Were gathered there for vengeance and I knew
> That if I dipped my hand the spawn would clutch it.[13]

However alliteratively lush and conventionally muscular the Hughesian texture of the poem ('The slap and plop were obscene threats. Some sat/ Poised
like mud grenades, their blunt heads farting') the details of the poem serve
to define the trauma of the perceiving consciousness.[14] The metamorphosis
in the flax-dam is a function, an index, of the child's discovery of a nascent
sexuality. One expects the absence of open irony, given Heaney's caution
above, yet the conclusion of the poem, with its suggestion of revenge for the
boy's innocent but culpable containment of the 'jampotfuls of the jellied/
Specks ... range(d) on window-sills at home', shares with Movement discourse a preference for the concluding moral.[15] The child, realizing his cul-
pability – as the reader realizes the irony – 'sickened, turned, and ran'.[16]

Morrison, as I have shown, has been an advocate for Heaney beyond the
bounds of his anthology. One essay opens with a fanfare for the commercial

success of Heaney's *North*, which was published by Faber in 1975: it won prizes; it was 'gushed over'; it sold better than Larkin or Hughes.[17] Heaney's transformation from the lyrical ruralist of *Death of a Naturalist* (1966) into the political poet of *North* seemed an answer to the demand that there should be work produced that was adequate to the 'troubles'. This is signalled in the very word 'north'; how one uses the apparently neutral geographical term indicates one's political and cultural alignment, whether one says Northern Ireland or the North of Ireland. However, Heaney's glimpses of actual terrorism are rare: 'Two young men with rifles on the hill,/ Profane and bracing as their instruments'.[18] Such men are transfigured and debased into functions of their weaponry. This ambivalence and irony is the vehicle of his more characteristically cautious approaches to contemporary Ireland through etymology (in particular of Gaelic place names) and history, particularly in the so-called 'bog poems', which use descriptions of the preserved bodies catalogued in Glob's *The Bog People*.[19] In 'Punishment' Heaney as persona deliberately enters the drama of ritual sacrifice, as Plath might have: 'I can feel the tug/ of the halter' (*CBP*, p. 29). The poem makes an analogy between the murderous ancient societies and the modern and contestable 'North' of his title, subtly connecting the ritual victim with the tar-and-feathering of Catholic girls who dated British soldiers: 'your/tar-black face was beautiful' (*CBP*, p. 29). The poem is almost a love lyric, suffused with the intimacy of an 'artful voyeur' (*CBP*, p. 29) but Heaney is weighed down with what he calls elsewhere his 'responsible *tristia*' (*CBP*, p. 32) as a Catholic with strong republican sympathies who accepts his complicity in the psychology, and even the mechanism, of retribution. The narrator is morally ambivalent, since he

> would connive
> in civilized outrage
> yet understand the exact
> and tribal, intimate revenge.
> (*CBP*, p. 30)

Such intimacy is double-edged, the poem finely balanced; outrage and revenge, civilization and tribalism, stand poised but suspended, an effect achieved partly through the piling up of qualifying adjectives, and partly by the ponderous shortlined accentual metre that Heaney employs. Morrison praises Heaney's exposure of 'a private world of divided feelings' as a means to both political statement and 'fine poetry'.[20] Yet I suspect that English liberalism – and its school teachers – prefers this suspension of politics in private feeling in which Heaney's Irish sense of the historical nature of his culture's divisions can be read (or misread) as a suitably engaged, yet comfortably distant, ironical defence. It is to turn Heaney into what Morrison and Motion claim for him, in effect: that he represents the latest stage of the development of a British orthodoxy. The orthodoxy operates as a normative set of practices that limits poetry production and reception, despite resistances in its leading figures. Heaney is in some ways an exception, although his objections to being in this 'British' anthology sit uneasily with his major status within the context of post-war British poetry.

While Heaney follows the Movement Orthodoxy by projecting an author-subject onto the world and enclosing and defining its objects in terms of the lyric ego's ironical desires – it combines the processes of Plath and the techniques of Raine – Tony Harrison, even though he reverses many of the Movement's social attitudes, maintains both its rational verse structure and the relentless social focus, the moral embrace of what Crozier calls its lyrical empiricism.

Indeed it was Blake Morrison who noted that Harrison 'may be the "first genuine working-class poet England has produced"'; Stephen Spender, who cites this, adds:

> One has the impression, underlying all else, of a deep-sworn vow, a passionate commitment to a family. [They are] members bound by a love whose very substance consists of their being working-class.[21]

Spender has in mind not the bravura displays of class and pride in its linguistic sources (as in 'Them and [uz]' or the longer public narratives such as *V,*) but the Meredithian sonnets that have been essential to his appeal, such as 'Long Distance II', a poem which ventriloquizes Larkin's 'Mr Bleaney' to an alarming extent.[22] Like Mr Bleaney, Harrison's mother (there is no disguising the author-subject here) is an absent presence, dead but still the determining motive for his father's habit-bound life: 'Dad kept her slippers warming by the gas.' (*CBP*, p. 48.) It is a world of self-deception , like Larkin's: 'He *knew* she'd just popped out to get the tea.' (*CBP*, p. 48.) More importantly, the discourse finally reflects on the narrator (or author-subject). He, too, is ironically complicit in that action. Indeed, like Larkin (though in lines rigidly end-stopped and ostentatiously rhymed), he risks a moral, though a blunter one than Larkin's:

I believe life ends with death, and that is all.
You haven't both gone shopping; just the same,
in my new black leather phone book there's your name
and the disconnected number I still call.

(CBP, p. 48)

Such a concluding irony is hard to believe and, as with so many contemporary British poems, one wonders what the motivation for such a discourse
is. It is content to publicize the frailties of others who are supposedly given
a voice, but in fact are denied one in this literary context, in such an intrusive discourse, incommensurable with the 'love' that Spender intuits.[23] Its
appropriation, its making the same of the other is, in strict Levinasian terms,
unethical.

I am not suggesting this relationship to 1950s Movement discourse is
imitative (as it clearly is in the case of Anthony Thwaite's anthologized
centre and absence narrative, 'Mr Cooper'), but just how pervasive and
persuasive the orthodoxy has been.[24] Perhaps the intrusiveness that I read
with discomfort has simply become a style.

The Return of the New

The arrival in 1993 of a second anthology called *The New Poetry* could be
seen as either an opportunistic, or an unimaginative, confirmation of Alvarez's
'negative feedback' paradigm, since it annexed not only the title but expressed similar claims to novelty as its predecessor of 31 years.

The New Poetry (the second) proposed a new generation of poets, a
term that was shortened in the marketing campaign for many of these poets
and others during 1994, the 'New Gen Poets', which involved nationwide
readings and promotions, a special edition of *Poetry Review*, the organ of
the Poetry Society, which administered it, as well as Radio 1 and other broadcast media coverage. *The Guardian* commented, 'Comedy was the new
rock 'n' roll; now poetry is staking that claim.'[25]

More significantly the anthology claimed to demonstrate the 'beginning
of the end of British poetry's tribal divisions and isolation, and a new cohe-
siveness', the end of negative feedbacks that Alvarez had proposed as the
cyclical progression of poetic development and change in the twentieth century.[26] Post-war poetry of an orthodox variety has internalized this view of

itself while perpetuating the poetic unconscious established in the 1950s. What is new here are the persistent claims to consensual inclusiveness.

The three editors rightly emphasize inclusiveness. Whereas *New Lines* contained only nine poets, *The New Poetry* 28, and *The Penguin Book of Contemporary British Poetry* featured only 20, the 1993 *The New Poetry* featured 55 poets born after 1940, selected from a list of 250 established by 'trawling exhaustively' through presses large and small (*NP93*, p.14). Not surprisingly the selection is eclectic, rather than 'cohesive'; but variety could be said to demonstrate consensus. This is oddly consonant with the rhetoric of New Labour, which was preparing itself for victory during the mid-1990s, in its apparent inclusiveness, its concern for the excluded; its embracing of a term once ridiculed by Margaret Thatcher, consensus, is striking.

On the other hand, diversity is maintained because 'the new poetry emphasizes accessibility, democracy and responsiveness ... and reaffirms the art's significance as public utterance' (*NP93*, p. 16). Its concern with identity politics is affirmed through the values and correctnesses of its time, whether that is a concern for marginalized communities and groups or the more political agendas of devolution (again to become a political reality under New Labour). For example, it is no longer a poetry of the metropolitan capital, nor of Oxford and Cambridge (or even of the university). Nor are the poets exclusively white and middle-class. There was a new sense of regionalism, 'a willing to challenge the centre' in a geographical sense, in Northern poets like Ian McMillan and a new sense of nationalism, particularly in the cultivated internationalism of the Scottish poets (*NP93*, p. 20).

'The idea of a centre is particularly fraught for those who feel marginalized' the editors remind us; (*NP93*, p. 18) with specific reference to post-coloniality and race they declare:

> By the 1980s, Britannia had long ceased to rule the waves; those in power, however, found it difficult to accept the fact. 'Inglan is a bitch', wrote Linton Kwesi Johnson'. (*NP93*, p. 16).

Although the new consensus is able to accommodate the powerful poetry of Johnson which 'has established the legitimacy of form-in-flux, of unsophisticated and fiercely targeted work that articulates the restlessness of the black diaspora', it has done so with this firm backhanded compliment (*NP93*, p. 19). That such a dynamic is implied to be 'unsophisticated' demonstrates that openness to Black British writing is not an unconditional acceptance of its oral-based aesthetic, and the use of the linguistic and cultural complexities of Nation Language and Black British vernacular in performance. It is only accepted (and acceptable) for its articulation of the dialect of an accommodated tribe, within a larger discourse of pluralism and representation *of* minorities.

The case of Jackie Kay is instructive, one of those permitted to 'preserve a relatively uncontaminated singleness of the first person'; (*NP93*, p. 23) the rhetoric of the introduction operates to assert her centrality by appeals to her (social and biographical) marginality. 'Kay's personal circumstances as a black British lesbian adopted and raised by a white Scottish family' guarantee her multiple membership of institutionalized marginalities central to the book (*NP93*, p. 18). This is emphasized by their selection from Kay's *The Adoption Papers*, from the section dealing with blatant racism.

Indeed, the notion of a 'marginality becoming central', a rare critical formulation in the editors' introduction, which they have borrowed from Terry Eagleton, becomes their metaphor for uniting their very wide range of poets in a rainbow alliance (*NP93*, p.18). Outside of the mainstream, of course, the emergent black poetries and women's poetries of the 1970s and 1980s had already staked their own claims to specificity. Ironically, the more specific, defined, they became, the more available for assimilation.[27]

Yet only 17 poets of the 55 are women, about a third. (Five out of 20 were women 'Contemporary Poets' in the *Penguin Book*: a quarter; in the 1962 *New Poetry* there were none, in the 1966 edition two, and in *New Lines* only one of the nine was a woman.) With the exception of Plath (one of Alvarez's pair), for the first time women writers like Carol Ann Duffy and Jackie Kay are commonly cited in critical studies; the former was even mooted as a possible Poet Laureate in 1999, when the post went to Andrew Motion. It must also be acknowledged that *The New Poetry* provides a better gender balance than many of the anthologies showcasing innovative work, and in my next chapter I will consider this disturbing fact.

In summary, it is the distinction of the editors, in their own opinions, that they have apparently been able not only to cease the cycles of negative feedbacks but to effect a judicious assimilation of various poetries in a spirit of what the editors describe credulously as 'total openness', to archive a healthy and democratic pluralism (*NP93*, p.14).

In support of such pluralism the editors state that the characteristic ironical strategies of the Movement are just as often replaced by a more playful 'scepticism' and a less defensive postmodernism than the ludic metaphoric tinges of the 1980s and *The Penguin Book of Contemporary British Poetry* (*NP93*, p. 27). Their poets' insistence upon a plural sense of world, action and self, through a suitable mingling of literary and non-literary styles, suits their social inclusiveness, but involves a strategically narrow definition of postmodernism. *The New Poetry* editors write loosely of 'the conception of culture as a collection of available props and an enjoyment of contradiction, discontinuity, randomness and excess' (*NP93*, pp. 23–24).

Perhaps Ian Gregson is nearer the mark in his book *Contemporary Poetry and Postmodernism* when he argues for a similar influence of postmodernism on British poetry of the 1980s and 1990s, in terms of a cultural 'melange', which 'reflects a genuine concern to oppose single-minded visions of experience with a self-conscious emphasis on diversity and mutability'.[28] Gregson speaks of British poetry's 'astonishing ability to domesticate such influences and accept them only in an altered form, and it is the hesitations between radically contradictory modes which make contemporary poetry what it is.'[29] This means that work collected in *The New Poetry*, in Gregson's analysis, is trying to effect a rapprochement between postmodernism (and modernism) and the native empirical tradition, in the name of a nuanced postmodernism.

This postmodernism – rather than the variety outlined in my introduction – can be conceived as narrowly complicit with the hyperreality of the media rather than resistant to it, as Fredric Jameson and others have argued.[30] Indeed, the media figures in these poets' thinking, as cause for ambivalence and anxiety.

David Kennedy's notion that the new public poetry of the new generation poets amounts to 'poetry as media', that it seeks a large audience while losing none of its specificity as poetry, as art (it fears it is 'open to criticism as elitist, obscure, eccentric and marginal'),[31] explains its many references to pop culture, and the desire for such poetry to be the new rock 'n' roll. Ian McMillan's 'Ted Hughes is Elvis Presley' turns on the absurdist contention that the former murdered the latter and took on his identity: one recluse, one Teddy Boy, for another. The poet as star remarks, 'At my poetry readings I sneer and rock my hips', comically, or possibly unconsciously, articulating the desire for show-biz fame of the New Gen poet (*NP93*, p. 253).

Yet it also masks a further anxiety, which involves the role of poetry in a contemporary world which is saturated by the media; the anthology is haunted by references to TV and newspapers.[32] Geoffrey Hattersley's 'Minus Three Point Six' presents the nightmare of being on a quiz programme that asks not trivial questions, but the large ones of 'Religion, Insanity, Suicide'. (*NP93*, p. 247). In Carol Ann Duffy's 'The Captain of the 1964 *Top of the Form* Team' the narrator lives his past glory as a childhood TV quiz star, mirroring national decline as he quizzes his wife and children with trivia about the premier of Rhodesia and the value of a florin; he is a victim of the media's industrial production of aural and visual simulcra. And yet the strange intrusion of Yeats's line, from the ironically relevant 'Among School Children', 'How can we know the dancer from the dance?' forces poetry into the equation. The immortality of Yeats's dancer seems compromised by the post-Gutenberg galaxy in which we cannot know the medium from the message. Postmodernist delight in the 'art' of the low cultural form of the headline, for example, is balanced by a fear of its delicious swallowing of reality and of poetry, as Carol Ann Duffy's 'Poet for Our Times' demonstrates.

At face value this is a satirical dramatic monologue of the hack headline sub-editor interspersed with parodic 'examples' of his typical endeavours (which *he* likens to haiku). They have particular targets or victims: sex is always a scandal, particularly in public political and media life, and is represented by the newspaper words 'romp' and 'bonk'; people performing such verbs are either doing it for money or are 'tarts' (*NP93*, p. 229). Homosexuality is vaguely salacious. Europeans are untrustworthy, telling tales or 'lies', or are inappropriate bed-mates (*NP93*, p. 229). Immigrants 'flood in', a typical propagandist locution, because unquantifiable, although it is only a 'claim'. A particularly clever touch by Duffy is the use of 'Heathrow Watcher' as the source of this news: an unrepresentative being who is almost given an official position in society by the baptism of this very headline, which illustrates the role of the press in the construction of our perceived social reality (*NP93*, p. 229). This is also a reminder of a real example; the narrator praises the jingoistic *Sun* headline on the controversial sinking of the Belgrano during the 1982 Falklands War: 'Gotcha!' (*NP93*, p. 229).

These would be telling points alone, about press hypocrisy, about the media's role in constructing reality, if it were not for the intrusion of this rivalry between headline writing and poetry writing. If poetry is news that stays news our newsman presents himself as a 'poet for our times', his headlines the 'poems of the decade' (*NP93*, p. 229). The anxiety of the poem is that if he is a poet then Carol Ann Duffy might not be. Poetry is the news that stays put in people's minds (and the hack's advice is not far from that of the bad creative writing tutor): 'You've got to grab attention/with just one phrase as punters rush on by.' (*NP93*, p. 229.) His art is a matter of 'knack' (*NP93*, p. 229). It bangs on as emphatically as his shout for more booze. The dream of this 'poet' is that his reportage will become memorized, will prove not to be ephemeral at all: 'Kids will know my headlines off by heart.' (*NP93*, p. 229.) Duffy finally hopes that the newsman is not a poet after all because his ambitions for his linguistic medium are debased by the medium itself, the 'instant tits and bottom line of art' (*NP93*, p. 229). In the poem's own 'bottom line', the author has the ironical last word. The fear is that the hack's words, even in Duffy's deliberate iambic doggerel and full rhyme, might spell the death of literary poetry, by becoming a more apparently adequate, though debased, index of the real.

Peter Forbes, writing in 1993, conjectured,

> It is a little known fact that the techniques of the persuaders – government spin doctors, media advisers, advertisers – are very closely allied to poetry. At a time when poetry is sidelined in our culture, a perversion of its techniques has become a powerful tool in shaping our perceptions.[33]

Whether or not this is strictly true, traditional poetic artifice can be found in media design and advertising copy. One answer to this anxiety is to attempt to become the media, as Kennedy argues, but this appears to only accentuate the anxiety, as the New Poets' obsession with the media and its relation to poetry demonstrates.

Larkin as Centre and Absence

Despite all the differences between Duffy and Larkin (particularly in terms of theme and attitudes) Justin Quinn, writing in *The Poetry Review*, remarked the Larkinesque features of 'Poet for Our Time'; 'the carefully timed vulgarity of Duffy's final line … recalls Larkin's use of the same device (… of ventriloquizing the voices of a speaker the poet despises …) in poems like "Sunny Prestatyn" and "Reading Habits".[34] Indeed, although he does not use the term, these features are generalized by Quinn, to suggest the persistence of the Movement Orthodoxy.

However, by the 1990s, that persistence was attenuated by the fact that the now unfashionable Larkin had become an optional centre and absence, like Mr Bleaney himself, of this contemporary discourse. The unofficial laureate had largely been toppled from his eminence not because of the limitations of his poetics, but for embodying social values inimical to *The New Poetry's* consensual political agenda. The posthumous revelations of his biography and letters suggested that 'to enter the poem' 'Mr Bleaney', was not 'to vote, with certain reservations, for the Labour Party at General Elections' as Jonathan Raban had supposed in 1971,[35] but something altogether more sinister.[36] These sources revealed a xenophobic racist, classist sexist consciousness unacceptable to the correctnesses of the end of the century. It was the vulgarity of the revelations, particularly in the *Letters*, edited by Anthony Thwaite in 1992, that struck readers most strongly, such as his epistolary celebration of the Conservative victory of 1970: 'Now Enoch for Home Secretary, eh? [...] Remember my song, How to Win The Next Election? "Prison for Strikers, Bring back the cat, Kick out the niggers, How about that?"' which Tom Paulin quotes in a letter to the *Times Literary Supplement*, complaining of the elisions which presumably mask more of this 'race hatred' in this 'revolting compilation which imperfectly reveals and conceals the sewer under the national monument Larkin became',[37] but as Terry Eagleton has argued such spleen is socially oriented and specific to national decline:

> Defeatist, lugubrious, implacably negative: in Philip Larkin, post-imperial Britain got the talent it deserved ... He was a death-obsessed emotionally retarded misanthropist who had the impudence to generalize his own fears and failings to the way things are.[38]

Such generalities are read back into the poetry as the false content of the empiricism. Although the core of the empiricism is not in fact touched by this just criticism, those who critically read his poetic pronouncements on mass civilization, working-class struggle, the loss of Empire, and the sexual revolution of the 1960s, would not have been surprised.

Yet, according to the introduction of *The New Poetry*, the poetry collected there, remains as oddly 'moral, representational' and 'empirical' as Movement verse had been. (*NP93*, p. 27) As Keith Tuma noted more generally of the anthology: 'Poetry for both the Movement and the New Generation poet looks very much the same on the page; ... with a distinct preference for the shorter, self-sufficient lyric or dramatic monologue.'[39]

A poem such as 'Night Shift' by Simon Armitage, admittedly a somewhat uncharacteristic work of its author, but nevertheless selected by the

editors of *The New Poetry*, signals the latest stage of the Movement Orthodoxy, and possibly its disintegration.[40] The vanished lover is almost as absent
as Mr Bleaney (and even Tony Harrison's parents) and revealed in an intimate
image of poignant regret within a domestic, claustrophobic setting:

> Upstairs, at least, there is understanding
> in things more telling than lipstick kisses:
>
> the air, still hung with spores of your hairspray;
> body-heat stowed in the crumpled duvet.
> (*NP93*, p. 338)

The empirical details constitute 'understanding'. It is precisely sense data
that supports the moral sense of precarious belonging. These people are
measured by how they live their lives, in a vicarious rhythm of 'lipstick
love-notes' and of spores and heat (*NP93*, p. 338).

There is even an echo of the Movement's characteristic moralism in the
line, subtly made forceful by its caesura, which prepares for the concluding
regret: 'We have found ourselves, but lost each other' (*NP93*, p. 338). Although the line is clearly personal ('we' are the lovers rather than humanity
in general) it has the rhythm, a ghostly iambic, and tone, of moral aphorism. That it is less certain of its social function perhaps suggests that the
artistic consensus of the 1990s was not the same as the communal and political consensus of the 1950s. Perhaps the orthodoxy's survival was now
posthumous, a haunting.

The introduction to *The Penguin Book of Poetry from Britain and Ireland since 1945*, published in 1998, offers a self-consciously millennial survey, consonant with that of *The New Poetry*, an anthology in which both
editors, Armitage and Robert Crawford, are featured. It pushes *The New
Poetry*'s central notion of plurality, consensus, or, as the editors prefer, 'the
democratic voice', back to 1945 in a revisionist reading designed to short-
circuit Alvarez's theories of generational feedback.[41] The positive aspect of
this anthology lies in its willingness to include in its consensus works written in the Celtic languages of the British Isles, and its openness to work from
the Republic of Ireland. It gives timely access to the work of Bunting, W.S.
Graham, and others, but like *The New Poetry*, it offers little room to the
figures of the British Poetry Revival or the Linguistically Innovative Poetries.

The democratic voice arrived as the obscurantism of the New Apocalypse waned. Not surprisingly, the Movement is identified as its originating

moment, and 'post-war poets' (Larkin among the list) 'wrote subtle, accessible and surprising poetry, communicating more directly with a wider public'.[42] But accessibility, communicability, is precisely a proximity with an audience that detracts from the dialogic nature of poetic openness as I have defined it, and analysed in terms of the dominant Movement Orthodoxy. Nobody would deny pluralism within these practices (indeed, its flexibility has allowed the orthodoxy to survive) but it is one achieved via a narrow definition of 'poetry'. Even the editors' attempts to decentre the Movement prove its very centrality.

> If older narratives of post-1945 poetry in these islands dwelt on the rejection of modernist aesthetics by the poets of The Movement (a group which crucially included Philip Larkin), then that now seems a dated and misleading oversimplification. Modernist interests in the run-down city, jazz and mixing unusual with demotic language, resurface in Larkin's work, for instance.[43]

This special pleading for Larkin as a proto-modernist is not convincing. To compare his patronizing depiction of devalued urban crowds with the re-explorations of Birmingham in the composite-epic of Roy Fisher is to contrast misanthropy, and worse, as I have shown, with a triumph of continual poetic renewal of the City of modernism in the de-Anglicized Midlands. Likewise Larkin's supposedly polyphonic verbal surfaces relate less to the hetereoglossia of Pound and more to uneasiness about social tone and the speaker's position in class structures.

It is with the example of jazz that Larkin's antipathy towards modernism becomes pronounced. 'After Parker ... After Picasso! After Pound! There could hardly have been a conciser summary of what I don't believe about art.'[44] Larkin suggests that a jazz writer who says that 'You can hear Bessie in Bird' may be sincere but that he rates his 'mental competence below zero'.[45] Those who hear modernism in Larkin catch the echo of an echo, and amplify the occasional French symbolist refrain into an anthem to the past.[46]

Notes

1   *The Penguin Book of Contemporary British Poetry*, eds. Blake Morrison and Andrew Motion (Harmondsworth: Penguin, 1982), p. 12. Subsequent citations of this volume will be marked *CBP* in the text.

2   *The New Poetry*, ed. A. Alvarez (Harmondsworth: Penguin, 1966), p. 15.

3   Blake Morrison, 'Young Poets in the 1970s', in *British Poetry Since 1970: a critical survey*, eds.

Peter Jones and Michael Schmidt (Manchester: Carcanet, 1980), pp. 141–56, at p. 143.

4   *Ibid.*, p. 143.

5   Answer to Questionnaire, 1982.

6   Quoted in Morrison, 'Young Poets in the 1970s', p. 154.

7   Blake Morrison, *Seamus Heaney* (London: Macmillan, 1982), pp. 14–15.

8   *Ibid.*, p. 18.

9   *Viewpoints: Poets in Conversation*, ed. John Haffenden, (London: Faber, 1982), pp. 73–74.

10   Morrison, *Seamus Heaney*, p. 30.

11   *Ibid.*, p. 13.

12   Seamus Heaney, *The Death of a Naturalist* (London: Faber, 1966), p. 15.

13   *Ibid.*, p. 15–16.

14   *Ibid.*, p. 16.

15   *Ibid.*, p. 16.

16   *Ibid.*, p. 16.

17   Blake Morrison, 'Speech and reticence: Seamus Heaney's "North"', in *British Poetry Since 1970*, eds. Jones and Schmidt, pp. 103–11, at p. 103.

18   Seamus Heaney, *Field Work* (London: Faber, 1979), p. 12.

19   P.V. Glob, *The Bog People* (London: Paladin, 1971).

20   Blake Morrison, 'Speech and reticence', p. 111.

21   Stephen Spender, 'Changeling', in *Tony Harrison*, ed. Neil Astley (Newcastle upon Tyne: Bloodaxe, 1991), pp. 221–26, at p. 221. (Morrison's own article 'Labour: Continuous' may be found on pp. 216–20 of the book, with the passage quoted by Spender on p. 216.)

22   Harrison's 'Them and [*uz*]' may be found in Tony Harrison, *Selected Poems* (Harmondsworth: Penguin, 1984), pp. 122–23; 'Long Distance' on p. 134, as well as in *CBP*, p. 48. *V* is published by Newcastle upon Tyne: Bloodaxe, 1985.

23   The rhetorical imposition upon the autobiographical is falsifying enough when the subject/object is the self, but when it is another person, and where the person may not speak, or testify, it surely amounts to an act of ontological violence, particularly as so many such poems do not attempt to fictionalize the circumstances as a novelist might. Tom Leonard has particularly harsh and apposite things to say about poetry that posits the poet as a professional 'spectator at someone else's experience' in his 'On Reclaiming the Local' in his *Reports from the Present* (London: Jonathan Cape, 1995), pp. 31–43, where he names Harrison.

24   Thwaite's 'Mr Cooper' may be found in *British Poetry since 1945* (second edition), ed. Edward Lucie-Smith (Harmondsworth: Penguin, 1985), p. 249–50.

25   Quoted in David Kennedy, *New Relations* (Bridgend: Seren, 1996), p. 236.

26   *The New Poetry*, eds. Michael Hulse, David Kennedy and David Morley (Newcastle upon Tyne: Bloodaxe Books, 1993), p. 16. Subsequent citations of this volume will be marked *NP93* in the text.

27   Women's writing can range between *One Foot on the Mountain: An Anthology of British Feminist Poetry, 1969–1979* ed. Lilian Mohin, (London: Only Women Press, 1980) and *Making for the Open: The Chatto Book of Post-Feminist Poetry*, ed. Carol Rumens (London: Chatto, 1985). Neither book contains linguistically innovative work. For defining black poetry anthologies, see *News for Babylon*, ed. James Berry (London: Chatto, 1984); *The New British Poetry*, eds. Allnutt et al, with a black poetry section ed. Fred D'Aguiar (London: Paladin,

1988); and *Hinterland: Caribbean poetry from the West Indies and Britain*, ed. E.A. Markham (Newcastle upon Tyne: Bloodaxe, 1989).

28 Ian Gregson, *Contemporary Poetry and Postmodernism: Dialogue and Estrangement* (Basingstoke: Macmillan, 1996), p. 5.

29 *Ibid.*, p. 251.

30 Jameson's famous essay 'Postmodernism and Consumer Society' in *Postmodern Culture*, ed. Hal Foster (London and Sydney: Pluto Press, 1985), pp. 111–25, defines a postmodernism complicit with advanced consumer capitalism, and sees the media as having a defining role in the process.

31 Kennedy, *New Relations*, p. 214.

32 Other poems which allude to the power of the media include Liz Lochhead's 'Bagpipe Musak, Glasgow 1990' (p. 125–27) (the title seems to refer to MacDiarmid's poem 'Glasgow 1960'); Peter Reading's 'Stet', pp. 112–13, 'From Ukulele Music', pp. 114–15 (though Reading's stance is confrontational); Tom Leonard's 'this is thi/ six a clock/ news' from 'Unrelated Incidents', p. 71 also confronts the media and, indeed, challenges its linguistic assumptions and its normative effects through a kind of anti-ventriloquism in that Glasgow dialect recasts the broadcast news into its own sociolect. Leonard seems to contest the media by ramming its words down somebody else's throat and letting him spit it back. Leonard is the only poet associated with the British Poetry Revival in *The New Poetry*. See note 23 above.

33 Quoted in Kennedy, *New Relations*, p. 214.

34 Justin Quinn, 'The Larkin-Duffy Line', *Poetry Review*, Volume 90, Number 3 (Autumn 2000) pp. 4–8, at p. 7. The Larkin poems, 'Sunny Prestatyn' and the correctly entitled 'A Study of Reading Habits' are to be found in his collection *The Whitsun Weddings* (London: Faber and Faber, 1964) at p. 35 and 31 respectively.

35 Jonathan Raban, *The Society of the Poem* (London: Harrap, 1971), p. 36.

36 The biography is Andrew Motion's *Philip Larkin: A Writer's Life* (London: Faber and Faber, 1992); the letters are *Selected Letters of Philip Larkin, 1940–1985*, ed. Anthony Thwaite (London: Faber and Faber, 1992).

37 Tom Paulin, Letter to *Times Literary Supplement*, 6 November 1992.

38 Terry Eagleton, 'A permanent casualty', *Socialist Review*, May 1993, pp. 22–23, at p. 23.

39 Keith Tuma, *Fishing by Obstinate Isles* (Evanston: Northwestern University Press, 1998), p. 199.

40 Armitage's poem was first published in *Zoom* (Newcastle upon Tyne: Bloodaxe, 1989), p. 14.

41 *The Penguin Book of Poetry from Britain and Ireland since 1945*, eds. Simon Armitage and Robert Crawford (Harmondsworth: Penguin, 1998), pp. ix–xxxii.

42 *Ibid*, p. xx.

43 *Ibid.*, p. xxvi.

44 Philip Larkin, *Required Writing* (London: Faber, 1983), pp. 292–93.

45 *Ibid.*, p. 295–96.

46 See Andrew Motion, *Philip Larkin* (London and New York: Methuen, 1982), p. 12. Motion makes the case for Larkin's use of 'strategies that derive from the modernists in general and the symbolists in particular' (p. 12).

6

Linguistically Innovative Poetry 1978–2000

Linguistically Innovative Poetry and Small Rooms in London

During the 1990s the clumsy term Linguistically Innovative Poetry began
to be used of much of the alternative British work of the era. It encompasses
a poetic of increased indeterminacy and discontinuity, the use of techniques
of disruption and of creative linkage, though its differences with the *creative* work of the British Poetry Revival do not constitute an absolute break.
However, the increased willingness of emerging poets to operate theoretically, in terms of post-structuralist and other theory, to even expound poetics more coherently, was in marked contrast to an earlier lack of such discourse. Ultimately, the definition of 'linguistically innovative' is not to be
found in the terms of its name. If anything, it is a term to constellate overlapping practices in the British alternative poetries from the 1980s onwards,
which operated under less propitious conditions than its predecessors. [1]

'Linguistically Innovative Poetry' had humble origins in the March 1988
issue of the magazine *Pages*. [2] Using the phrase to specify work 'for which we
haven't yet a satisfactory name', it was the way poet and critic Gilbert Adair
described the kinds of British poetry he believed had been 'operating since
1977' in 'fragmentation and incoherence'. [3] The choice of date is decisive; it
marks the Arts Council's takeover of the Poetry Society and the atomizing
of the community of British Poetry Revival writers. Adair, possibly looking
at it with a London bias and from the perspective of one who had not been
a member of the British Poetry Revival, declared that there had been a
'public invisibility of the poetry' and 'ditto of a theorizing discourse'. [4]

Adair's identification of the post-1977 conditions of the poetry include
'decreasing publishing opportunities; wide gaps in continuations of public
… discussions', and, looking towards the Movement Orthodoxy and the
broader literary world, 'a one-way "dialogue" with oppositions that largely

expunge us from more public discussion, … movement in a less visible, less real poetic community'.[5] This contrasts with Eric Mottram's already discussed survey 'The British Poetry Revival 1960–1975', which celebrates reputations, achievements and opportunities. Yet as republished in Hampson and Barry's volume *New British Poetries* in 1993, it carries an appendix, dated 1978, which narrates the end of the Poetry Society adventure.[6] This was the 'fragmented and incoherent' backdrop to the despair of the early 1980s, one echoed by Allen Fisher's identification, in the introduction to his 1985 *Necessary Business* essay, of those years as 'a period of entrenchment and awe … speaking in a considerably small room'.[7] Politically, a bumbling 1970s social democracy had been replaced by a right-wing ideology that wanted to change human consciousness, and nearly succeeded, 'a culture fascinated with change, ruthless curtailment of job reliabilities, share-owning, and the legitimating professionalism', as Adair put it in language redolent of common anti-Thatcher rhetoric of the era.[8]

The gesture of the 1988 anthology *The New British Poetry* to separate a section of British Poetry Revival work edited by Eric Mottram, entitled 'A Treacherous Assault on British Poetry', from the section 'Some Younger Poets', simultaneously acknowledges the proximity and difference of the two strands. Yet Ken Edwards, the editor of the latter section, notes both the sense of a revolution having been lost in the late 1970s, and the sense that his poets

> have the previous generation's work to refer to: a body of specifically British but non-parochial writing that has remained, thanks to the small presses, available and alive. Many of the poets at the younger end of this selection have *started* by discovering the work of Prynne, Mottram, Raworth, Harwood, Cobbing or Roy Fisher

before American or European works.[9]

Cris cheek recalled these troubled years, and again, taking a specific London perspective, noted:

> Rapid deterioration began. For the best part of a decade from 1980 there was only really occasional Kings' readings (put on by Eric Mottram), the Sub Voicive series curated by Gilbert Adair, and Bob Cobbing's Writers Forum workshops. Allen Fisher ran workshops at Goldsmiths' College which generated a focus and produced the Robert Sheppard, Adrian Clarke axis, and there were occasional programmes such as the RASP sessions in South London put together by Reality Studios and Spanner [the presses of Ken Edwards and Allen Fisher respectively]. But really the scene, which had been a steaming scene, went flat.[10]

While cheek saw these years as an interregnum between the British Poetry Revival and the rise of 'performance writing', I believe that these London based activities (and I was a participant, as the above proves) were
important for consolidating Linguistically Innovative Poetry, and were not
as flat as cheek suggests. They were notable for including poets who had
either not been bruised by the affairs of the 1970s, or who recognized that
the entryism of the Poetry Society could have only been temporary. Cheek
ignores a vigorous though admittedly smaller nexus of magazines than there
had been in the 1970s; Hampson and Barry itemize the following:

> Rod Mengham and John Wilkinson's *Equofinality*, Tony Baker's *Figs*, Martin
> Stannard's *joe soap's canoe*, John Welch's *The Many Review*, Tony Frazer, Ian
> Robinson and Robert Vas Dias's *Ninth Decade*, Robert Sheppard's *Pages*, Ken
> Edwards' *Reality Studios*, Paul Green's *Spectacular Diseases*, and Ric Caddel's *Staple
> Diet*.[11]

To which may be added, for the 1990s: Drew Milne's *Parataxis*, Anthony
Mellors' (and Andrew Lawson's) *Fragmente*; a revitalized *And*, edited by
Adrian Clarke and by Bob Cobbing (who had edited its first issue in 1954);
Angel Exhaust (edited mainly by Andrew Duncan, but with serial co-edi-
tors including Adrian Clarke, Scott Thurston and Simon Smith); *Object
Permanence*, edited in Glasgow by Robin Purves and Peter Manson; Tony
Frazer's *Shearsman* and Ian Robinson's *Oasis*, both slim regular magazines
after their collaborative effort. Even slimmer but more regular (though short-
lived) was Tom Raworth's *In Folio*, which miniaturized the little magazine
to a single folded A5 card, which was sometimes published daily! The fugitive nature of this last publication should remind us of the rebellious and
contentious nature of small press publishing.[12]

King's Readings (based at Mottram's college, where he became professor
of American Literature) ran between the late 1970s and the mid-1980s, dove-
tailing on alternate Tuesdays with Gilbert Adair's and Patricia Farrell's Sub
Voicive readings, which began in 1980 and continued under different
convenors. Adair was a research student of Mottram's, but Sub Voicive was
developing a new set of poets. There was a tendency for the British Poetry
Revival poets to read at King's, for example: Allen Fisher, Wendy Mulford,
Cobbing and Paul Evans, all of whom were in the 'Treacherous Assault'
section of *The New British Poetry*, whereas Edwards' 'Some Younger Poets'
– for example, Maggie O'Sullivan, Geraldine Monk, Kelvin Corcoran, Gavin
Selerie, and Edwards himself, tended to read at Sub Voicive. While both

were literally 'small rooms', King's Readings took place in an austere lecture
theatre, whereas Sub Voicive was located in a series of hired rooms above
pubs. It could be argued that the smaller audiences at Sub Voicive fostered a
stronger community of writers, and newcomers were given a chance to read;
often they took the opportunity to extend reading into performance. Writing
in 1991, Adrian Clarke and myself stated that many Sub Voicive poets

> have at one time performed their texts rather than simply read them, whether this
> has involved tapes, music, multiple voices, elements of drama and performance art,
> the creation of environments or the use of visual art.[13]

Clare Buck describes *The New British Poetry* as 'the first (anthology) to
map the challenges in the 1970s and 1980s to the myth of a new postwar
cultural consensus'.[14] It was general edited by John Muckle, who himself
read his fiction and poetry at Sub Voicive. Muckle saw the opportunity to
produce an anthology containing the alternative British poetries: black, feminist and two generations of experimental writers. The strict division of the
work in representative sections reflected a moment when there was no cross-
over between poetry 'scenes' and no critical work to make such links.[15]

While Mottram, as a former editor of the *Poetry Review*, was an obvious
choice to edit a section of British Poetry Revival work, Edwards was selected because he was by the mid-1980s editing what was the most important magazine publishing Linguistically Innovative Poetry, *Reality Studios*.
Beginning in 1978 as a few stapled sheets, distributed with another magazine,
Hampson and Barry's *Alembic*, it developed into a perfect-bound paperback
magazine with a print run of 500. The last volume appeared in 1988.

Reality Studios was important as a vehicle for poetics. The May–June
1980 issue, entitled 'the death of a referent?' was the first attempt to introduce the most recent American avant garde, the language poets, to a British
audience. Edwards himself explained the poetry in a typically British politicized way as 'reacting effectively to cultural/political enforcements ... by
exposing the mechanisms whereby language is employed to naturalize historical determinations'.[16] The use of the term 'naturalization' suggests that
Edwards was attempting to rearticulate language theory using Forrest-
Thomson's British poetics.[17]

A number of theoreticians of the language movement have argued for a
strictly 'non-referential' poetry, to completely break 'the referential qualities
of language that have been over-emphasized in modern societies' and its

poetry.[18] Some, such as Ron Silliman, have argued that reference in language is akin to commodity fetishism, and should be subverted or deregulated; politics is located within the play and clash, of indeterminate signifiers.[19] Others, such as Charles Bernstein, writing in the *Reality Studios* issue, argue, not for the 'death of a referent', but for 'a recharged use of the multivalent referential vectors that any word has, how words in combination tone and modify the associations made for each of them, how "reference" then is not a one-to-one relation to an 'object' but a perceptual dimension.'[20]

Early language poetry theory (before about 1982) was necessarily very strict in order to keep the object of its attention clear. Work from the 1970s by Bruce Andrews, Bernstein's co-editor of the influential magazine *L=A=N=G=U=A=G=E*, often contrasts a mainstream aesthetic of linguistic transparency with the structuralist analytic of opacity and difference, and extends this theoretically to the 'third paradigm' of his own work,[21] where the linguistic system is worked over to produce 'a political writing practice' that avoids complete opacity, and 'unveils or demystifies the creation & sharing of meaning ... to stress (words') use value & productivity in the face of mechanisms of social control'.[22] Language poetry was a general influence, one which encouraged the development of poetics as a discourse, and one which encouraged innovation in formal and linguistic structures, but few British writers have characterized themselves as operating exclusively in the area between the signifier and signified.

In the final issue of *Reality Studios*, Adair reviews Bruce Andrews' poetry, and writes with a political edge that matches Edwards, but with an attention to Andrews' awareness of language as an element of social control: 'The proliferation of Andrews' writing' (and Adair names a group of both US and British writers who share this sense of proliferation, and it seems reasonable to assume this poetics for his own work)

> is, it seems, a capitulation to the overproduction of message, commodity and rhythm in the consumerist urban environment, which nevertheless resists that by coupling quantity with the quality of each linguistic unit. It apes but contests the shit machine.[23]

That a younger London writer was assimilating language poetry, and speaking of it in terms borrowed from Deleuze and Guattari to describe what they would call a 'machinic' mode of literary production, is emblematic of a dual interest around the mid-1980s in the theory of language poetry and the more radical edges of critical theory.

The British connection with language poetry seems obvious because 'Linguistically Innovative Poetry' could be a synonym for this term. But Bruce Andrews, in his introduction to the anthology *Floating Capital: new poets from London* (1991), demands we should forget national differences and speak of 'this more inclusive field of so-called English language writing', which shows the 'same barriers being dismantled'.[24] However much this is desirable, I have decided to stress the less evaluated British context in this study. It has become common to remark the influence of the Vietnam War on the post-war baby boom generation of North American language poets. Questions of 'ideology, discourse, social rules, & epistemological paradigms or opacity or "sense"' raised by Bruce Andrews' academic work on US foreign policy found a place in his poetics.[25] Protest at this war had been present in British Poetry Revival work but 1980s Thatcherite Britain afforded a different situation. A foreign policy dominated by a fortuitous war in the South Atlantic and by a frantic last minute cold war before the Berlin Wall fell, was combined at least with an anti-nuclear official opposition in parliament, however unelectable. Outside of parliament inspirational protest, such as the Women's Peace Camp at the American nuclear base at Greenham Common, bred a grim optimism in direct action. To be engaged in leftist politics in Britain in the 1980s was not the act of despair it was in 1970s America. The enemy and the evil were identifiable in all their absurd manifestations, as Tom Raworth noted in the poem *West Wind*, which might be thought typical of the combative political work of the 1980s, with its attacks on a 'colourless nation/ sucking on grief'.[26] Linguistic innovation still held to the utopian resistance to the reality principle found in earlier British Poetry Revival work rather than operating in terms of Andrews' third paradigm of linguistic de-regulation.

When Adrian Clarke and I edited the anthology *Floating Capital* in 1991, this anger formed its political background, although the aesthetic aim was to bring 'linguistically innovative work' into focus, and to foreground its utopian resistance.[27] Its opening section contained the work of two poets, Bob Cobbing and Allen Fisher.

We celebrated Cobbing's 'exemplary journey of discovery and innovation', the inspiration of Writers Forum and New River Project publications and performances.[28] The project met in a large railway shed, the headquarters of the London Musicians' Collective, whose members trickled over into some of the performances: the free jazz singer Phil Minton performed with

Clive Fencott, and worked with Cobbing (as did David Toop and Paul Burwell, and – later – Lol Coxhill, from the same experimental grouping). The *Interface* issue of *Reality Studios 6* (1984) featured visual poetries and non-linear poetries, much of it showcased in performance for one or more voice at venues like the New River (and SubVoicive). This included a framed set of still images from Maggie O' Sullivan, and pages from Gilbert Adair's *Frog Boks*, a work later published by Writers Forum as a box of pages, most of which combine text and design, in which 'frog' acts as a kind of empty sign in a process of aping and contesting the shit machine. Clive Fencott and Steve Moore's *The Manual of the Permanent Waver*, a visual performance text generated by computer program from phrases of a hairdressing manual of the 1930s, is an early example of cyberpoetics. One of the first poems from Allen Fisher's *Gravity* project, 'African Twist', appeared too, parts of which Fisher read to slides of his own paintings at Sub Voicive.

'Allen Fisher is … prolific and extraordinary,' Clarke and I wrote of our second chosen poet, adding that the 'extensive project called GRAVITY AS A CONSEQUENCE OF SHAPE … has been of some importance to a number of writers reaching maturity in the mid 80s.'[29] Our introduction pointed to one differentiation with British Poetry Revival work, made visible in the shift in Fisher's poetry and poetics, from the notional poetry of place (analysed in Chapter 2) to the creative linkages of the *Gravity as a Consequence of Shape* project (to be examined in Chapter 8). The appearance of this project

> both confirmed and accelerated a shift away from ideals prevalent in the 60s and 70s in favour of approaches that attend more closely to the paving slabs than to 'open field' poetics … and the … deadening … obsession with 'place'.[30]

Instead of the post-Olsonian open field poetics favoured by Mottram, Clarke and I affirmed a Lyotardian postmodern poetics, with its 'willingness to deal with the materials that are readily to hand or impose themselves in the act of writing'.[31] Fisher's interview-essay *Necessary Business* is crucial in its attempt to articulate a poetics of a new pertinence that emphasizes activating readers through habit-breaking unpredictability and plurivocal structures. It was the best example of the theorizing discourse that Adair had demanded:

> Allen Fisher calls attention to art as 'necessary business'…. Cutting across formations categorized as discrete, 'discontinuity' is so only if it makes other relations; or else it is mimesis of actual informational chaos.[32]

The work of Adair and Edwards in *Floating Capital* may be contrasted in terms of technique. In Edwards' texts from *Drumming and Poems* (1982), a collection which prefigures many of the developments of the 1980s, 'Notation and narrative are combined with experiments with chance procedures, phrasal permutations ... sudden changes of direction ... [they] produce a ... disrupted, unsettled poetic surface'.[33] The effects of creative linkage, achieved through collage techniques, such as cut-up, are surreal.

> 2 pints of lager
> was laughing in your sleep,
> flutes of your bones
> picking the ball out of the back of the net,[34]

introduces us to the dream-world of the 'down & out' who addresses 'the Daily Mail lady' on the 'Poster, Walworth Rd, winter '80' of its title: 'In autumn you bathe in oatmeal'.[35] Edwards presents a sardonic glimpse of complacent wealth:

> Look at the
> valuable kitchen accessories;
> new they suddenly united,
> snorting. The colours
> are branded goods,
> products which recognise & respond to
> human needs.[36]

The superior snorting undermines the claim to agency and response of the heavily represented world of consumerism. The inessential 'accessories' are valuable only through their colour-coded brand names.

Adair is more theoretical in his text *Hot Licks* (1987), more likely to court informational chaos in the service of his analysis, to both ape and contest the social reality, to create discontinuity so that new connections may be made in its creative linkage. Yet what is striking is the same political anger; the reader, too, is out on the streets, courting the sinister hidden order amongst the *social* discontinuities:

> it's a bus queue
> too drunk to form up
> chamber of tongue
> eyes   hold   from holes hold
> held by a fury body-lens

> *militarisation of entire culture*
> joy of plague reasons mob interior
> de-educate contain the unoccupiable for use
> police the wastes[37]

Paul Virilio waits for the night bus, it seems, as the mob internalizes its own repression, as hopelessly as the down and out peering at a society that attempts to totalize control insidiously through its billboards. These poems, in different ways, replicate the constrained paranoia of the left during the Thatcher years, as well as demonstrating the technical resources of London's Linguistically Innovative Poetry, to which I shall return in Chapter 8.

Cambridge: Towards a Community of Risk

'London writers,' declared Keith Tuma in 1998,

> are sometimes supposed to be at odds with writers affiliated with another cultural centre, Cambridge. Such tensions ... were no doubt exacerbated by an issue of the magazine *Angel Exhaust* containing ... editor Andrew Duncan's essay 'The Cambridge Leisure Centre: Traits' ......[38]

Another American commentator, Charles Bernstein, co-editor of *L=A=N=G=U=A=G=E* magazine, noted in 1994 a split between London's Linguistically Innovative Poetry and a Cambridge poetry which he negatively characterized as 'renovations (or refashionings) of lyrical and pastoral (or postpastoral) forms',[39] and noted that 'a particular range of aesthetic procedures seems to be propped up by a patrician decorum and Oxbridge authoritativeness that barely covers over the thematic renunciation of these values'.[40]

Duncan's article attempted taxonomy of the Cambridge tribe as yet another 'lit room' for 'the ambient medium of society'.[41] Duncan discerns three factors, the first being the pervasive influence of Prynne. Ben Watson has written that the annual Cambridge Conference of Contemporary Poetry (which began in 1991), 'was founded by Prynnians, but (Prynne)'s such a crucial figure to the attenders, he himself cannot attend (as Ian Patterson, one of Prynne's proselytisers put it, "he's made himself the Pope, so now he can't be there.")'.[42] Secondly, Duncan notes, the 'reputation of the group is for hermetic complexity'; certainly Prynne's poetry is difficult and allusive, mannered and gestural in a way that may be imitated, but there is a contrary tendency to follow the example of Peter Riley.[43]

Duncan thirdly detects 'a remarkable density of serious Marxist politics' (yet he also acknowledges 'an undocumented strand of Far Right thought in another groupuscule'); he has in mind the younger generation of theorists and poets, such as the 'Material Esthetix' of Watson, or the thinking of Drew Milne.[44]

Milne was editor of the influential magazine *Parataxis* between 1992 and 1996, a journal whose subtitle, 'modernism and modern writing' announced its resistance to postmodernism and suggested the Adornoesque high modernist line of its critical content. In the third issue, in 1993, Milne's article 'Agoraphobia, and the embarrassment of manifestos: notes towards a community of risk' sought 'to ventriloquize a utopian collective',[45] 'a community of writing which liberates its possible readers',[46] and a poetics of 'the residual and emergent avant-gardes of contemporary poetry'.[47] He identifies conditions which militate against the collective. He attacks the exclusivity of the Cambridge poetry scene; Duncan suggests that the 'coterie smugness of the poets', which Bernstein sees as aesthetically self-defeating, is a remedy against the 'encircling chill' of the atmosphere of Cambridge University.[48] 'An embarrassment with direct statement', both in poetry and poetics, combines, for Milne, with 'hostility to traditional literary criticism and literary theory',[49] the refusal to theorize that Adair had noted; Adair and Milne (in their different ways) were both poets who fought this tendency in their own creative and critical work. The 'embarrassment of manifestos' is a clear plea for the development of poetics. Milne's argument pays scant attention to the development of this discourse in the London grouping, and he has been a resistant but perceptive critic of language poetry theory; his focus is Cambridge, yet he expresses his annoyance at both Peter Riley and Denise Riley for denying the term 'Cambridge poetry':

> The fear of labels is an endemic and edenic aspect of poetry, and the non-identity of such communities, perhaps best described as the Cambridge axis, indicates the need for a poetics of community, a poetics which, if successful, would have considerable and more general political value.[50]

Apart from nostalgia for the stridency and intimacy of *The English Intelligencer* of the 1960s, he finds little to fulfil his wishes in 1993, though *Parataxis* itself preserved some form of community. Indeed one result of perceived insularity is the detailed way Cambridge poets critique one another. Like the writings of the American language poets these are no mutual back-slapping exercises. This contrasts with the paucity of critical writing in the London grouping, despite the examples of Fisher and Adair.

Probably the most extraordinary Cambridge activity, though, is Rod Mengham's small press Equipage which has, with great frequency, brought out pamphlets, often from the now wide age range, of Cambridge poets, from Prynne and Chaloner, to Wilkinson and Drew Milne, to the active young editor of *Quid*, Keston Sutherland, but also of outsiders, such as Allen Fisher and Ulli Freer. By 2000 he had published over 60 pamphlets.

Throughout the late 1980s and 1990s, Iain Sinclair was clearly collecting this series, and when he was commissioned to edit an anthology, this 'mass of instant-printed pamphlets that pile up around my desk' was readily to hand, and furnished many of his selections.[51]

Conductors of Chaos: **Crusty Revenants and Uppity Newcomers**

Sinclair edited *Conductors of Chaos* in 1996; as Poetry Consultant at Paladin, after John Muckle, he had attempted to obtain the same visibility for marginal poets that he has achieved himself, chiefly as a novelist.[52] However it is odd that his introduction should not mention *The New British Poetry*, particularly since much of his introduction is exhausted critiquing 'the absolute betrayal of the programme they presume to promote' of the 'ice-floe of meaningless anthologies' that have appeared since the 1960s (*CC*, p. xiii). He correctly suggests that, after Michael Horovitz's *Children of Albion*, they had become an institution for 'the suppression of a more radical and heterodox body of work' (*CC*, p. xv).

My characterizations of the little press scene lack the panache and imaginative gloss provided by Sinclair's introduction. The gifts that have justly made Sinclair an acclaimed novelist, the depiction of a gritty hyperreality, an arcane and conspiratorial world, as evinced in *White Chappell, Scarlet Tracings* (1987), are deployed to create a vampiric world of poetic parasitism and backbiting. Its

> special-needs citizen[s] … correspond compulsively and at length, dispatching multiple photocopies of their poison-pen squibs to the relevant small-press editors. A private world: their reports, scratched on glass, are of events that happen elsewhere, outside, beyond their sphere of influence. (*CC*, p. xviii)

The introduction is unfortunately entitled 'Infamous and Invisible' but the mythic infamy only contributes to the continued invisibility. Boldly subtitled

'A Manifesto for Those Who Do not Believe in Such Things', Sinclair's introduction presumes to speak for his 36 various poets (or 'pick-'n'-mix shambles of has-beens, headcases and emerging chancers' as he prefers) (*CC*, p. xiii). As a manifesto it is lacking; Sinclair has no theory of textual complexity, no appeals to a poetics, other than asserting the work's right to be difficult: 'The work I value is that which seems most remote, alienated, fractured. I don't claim to "understand" it but I like having it around.' (*CC*, p. vii). His assertion that 'these apes from the attic ... are the ones that have been locked away, those who rather enjoy it', seems perverse given the involvement of many of the contributors in publishing and performing ventures, such as Brian Catling, whose performance *The Blindings* at the Serpentine Galleries in 1994, consisted of him reading for 8 hours a day for the length of the show (*CC*, p. xvii).[53]

It is, however, this sort of performance work that Sinclair has in mind when he admits 'that something, at last, is *happening* out there: crusty revenants conspiring with uppity newcomers'. (*CC*, p. xviii) The anthology is mainly a mixture of these new performance writers and work of the Cambridge axis, along with established writers, such as Harwood, Allen Fisher and Griffiths (and some New Apocalypse and modernist poets of the past).

J.H. Prynne is represented by one of his baffling texts of the 1990s, 'Her Weasels Wild Returning'; its seven sections of 24 lines suggest the measures of time itself, while focusing, not on an 'I', however fractured, but on an obsessively tracked 'she, she, she, and only she', almost quoting one of Coleridge's complaints to Asra (*CC*, p. 351). Whereas earlier work had used specific specialized discourses, such as geology, this text seems to connote simultaneously the language and worlds of consumerism, and scarcity, physical attack, even rape, in a knot of reference that, following Forrest-Thomson, might be called an 'image-complex', which leads to the condition of 'suspended naturalization'.[54] The connotations that radiate from the word 'slashed', invite the sceptical judgement that follows:

> Her step pervades
> the slashed shelf life here to utter startled bleeding, that
> can't be right, loaded entry starvation gives over at last
> these new particulate verticals.
> (*CC*, p. 351)

The text intertwines its discourses so that on different readings different connections seem prominent. The loading bays of supermarkets which promise starvation may indeed 'give over' to other readings in which 'particulate verticals' may suggest rainfall, scientific discourse, or return the reader to supermarket shelves, or even the shelf upon which 'she' is left. Even then there is the suspicion that 'that can't be right', semantically or morally.

The influence of this dense multiple referentiality can be detected in the works of John Wilkinson and Drew Milne. In one example of the harsh mutual-critiquing of the Cambridge poets, Drew Milne usefully defines Wilkinson's differences from Prynne in terms of semantic containment and dispersal.

> Whereas Prynne's work often seems constrained by the authority of an almost literal, stoic fidelity to relations between cognition and semantics, Wilkinson's work is more restless … in a perpetually renewing struggle for recognition which is reluctant to eschew the possibility of a freer subjectivity.[55]

Part of this restless struggle can be seen in 'Cabling the Suburbs' from *Conductors of Chaos*; the title alludes to the installation of underground communication cables connecting a domestic margin to an absent centre.

> The valleys echoed cathedral with mechanical
> azaleas, roseate petals smudged down the pathway,
> cones were set out, varicose cables trenched
> off the head station, little magnetic workers
> trudge down their powerful lines blowing & refute.
>   (*CC*, p. 468)

Although there are some visual images here (varicose, for example), 'Wilkinson's work affords many such uncanny encounters with our polluted life-world, drawing out figures of lyric form from a distress which is at once social and political', as Milne says.[56] The mechanical azaleas, the magnetic workers are not simply the metal cable being laid, but have become autonomous metaphors. The lyricism of this is indeed conducted through figurative devices, a semantic dispersal that Wilkinson characterizes as 'metastatic'. This is a way of describing a dispersal of linguistic elements, that are also subjective counters, throughout the body of the poem (metastasis literally describes the spreading of cancer cells) through 'a set of linked and transforming entities, which can be syntactical gestures, vowel and consonant patterning, imagistic or discursive modes'.[57]

The metaphors take over the power of narrative and argument without becoming either, the struggle for recognition of its subjective agency and efficacy. A state of stillborn economics where riots are emphatically at home, offers the 'Birth stagflation riots in the nest in their nest' of the poem's opening, with its strange repetition that reminds us that 'they' own the nest (*CC*, p. 468). This improvisatory method of composition, a series of transformations and dispersals, brings it closer to the practice of Allen Fisher and others than the resultant hard surface might suggest.[58] Interestingly, Wilkinson takes up Milne's term risk to discuss his method 'at the micro-level ...'

> Risk in poetry is found where the accepted word would join the poem in an unanticipated way to the world ... It's hard sometimes to know the difference between risk and defence. If I vandalize a lucid but banal passage am I taking a risk (with a reader's willingness to follow) ... ?[59]

Perhaps the passage I quote above originally contained the banality of the empirical but was editorially 'vandalized' out of easeful lucidity. The asyntactical and unanticipated '& refute' refutes the visual images of workmen digging that lie behind the metaphors. By the time the poem ends the suburban has become a desert; identity is dispersed and desperate, multiple yet collectively narcissistic:

> Reprobates they cry, then a devolved cost rifle
> pans out as We. We where the child pinkish like
> from an exhaust, We passing for collective in
> multiplex repeat but through carbon foil, we
> whether we like it or not, wringing the crusts.
> (*CC*, p. 469)

A series of metastatic figures works alongside the first person plural here: the exhaust, the carbon, reminders of the ecological vandalism that supports the multiplex, the social emerging from the lyrical trajectory.

While Milne sees the political shining through the lyric resources, Wilkinson sees the opposite in Milne. In his introduction to Milne's *Conductors of Chaos* selection, he writes, 'Milne's use of poetry as a critical instrument is not reduction of its lyrical potency.' (*CC*, p. 253.) Repetition is more controlled for Milne: each of the 12 15-line poems of his sequence begins with the word 'Clamour ...' and the effect is not of dispersal but of confinement. The title 'Foul Papers' is focused for the reader by a characteristic epigraph from Hegel: 'Reading the morning paper is the realist's morning prayer', but Milne seeks to deconstruct what he finds; the text is a reading through the Daily Clamour of newsprint:

> a flurry of front page glorie
> and nemesis time on the footsie,
> when ten thousand chickens died, we're told,
> in a fire started on purpose.
>
> (CC, p. 255)

The 'we're told' is not parenthetical but chillingly central: the paper's 'foul' news punning away the 'fowl' news, and the casual, even flirty, abbreviation of the Financial Times Share Index (FTSI), whose index involves the nemesis of the financial loss of such news. The juxtapositions here reflect the juxtaposition that news itself offers. The section finishes:

> though
> I suppose it's the marine in me
> says go if the hearing continues.
>
> (CC, p. 255)

This would be funny if it were not the sudden intrusion of an individualized militarism that can threaten and act against the impositions of a legal proceeding, such as a public 'hearing', inquiry or inquest.

While the poem is polyphonic ('Voices rather than voice, then, and as writing' as Milne writes elsewhere), [60] the gesture requires an Adornoesque belief in the resistance inherent in the autonomy of the art object, but Milne rejects the emptiness of Ackroyd's theories of autonomy, and the utopian ease of Marcuse. Yet the text hovers around a skeletal argument in its elaborate punning: 'word without bend/ in a maze of blight' (world without end in a blaze of light) (CC, p. 257) that is constantly refunctioning the 'wisdom' of the cliché, a borrowing that is precisely 'debit where debit is due' (CC, p. 254). There is a savage indignation that instructs us at its end to 'stand toxic, tall and tousled, as we/ go forth coldly into the dark page', (CC, p. 259) which is a call to use poetry as a critical instrument upon the real, which, despite the worked surface, recalls Adair's anti-Thatcherite bus stop resistance.

Peter Riley represents the lyrical, even pastoral, side of Cambridge poetry in his long poem *Alstonefield*. Whether his work amounts to the 'renovations' detected by Bernstein, he courts the evocation of a fragile pastoral balanced against the modern world, exequy against decay, Blake's echoing green echoed again in an image of community that harbours sinister secrecy:

> But a pastoral substantive, where the story
> gathers to a close the community accedes to what
> 'must be' in secret delight. Here the maidens
> dance on the darkening green to the end of day
> a torse in history that rights itself by
> candle lanterns, as the soul is timed to
> exequies. Bow to it and cross the glowing river
> on a wooden footbridge into urban decay.
>   (*CC*, p. 409–10)

But the torse of the past can also involve the textual materials of another of Riley's projects, *Excavations*, which collages the writings of J.R. Mortimer on his exhaustive and actual excavations of burial mounds, with Tudor songs, to present a reconfiguration of our knowledges of what lies under urban decay:

> hollows in the earth, **the secrets of our hearts** declaimed from ridge to ridge as white
> tumuli, writing the edge of belonging on a winter arch.
> (*CC*, p. 405)

These conductions of order, rather than chaos, this writing of such an edge in *Excavations* brings the text closer to the historical found poetry of Bill Griffiths or to Linguistically Innovative Poetry than its author would acknowledge. Tom Lowenstein calls the first two parts, published as *Distant Points*, by Reality Street,

> a recalcitrant, somewhat rebarbative text. Dislocated and restless, the eye forks over
> the paragraphs in search of connections that make sense, greedy for the threads,
> veins, intercalations offering a route through the labyrinths of discord. And is this
> not the nature of excavation?[61]

Sinclair's anthology also reflects the growth of a specific 'performance writing'. Not to be confused with the populist performance poetry to be found in most cities and towns (a distant descendent of the British Beats of the 1960s), this emergent practice developed out of the performance contexts of British poetry in the 1970s and 1980s analysed above. It found a temporary institutional home at Dartington College of the Arts, in Devon. Aaron Williamson, for a while a research fellow there, was witnessed in performance by Susan de Muth of the *Independent* in 1995:

When he bursts through the glass doors, it is like an explosion of noise. People step back, tread on each others' toes, stumble; we're assaulted by the violent cacophony of his roaring, screaming, jibbering, weeping and moaning.[62]

Indeed 'Cacophonies' is the title of one sequence excerpted in *Conductors Of Chaos*. The poems are exacting explorations of the condition of profound deafness.

Stamping so that the floorboards resound, Williamson strikes a balletic pose and suddenly, from the echoes of this aural anarchy, brings forth a serene and lucid stream of poetry. The feedback from his wayward hearing aid produces an eerie accompaniment which could be the music of the spheres. Some people cry. The experience is overwhelming.[63]

When Williamson says, 'The words themselves, the modes of saying, are as significant as meaning,' he is opening up his practice to 'a more physical currency of accord' that would try to avoid thematizing the text by re-casting it in a more performative mode.[64] On the page the 'Cacophony' is a text of misheard 'confused loads', of corrections ('yes that one'), and the existentially chilling, 'you've lost me' of the deaf (*CC*, pp. 481–82). The text stutters, tongue-tied, breaks up language, lards the interstices between words with other words, word-parts and anagram, uses enjambement to prise open lexical items and suggests performance in its notation, in a manner reminiscent of Maggie O'Sullivan's work.

> Contin-
> uses contingent on con-
> -tract, facts tussle 'twixt centre and
> everywidewhere ELSEWISE
> or 'role', or 'participant'
> 'lore', 'rawstate', 'poor'
> litigant, COMP
> -pet-eat-height-or, MANAGERing – birthing
> as U-Factor
>
> (*CC*, p. 482)

The nature of identity, of the 'U', and the 'participating hazards' of identifying with a centre that seems defined by laws rather than roles and lores is contrasted to the 'everywidewhere' of elsewhere. Between these extremes, the facts, like the text in performance, tussles.

The similarly centred lines of 'Stranger' by cris cheek look so fixed

upon the pages of *Conductors of Chaos*, that it is a surprise to hear performance variations on his own *Skin Upon Skin* studio CD, also released in
1996.[65] Indeed one can hear the process of word transformation, as 'tactic'
becomes 'tic tac' in the passage below, and one can then see how 'stranger'
became 'stringer' in the printed text. Oral improvisation, transcription,
computer screen design, and subsequent performance, are the acknowledged stages of creation. Yet it is also a meditation upon estrangement
and alienation, focussing at times on the island of Madagascar, sometimes on its own processes and orderings. The recasting of Felicia Hemans'
famous lines of maritime catastrophe is only one of the most obvious
verbal transformations, one which introduces the theme of nomadic movement:

> The toy stood on the turning Wreck
> Of climax and Closure.
> To distract from a diversionary
>
> Because to sequence the modern and get it 'right' in that
> Sequence is not Necessarily order, right?
>
> To distract from a diversionary modern tic tac
> Or there isn't time for letters and you can't afford to phone – country road
> – Going home.
>
> (*CC*, p. 35)

Vocal techniques – breathing and throat sounds (reminiscent of the sound
poetry of Henri Chopin), half-singing, full song (as in the lines from a
country song above) – are heard against an intermittent chant and violin
drone. The intonation patterns are not those of ordinary speech. Such effects are improvised from the text (or some variant) and range between the
mimetic (the quoted song) and the random (sudden dips of tone or squeaky
falsettos). The 'text' is also its performance and its subsequent transformations. The risk is that it might be performed or re-inscribed in less, as well
as more, interesting ways, that climax and closure might not become inte-
grated. But the text itself poses a question that (given its serial transformation) is oddly rhetorical among such transitions.

> Now – is poetry then
> a process of arresting
> or of Moving?
> (*CC*, p. 36)

If we equate arrest with the Levinasian said and movement with the saying, this poetry opts for the constant promise of re-invention imposed by the transformations. But the poetry of moving must embrace the arrest (which is only a rest) in the material text upon the page, and even as sound traces on the CD.

Caroline Bergvall delivered a keynote paper at a 1996 conference concerning performance, at Dartington College, when she was the director of the performance writing programme. The questions she asks about the 'concerted excavation of the intradisciplinarity of much textual work' push the possible boundaries of what might be considered performance beyond the two examples above:[66]

> Is it not Performance Writing to site some text in a space or on a wall or on electronic boards? ... Is it not Performance Writing to treat spoken writing as part of a sound composition ... to inscribe words on a canvas, spray them on a wall, layer text into photographs or carve them into wood, steel or other solids ... ? to use text as part of a body-related piece ... ? to bleed a word into flesh ... ? Is it not Performance Writing to generate text for the page ... ?[67]

This is a stance that acknowledges that writing itself *is* performance, which is at once liberating and limiting for the question remains: what will *not* be performance? If everything is, what value and specificity can the category have? To include under this rubric, writing 'activated for and through a stage, for and through a site, a time-frame, a performer's body, the body of a voice or the body of a page' authorizes experimentation in dozens of ways out *from* writing, but simultaneously directs attention to a kind of total artifice that emphasizes the materiality of any aspect of language and its propagation, since

> everything about a piece of work is active and carries meaning. Any treatment, any font, any blank, any punctuation, any intonation, any choice of materials, any blob, however seemingly peripheral to the work, is part of the work, carries it, opens it up, closes it in, determines it.[68]

Williamson, cheek and Bergvall herself have explored performing with musicians and dancers, but also have investigated site-specific installation work, and cheek has been exploring hybrid forms of writing.[69] Brian Catling, for example, is also a sculptor, performer and book artist.[70]

Sinclair's anthology showcases Bergvall's splendidly funny, typographically extravagant, post-porn ('leg over') (*CC*, p. 6) piece for two 'kissers': ('come legs over legs suck armpits with tongue/ come legs over neck press belly on butt') (*CC*, p. 7). The accompanying marginal gloss reads: 'on remembering one's past suddenly' (*CC*, p. 7). It is this bodily memory of sexual experience that informs what Drew Milne has called her 'queer poetics'.[71] The text (it is not easy to see what performance would unravel from the page) ends:

> muscle-constructions do the archaeology of sex in one hundred and twenty situations [the text is entitled *In Situ*] and ah ah where you have just come from disperses in the growing background: so I'll ask you once again what do you remember of what you know. (*CC*, p. 10)

Out of Everywhere: Being a Woman Poet

The absence of women writers in the British Poetry Revival has been noted; Horovitz's *Children of Albion* was 'no more hospitable to women than [Alvarez's] *The New Poetry*' as Claire Buck says, but little has been suggested as to why this was so.[72] One of the five women among the 63 poets of *Children of Albion*, Libby Houston, remembered being involved in Horovitz's proto-Beat scene and recalled being the only woman to attend readings, a view echoed in Michelene Wandor's memories of a slightly later period;

> In the late 1960s–early 1970s I had read my poetry at the very many poetry-reading venues there were but had stopped by choice, since I felt uncomfortable at being (mostly) the only woman poet – the other women around were wives or groupies, and I always felt a bit odd in relation to both camps.[73]

Female audience members clearly were defined in relation to male audiences and male poets. The word 'groupie' suggests not just an importation of pop argot, but the adoption of its macho ethos. A groupie is there to have casual sex with the poetry star. Such a scene – and the poetry reading was as vital to the survival of the poetry as print – would be prohibitive for a woman writer or audience member. Readings were often held in pubs, traditional male territory; the potential childcare problems of attending readings, let alone going on 'tour', must be recalled too. A telling anecdote of Houston suggests that women were expected to play other familiar roles.

> I could flash a smile, dress up, being a woman part of the act which belonged there. When Horovitz and [Pete] Brown set about starting a reading agency, *Poetry in Motion* … eyebrows were raised at me, the woman … to run it.[74]

If sexism was rife through the underground – and even if it was not – it is not surprising that aspiring women poets of the 1960s and 1970s turned to the women's movement for an audience, although the movement was not unequivocally receptive. Wandor recalls political attacks on poetry as 'moribund',[75] so it is small wonder that, as Claire Buck states,

> The poetry that flourished within the context of the new women's movement was characterized by a clear fidelity to its political ideals translated into a poetics concerned with cultural critique, an accessible language and form, and the expression of women's personal experience.[76]

Clearly distinct if not distant from the poetry dealt with here, some of this work was collected in *The New British Poetry*. While its feminist section was slim on the grounds that women were also represented in the black writing section and the two sections which are my concern here, Mottram's British Poetry Revival section has only 2 women poets out of its 25, Denise Riley and Wendy Mulford. Linguistically Innovative Poetry by women has not fared much better; Edwards' section, 'Some Younger Poets', has 4 women out of 18 poets, and *Conductors of Chaos* showcases only 5 women out of 36 contributors.

However, there seemed a genuine paucity of women writers. When Maggie O'Sullivan, who was only too keen to redress this imbalance, edited *Out of Everywhere: Linguistically Innovative Poetry by Women in North America & the UK* in 1996, she could only find nine British poets to join the 21 from across the Atlantic.[77]

Out of Everywhere therefore features a large selection of North American, mostly language, poetry. It is interesting to see that, by 1996, it was possible to place British work alongside North American work in the same context; for example, to put Bergvall's performance work next to Rosmarie Waldrop's extraordinary series of prose texts 'writing back' to other texts.[78] Such work is located outside of most gatherings, and discussions, of women's poetry, despite its importance for certain questions concerning women's writing, such as French feminism's identification of a specific *écriture féminine*.[79] O'Sullivan's introduction quotes the words of 'an unidentified audience member' at a Waldrop talk who noted how such linguistically innovative work by women is *doubly* excluded from the institutionized marginality of feminist poetry or from Gilbert and Gubar style anthologies.[80] The comment provides O'Sullivan's anthology with its title: 'There's an extra difficulty being a woman poet and writing the kind of poetry you write:

you are out of everywhere (laughter).'[81] This ambivalent evocation of both inclusion and exclusion is apposite. O'Sullivan points out, perhaps a little too stridently, that

> Excluded from 'women's canons', such work does, however, connect up with linguistically innovative work by men who have themselves also transcended the agenda-based and cliché-ridden rallying positions of mainstream poetry.[82]

As early as 1984, O'Sullivan and Geraldine Monk launched an attack in an article which prepared the ground for *Out of Everywhere*. They argue that feminist poetry, far from raising consciousness, is often 'versified propaganda' and, more importantly, is being falsely 'validated as the poetry that speaks for women'.[83] In terms that mirror Buck's analysis, they argue that

> the most effective chance any woman has of dismantling the fallacy of male creative supremacy is simply by writing poetry of a kind which is liberating by the breadth of its range, risk and innovation ... to exploit and realize the full potential and importance of language.[84]

Caroline Bergvall, Maggie O'Sullivan and Geraldine Monk, are featured in both the 1996 anthologies, as is Denise Riley. Claire Buck argues that Riley, too, was 'out of everywhere', because her 'focus on the poststructuralist concerns of language and sexual difference place her ... in opposition to the main trajectory of feminist poetry in both the 1970s and the 1980s.'[85] After some years of poetic silence, the genuine and distinctive voice of Riley rose to prominence, with two Reality Street collections, one of new poems, *Mop Mop Georgette* in 1993, and her *Selected Poems* in 2000. Among the formal experimentation of *Out of Everywhere*, her work (which, in any case, has also found itself in the *Penguin Modern Poets* series), seems muted, the ironical play with voice and self more often attenuated by traditional rhetorical figures; she is often seen as another member of the Cambridge axis. However, the texts are full of evanescent presentations of a far from stable female ego, a voice in which the promises of identity divide and dissolve into the 'I' provided by the lyric poetry tradition. Like Milne, she articulates voices (not 'voice'); most of them want to act out a self-absorbed otherness:

> in sleep alone I get articulate to mouth the part of
> anyone and reel off others' characters until the focus
>
> of a day through one-eyed self sets in again: go into it.
> I must.
>
> (*CC*, p. 393)

The weaving of song lyrics into the text (so that what is quotation and what
is not, what is expressive and what is ironic, is unclear) enacts the ambivalent remembering and misremembering of a nostalgic and narcissistic content that the poems themselves appear to offer, as in 'Lure 1963':

> Oh yes I'm the great pretender. Red lays a stripe of darkest
> green on dark. My need is such I pretend too much. I'm
> wearing. And you're not listening to a word I say.[86]

Fashion and emotional excess are intertwined in the word 'wearing'. Such
sartorial disguise and the deference to the ventriloquial articulations of popular song result in the ego singing, rather than talking, to itself.

Anthologies and Assemblages

A confident editorial route taken by poet Richard Caddel and critic Peter
Quartermain in editing *Other: British and Irish Poetry since 1970*, is to follow the North American fashion for teaching anthologies, an academic
option one might imagine Sinclair, for example, deploring. As a number of
poets enter the academy as teachers of literature or of creative and performance writing; as books such as former *Alembic* editors Hampson and
Barry's *New British Poetries*, and indeed, the present study, are published;
as conferences, such as Hampson's at the University of London, are organized; as even a Centre for Contemporary Poetics is convened; the
academicization of poetry is inevitable. Even the late 1990s Sub Voicive
Colloquia have been held in academic institutions.

Indeed the occasion for *Other*, which was published by Wesleyan University Press in New England, in 1999, may have been the University of
New Hampshire conference *Assembling the Alternatives*. Another event of
1996, this conference assembled 'alternative' British, North American, Irish
and Antipodean poets side by side. British writers such as Tom Raworth,
Allen Fisher, Ken Edwards, cris cheek, Miles Champion, Maggie O'Sullivan
and Denise Riley, appeared alongside the leading language poets to both
read and discuss poetics. Given the historical reluctance to theorize in Britain, and the lack of celebrity enjoyed by these writers, this event may be
thought of as an international academic validation of this British writing.
However, the fact that, like the anthology, it was not British in origin, tempers
the celebration.[87]

Other also placed these writers alongside some Irish counterparts who attended the conference, such as Catherine Walsh and Maurice Scully, whose poetry may be read about elsewhere.[88] Caddel and Quartermain – both Bunting scholars – might also have been expected to include post-Objectivist writers, such as John Seed, Tony Baker, and Caddel himself, who have been dealt with only slenderly in this study, as have the black writers collected there, such as Linton Kwesi Johnson, Grace Nichols and Fred D'Aguiar.

Such omissions are, I hope, understandable in assembling the kinds of alternatives I have been attempted to outline in Chapters 2 and 6. Recent younger writers have particularly faced exclusion.[89] Such imposition of silence upon those various sayings amid the noisy thematizing of such history, is forgivable only because such a beginning is only a beginning. Indeed, omissions are testimony to one of my main claims about this poetry through the decades: that it is multifarious and complex. The editors of *Other*, for example, anthologise 55 poets but name a further 55 in their introduction. The imperative, for myself, and for others, as academics, critics, editors, publishers, and writers of poetics and poetry, is to feed both the poetry's histories and its futures.

Notes

1   The term is found most prominently in the subtitle of Maggie O'Sullivan's *Out of Everywhere: linguistically innovative poetry by women in North America & the UK* (London and Saxmundham: Reality Street, 1996), yet its original intention to specify a British (and possibly Irish) poetry is often ignored.

2   Gilbert Adair, 'Dear Robert, "Linguistically innovative poetry" for which we haven't yet a satisfactory name', *Pages* 65–72 (March 1988), p. 68. That I was the editor of that publication and Adair's remarks were addressed to me must be acknowledged.

3   *Ibid.*, p. 68.

4   *Ibid.*, p. 68.

5   *Ibid.*, p. 68.

6   Eric Mottram, 'The British Poetry Revival, 1960–75', in Robert Hampson and Peter Barry, eds., *New British Poetries* (Manchester: Manchester University Press, 1993), pp 15–50.

7   Allen Fisher, *Necessary Business* (London: Spanner, 1985), p. 163.

8   Adair, 'Dear Robert', p. 68.

9   *The New British Poetry* eds. Gillian Allnutt, Fred D'Aguiar, Ken Edwards and Eric Mottram (London: Paladin, 1988), p. 267. Indeed, the desire to anthologize new work coincided with the desire to collect and select older work at this time, for example: Lee Harwood, *Crossing*

the Frozen River: selected poems (London: Paladin, 1988), and Tom Raworth (second edition) *Tottering State; Selected Poems 1963–1987* (London: Paladin, 1988). Like *The New British Poetry*, they were general edited by John Muckle. (The Carcanet anthology of Cambridge poetry, *A Various* Art (1987), was reissued by Paladin in 1990.)

10   Quoted in Keith Tuma *Fishing by Obstinate Isles* (Evanston: Northwestern University Press, 1998), p. 212. Even here there are strange assignations. I had nothing to do with the Goldsmiths' workshop, though Clarke did. Hampson and Barry write similarly of 'the poetry workshop run successively by Paul Brown, Allen Fisher and Robert Sheppard' ('The scope of the possible' in Hampson and Barry, *New British Poetries*, pp. 1–11, at p. 9); the first two ran the official Goldsmiths' course; I convened informal, deliberately unnamed meetings, at my house.

11   Hampson and Barry, 'The scope of the possible', p. 9.

12   Wolfgang Gortschacher, *Little Magazine Profiles* (Saltzburg: University of Saltzburg, 1993) is a full-length study of the phenomenon of little magazines. Geoffrey Soar and R.J. Ellis, 'Little Magazines in the British Isles Today', *British Book News* (December 1983), pp. 728–33 is a good general introduction. R.J. Ellis, 'Mapping the UK little magazine field' in Hampson and Barry, eds., *New British Poetries*, pp. 72–103, is a full academic account. David Miller and Geoffrey Soar, *Little Magazines and How They Got That Way*, Exhibition Guide, 27 September–25 October 1990, Royal Festival Hall, London, draws on the Little Magazine Collection at University College, London, started by Soar and, for a while, maintained by Miller.

13   Adrian Clarke and Robert Sheppard, 'Afterword' in *Floating Capital; new poets from London*, eds. Adrian Clarke and Robert Sheppard (Elmwood: Poets and Poets Press, 1991), pp. 122–23. Both Clarke and myself were frequent attendees and readers at Sub Voicive.

14   Claire Buck, 'Poetry and the Women's Movement in Postwar Britain' in *Contemporary British Poetry*, eds., James Acheson and Romana Huk (Albany: State University of New York Press, 1996) , pp. 81–111 at p. 82.

15   One exception is in Hampson and Barry *New British Poetries*. The chapter 'Have you been here long? Black poetry in Britain' (pp. 51–71) by *The New British Poetry* editor Fred D'Aguiar is a excellent survey of its subject.

16   Ken Edwards, '$L=A=N=G=U=A=G=E$ / "language" / language: three attempts at an introduction', *Reality Studios*, vol. 2, no. 4 (May–June 1980), pp. 63–65, at p. 65.

17   Without outlining in detail the convergences and divergences of the British Veronica Forrest-Thomson's *Poetic Artifice* (Manchester: Manchester University Press, 1978) and American Charles Bernstein's 'The Artifice of Absorption' (1986) (in *A Poetics* (Yale: Yale University Press, 1992)) it is clear that language poetry (or its more recent theory) has moved towards a more open notion of artifice as 'devicehood'. See Alison Mark, *Veronica Forrest-Thomson and Language Poetry* (Tavistock: Northcote House, 2001), particularly the chapter 'language, Language, $L=A=N=G=U=A=G=E$', pp. 111–31; see also my 'The Poetics of Poetics: Charles Bernstein, Allen Fisher and "the poetic thinking that results"' in *Symbiosis*, vol. 3, no. 1 (April 1999), pp. 77–92.

18   Peter Middleton, '80 Langton Street Residence Program 1982/The $L=A=N=G=U=A=G=E$ Book', *Reality Studios*, vol. 6 (1984), p. 85.

19   Ron Silliman, 'The Politics of Poetry' $L=A=N=G=U=A=G=E$, 9/10 (1979).

20 Charles Bernstein, 'Semblance', *Reality Studios*, vol. 2, no. 4 (May–June 1980), pp. 66–68, at p. 66.

21 Bruce Andrews, *Paradise and Method: Poetics and Praxis* (Evanston, Northwestern University Press, 1996), p. 26.

22 *Ibid.*, p. 19.

23 Gilbert Adair, 'Bruce Andrews: Give Em Enough Rope', *Reality Studios* 10, pp. 101–10, at p. 108.

24 Bruce Andrews, 'Transatlantic', in *Floating Capital*, eds., Clarke and Sheppard pp. i-v, at p. i. Reprinted in Andrews, *Paradise and Method*, pp. 246–50 at p. 247.

25 Andrews, *Paradise and Method*, p. 79.

26 Tom Raworth, *Tottering State; Selected Early Poems 1963–1983* (Oakland: O Books, 2000), p. 216.

27 Our full title was *Floating Capital; new poets from London*, eds., Clarke and Sheppard, p. 123. Our featured writers were Cobbing, Fisher, Adair, Paul Brown, cris cheek, Clarke, Kelvin Corcoran, Edwards, Virginia Firnberg, Peter Middleton, O'Sullivan, Val Pancucci, Hazel Smith, and myself.

28 *Ibid.*, p. 122.

29 *Ibid.*, p. 122.

30 *Ibid.*, p. 122.

31 *Ibid.*, p. 122.

32 Adair, 'Dear Robert', p. 68.

33 Robert Hampson, 'Producing the unknown; language and ideology in contemporary poetry', in Hampson and Barry, *The New British Poetries*, pp. 134–55, at p. 148.

34 In Clarke and Sheppard, eds., *Floating Capital*, p. 59. The poem was first collected in Ken Edwards, *Drumming and Poems* (Newcastle upon Tyne: Galloping Dog Press, 1982), pp. 13–14.

35 Clarke and Sheppard, eds., *Floating Capital*, p. 59.

36 *Ibid.*, p. 59.

37 *Ibid.*, pp. 28–29. The poem was first published as Gilbert Adair, *Hot Licks* (London: Sub-Voicive, 1987).

38 Tuma, *Fishing by Obstinate Isles*, p. 201. The issue of *Angel Exhaust* is no. 8 (1992), entitled 'The Bloodsoaked Royston Perimeter'. Royston is a stop on the Cambridge–London railway line. Duncan's essay is 'The Cambridge Leisure Centre: Traits' (pp. 5–14.) Adrian Clarke supplies 'Underground Terminal' (pp. 15–17), his account of the London tribe.

39 Charles Bernstein, 'Leaking Truth: British Poetry in the '90s', *Sulfur* 35 (Fall 1994), pp. 204–12, at p. 206.

40 *Ibid.*, p. 205. Not everybody is in agreement with this absolute split, of course. In writing an appreciation for Bob Cobbing's 75th birthday in 1995, in *And,* Adrian Clarke writes of 'Bruce Andrews' observation to Gilbert Adair in 1987 when he was exploring English 'Linguistically Innovative Poetries' that were Schools of Prynne, Mottram and Cobbing. I can imagine the scorn with which associates of J.H. Prynne and the late Eric Mottram would seek to reject that attempted taxonomy, while the 'School of Cobbing' is characterized by a total absence of graduates.' *And* 9 (1995) n.p.

41 Duncan, 'The Cambridge Leisure Centre', p. 5.

42   Ben Watson, 'The Poet Prynne', *Modern Painters*, vol. 13, no. 2 (Summer 2000), p. 27.

43   Duncan, 'The Cambridge Leisure Centre', p. 5.

44   *Ibid.*, p. 5. Ben Watson is also the poet Out to Lunch, but as Watson he has published *Art, Class and Cleavage: A Qunantulumcunque Concerning Materialistic Esthetics* (London: Verso, 1999). This reading of culture is indebted to the thinking of V.N. Vološinov. Reading chapters of this book in proof influenced my use of Vološinov. Milne is a more orthodox Marxist.

45   Drew Milne, 'Agoraphobia, and the embarrassment of manifestos: notes towards a community of risk', in *Parataxis* 3 (Spring 1993), pp. 25–39, at p. 25.

46   *Ibid.*, p. 27.

47   *Ibid.*, p. 26.

48   Duncan, 'The Cambridge Leisure Centre', p. 7.

49   Milne, 'Agoraphobia', p. 27.

50   *Ibid.*, p. 30.

51   *Conductors of Chaos: a poetry anthology*, ed. Iain Sinclair (London: Picador, 1996), p. xvii. Subsequent citations of this text are marked in the text as *CC*.

52   Sinclair's major trilogy (for a number of years it looked as if the third might never appear) consists of the books *Lud Heat* (London: Albion Village Press, 1975), *Suicide Bridge* (London: Albion Village Press, 1979), dealt with in Chapter 2, and *White Chappell, Scarlet Tracings* (London: Paladin, 1988). The success of the novel led Paladin to issue a selected poems, *Flesh Eggs and Scalp Metal* (London: Paladin, 1992) and Penguin to feature him in its *Modern Poets* series, number 10, with Douglas Oliver and Denise Riley (another event of 1996). These are valuable for collecting his short poems of recent years, notable for their terse 'street detail' (to use the title of one) of East End lowlife. The poems seem occasional as though his greatest energies are now reserved for fiction. See my forthcoming monograph *Iain Sinclair* (Tavistock: Northcote House).

53   See *Bookworks: A Partial History and Sourcebook*, eds. Jane Rolo and Ian Hunt, (London: Bookworks, 1996), pp. 77–79 for an account of the work.

54   Veronica Forrest-Thomson, *Poetic Artifice* defines the 'image-complex' as that which tells 'us how to apportion our attention between synthesis on the scale of relevance, where we use external contexts and move up through the various levels of the poem towards the naturalization of a thematic synthesis, and the scale of irrelevance, where we accumulate all the patterns and features which are irrelevant to this thematic synthesis and which combine to form what I shall call a "suspended naturalization"' (p. xiii).

55   Drew Milne, 'John Wilkinson: Swarf Fever', *Pages* 301–21, pp. 314–319, at p. 317.

56   *Ibid.*, p. 314.

57   John Wilkinson, 'The Metastases of Poetry', *Parataxis*, 8/9, p. 49–55, at p. 54.

58   I am indebted to Scott Thurston's thesis 'Rescale: Method and Technique in Contemporary Poetry and Poetics', on Wilkinson, (PhD thesis, University of Lancaster, 2001), in particular the interview with Wilkinson and chapter 7: 'John Wilkinson'.

59   John Wilkinson's reply to 'Risk, O Risk, O Careless Risk (Reader Inquiry Feature)', *Gare du Nord*, vol. 2, no. 2 (1999), p. 23.

60   Drew Milne, 'Contributor's Statement' *Angel Exhaust*, 9 (Summer 1993), p. 66. Reprinted as 'A Statement on Purpose' in *Foil: defining poetry 1985–2000* ed. Nicholas Johnson

(Buckfastleigh: Etruscan Books, 2000), p. 383.

61 Tom Lowenstein, 'Excavation and Contemplation: Peter Riley's *Distant Points*'in *The Poetry of Peter Riley*, ed. Nate Dorward, *The Gig* 4/5, November 1999/March 2000, pp. 185–95, at p. 194. This collection of interview, articles and poems (by Riley) is an excellent introduction to the many projects Riley has undertaken. See also *Passing Measures: A Collection of Poems 1966–1990* (Manchester: Carcanet, 2000) for Riley's selected poems, and the collection *Distant Points* which was published by Reality Street Editions in 1995. Peter Riley has also been important as an advocate of unfashionable writers, particularly Nicholas Moore. Moore is one of the non-canonical writers of the past featured in *Conductors of Chaos*. J.F. Hendry, W.S. Graham, David Jones and David Gascoyne are the others.

62 Susan de Muth, 'Aural anarchy from the sound of silence', *The Independent*, Wednesday 1 March 1995, p. 23.

63 *Ibid.*, p. 23.

64 *Ibid.*, p. 23.

65 Cris cheek, *Skin upon Skin* (Lowestoft: Sound and Language Publishing, 1996) SLCD0300spokenword. Another version of the text appears in *Anthology of Twentieth-Century British and Irish Poetry*, ed. Keith Tuma (New York: Oxford University Press, 2001), pp. 857–65.

66 Caroline Bergvall, 'What do we mean by Performance Writing?'. *www.dartington.ac.uk/Performance_Writing/keynote.html*, accessed 23 October 2000.

67 *Ibid.*

68 *Ibid.*

69 See his unpublished '*Hybridising Writings and Writing Technologies*: To research, examine and contextualize key influences, of emergent technologies and those additional convergent agencies cogent to poetic writing practices, in England between 1994–2001, that hybridize writings,' PhD thesis, University of Lancaster, 2004.

70 For aspects of Catling's work and for a good introduction to book art see *Bookworks: A Partial History and Sourcebook*, eds. Rolo and Hunt, pp. 72–80.

71 Drew Milne, 'A Veritable Dollmine: Caroline Bergvall, *Goan Atom, 1. Jets-Poupee*', *Quid* 4 (2000), pp. 6–9, at p. 7.

72 Buck, 'Poetry and the Women's Movement in Postwar Britain', p.101.

73 Michelene Wandor, 'Masks and Options', in *On Gender and Writing*, ed. Michelene Wandor (London: Pandora Press, 1983), pp. 1–9, at p. 6.

74 Libby Houston, 'On Being a Woman Poet' in *On Gender and Writing*, ed. Wandor, pp. 42–50, at p. 44.

75 Wandor, 'Masks and Options', p. 6.

76 Buck, 'Poetry and the Women's Movement in Postwar Britain', p. 87.

77 The 'Postscript' to the anthology suggests another 23 names, but only four are British, one Irish (p. 252).

78 Most memorably, she writes back to Wittgenstein, which I have mentioned in relation to Roy Fisher's *Interiors*. Some of her other work was, as I shall show, an influence on Adrian Clarke.

79 It is beyond the scope of this chapter to consider whether *écriture feminine* exists, as that is articulated by Cixous and others, but if it does then it arguably resides not in the thematized

works of Jackie Kay or Carol Ann Duffy, but in this work, both North American and British, which uses techniques of non-linearity and impaction.

80   *Out of Everywhere*, ed. O'Sullivan, p. 9.

81   *Ibid.*, p. 9.

82   *Ibid.*, p. 9

83   Joint article by Maggie O'Sullivan and Geraldine Monk, *City Limits*, July 13–19, 1984, quoted on Galloping Dog Press flier, Spring 1986.

84   *Ibid.*

85   Buck, 'Poetry and the Women's Movement in Postwar Britain', p. 96. See also Denise Riley, *'Am I That Name?' Feminism and the Category of 'Women' in History* (Basingstoke: Macmillan, 1992) for some of Riley's feminist theory.

86   This poem is collected in *Out of Everywhere*, ed. O'Sullivan, p. 86, *Other; British and Irish Poetry since 1970*, eds. Richard Caddell and Peter Quartermain, (Hanover: Wesleyan University Press, 1999), p. 211, and in *Anthology of Twentieth-Century British and Irish Poetry*, ed. Tuma, p. 279.

87   My account of the conference and my involvement in it as poet and critic are described in 'Re-Tooling for the Alternatives', *PN Review*, vol. 23, no. 4 (March–April 1997), pp. 12–14.

88   See Trevor Joyce, 'New Writers' Press: The History of a Project', *Modernism and Ireland: The Poetry of the 1930s*, in eds., Patricia Coughlan and Alex Davis (Cork: Cork University Press, 1995), pp. 276–306. See also *For the Birds: Proceedings of the First Cork Conference on New and Experimental Irish Poetry (26 April 1997)*, ed. Harry Gilonis (Sutton and Dublin: Mainstream/hardPressed Poetry, 1998); Alex Davis, 'Deferred Action: Irish Neo-Avant Garde Poetry', in *Angelaki*, Vol 5, No. 1 (April 2000), pp. 81–93. John Goodby's book *Irish Poetry Since 1950* (Manchester: Manchester University Press, 2000) is a broad survey and features the work of Trevor Joyce, Geoffrey Squires, Maurice Scully, and Catherine Walsh. Goodby criticizes Iain Sinclair's *Conductors of Chaos* for ignoring the alternative Irish poetries, and he offers a useful summary of its history, particularly on p. 302.

89   For attempts to anthologize new writing see the Reality Street series of *Fourpack* anthologies, begun in 1996, with *Sleight of Foot*, which featured Scott Thurston, Harriet Tarlo, Miles Champion, and Helen Kidd. See also *Foil: defining poetry 1985–2000*, ed. N. Johnson (Buckfastleigh: Etruscan Books, 2000).

7

What Was To One Side or Not Real:
The Poetry of Tom Raworth 1970–1991

The Speed of Writing

In 1989 Tom Raworth commented on the focus and purpose of his poetry:

> At the back there is always the hope that there are other people … other minds, who
> will recognize something that they thought was to one side or not real. I hope that
> my poems will show them that it is real, that it does exist.[1]

The implications of this poetics will be felt throughout this chapter, which
traces Raworth's career as it navigates both the years of the British Poetry
Revival and of Linguistically Innovative Poetry; his work has been of importance to both groupings. Marjorie Perloff additionally reminds us that
Raworth has been 'a kind of elder statesman' to the American language
poets.[2]

After writing the poems examined in Chapter 2, Raworth worked through
the implications of attempting to expand his range, in serial texts that are
less immediately phenomenological and more imbedded in the language as
it is produced than the early work. They are meditative, logopoetic in Pound's
sense: of the intellect moving among words, as well as being self-referential
and self-definitional. 'Tracking (notes)' states

we
    are
        now [3]

The isolation of each word questions the assumptions ordinarily placed
upon the plural personal pronoun, the important verb 'to be', and the nature of time. The last of these haunts a number of Raworth's works of the
early 1970s, not least of all because spontaneity and process raise issues about
temporality. The poem seems to be asking where 'are we now?', a question

that he elsewhere poses in social and aesthetic terms:

> *things* of your time are influenced by the past. the artist can only go on from there
> and see the situation *as it is*: anything else is distortion ... i stick with de Kooning
> saying 'i influence the past' – and it is not important for the work of a time to be
> available in the mass media of its time: think of dickens on film, dostoyevsky on
> radio. (*TS88*, p. 91)

Rather than worshipping the past as a hallowed tradition, it can only be
activated by, realized in, the present. Raworth reverses, and makes egalitar-
ian, Pound's notion that artists are the 'antennae of the race',[4] not by some
reductive suggestion that everybody is, or should be, an artist, but by arguing that the nature of education should open everybody to the age's aesthetic messages, whatever the medium:

> within everyone is an antenna sensitive to the messages of the time: art is beamed to
> these antennae. education should tune them : instead they are smothered with phony
> 'learning'. the past has no messages (yes it has – whispering smith's harmonica and
> a dog howling in the night). (*TS88*, p. 90)

Characteristically, Raworth interrupts his own arrogance when it threatens
to elevate the 'now'; the epiphany of the narrator's memory is comic but
decisive. He also expresses a refinement of his earlier insistence upon the
intuitive as against the intellectual (or intelligence), as long as it is recalled
that inert factual learning, or research, is different from the vitality of the
'beamed' art.

> not rejecting *knowledge* but what (as in research) passes for knowledge and is but an
> illusion. the words (knowledge, intelligent etc.) must be redefined, or new words
> coined. (*TS88*, p. 90)

In a slightly later sequence, 'The Conscience of a Conservative', one section
reads:

> imagine
> being
> and not
> knowing
> (*TS2000*, p. 109)

The ironic impossibility of imagining a state of non-knowing is not stated
but felt in the segmented lineation. Amid these 'snapshots that are interiorized
both in their presentation of experience and their dissection of the phrase

or even the single word', as Geoffrey Ward calls them, Raworth's prose meditations on poetics implicitly demonstrate the inadequacy of the notational mode which they interrupt.[5] They interrogate the difficulties of poetic expression in a world in which the discursive is undercut by the speed of contemporary technology and in which development of ideas is replaced by immediacy of image. Yet even the famous ideogrammic method of the juxtaposition of fragments, of Pound, or the open field poetics of Olson, which serve Lee Harwood well in *The Long Black Veil*, is rejected:

> the connections (or connectives) no longer work – so how to build the long poem everyone is straining for? (the synopsis is enough for a quick mind now (result of film?) you can't pad out the book). (*TS88*, p. 91)

That celerity and quickness might be part of the answer rather than the problem for Raworth is intuited:

> all week i've (week) felt
> the speed of writing
> explanation rejects my advance
> (*TS88*, p. 94)

Practice, this implies, outstrips explanatory poetics but it also recognizes that velocity as a scriptural equivalent of mental celerity might ground the poetics of 'what is to one side'.

Feeling Speed of Thought Take it Off

This apprehension of velocity led to the production, between 1973 and 1983, of a significant series of long poems that Raworth had clearly been 'straining for' for some time: *Ace* (written in 1973), with *Bolivia: Another End of Ace* appending itself soon after; *Writing* (the longest, composed between 1975–77); *Catacoustics* (composed between 1978–81, the longest in gestation); and 'West Wind' (1982–1983).[6]

In *Ace* we see the birth of a method. One definition of the word 'ace' is unit; in this poem, one or two words (occasionally more if monosyllabic) establish the unity of the line. Each line's 'frame' is also part of the 'film' of the poem. This cinematic analogy often arises in descriptions of these strip-like poems and it has a clear but limited use.[7] It is useful in describing the relationship of line to text: the animating of the aces through the kinetics of reading. The units unite and disintegrate to create a processual but also, sometimes, provisional meaning. This is obvious in performances by Raworth, which are at tremendous speed. It is almost as if words have to be 'projected' at a certain speed to create the illusion of movement from frozen stills. But it could also be argued that this self-interruption of the text resists 'the intelligence almost completely', as Wallace Stevens wished of his poems.[8] As a listener to such texts, Ken Edwards notes Raworth's 'insistence ... that each image should enter and exit from the brain faster than it was possible to process the information sequentially', that the cinematic analogy must be refined; the experience of reading is more like watching a film containing flashes of subliminal messages.[9] But Edwards reminds us: 'The images, were, incontrovertibly, words.'[10]

The opening of *Bolivia: Another End of Ace*, one of the few short lyrics in this mode, usefully comments on this process:

feeling
speed
of thought
take
it off
make
it firm
lay back
play back
cracked energy[11]

With lines this short, the eye has to keep jumping in a way quite alien to the common reading experience. 'Take it off' suggests, oddly, a parodic impersonation as well as a launching into necessary flight. 'Make it firm' might be a reworking of the 'Make it new' of Modernism, if we read the reference of 'it' as the 'ace' or unit; the firmness will be the temporary apprehension of fixity of each line against the fluidity of the entire poem. The one letter difference between 'lay back' and 'play back' equates a relaxed frame of mind with the ability to recapitulate the performance. The final line records the elapsed moment of creativity, when improvisation breaks down.

Writing is a poem haunted, as its title suggests, by the scriptural, by acts of inscription and re-inscription. When Perloff notes of the sonogram (literally 'writing with sound') of Tom Raworth's voice saying 'writing' (part of the frontispiece to the original publication), this 'visual representation of vocality has a nice irony for, as the poem itself will suggest, the poet's voice is constantly displaced by the process of writing itself'.[12] Raworth is playing with the ironies of the writing of speech, the speech of writing: as in the colloquial transcription: 'what/you trine/ado'. (*TS2000*, p. 175) This is reflected in *Writing*'s Biblical dedication: 'to the moles and the bats', two notoriously blind mammals; indeed a bat uses sound to 'read' its environment.[13]

> see the words try
> to explain what
> is going in there
> an imagined book
>   (*TS2000*, p. 138)

Indeed, a series of imaginary books interrupt the poem: 'we imagine at/ page one the title' (*TS2000*, p.139). The shortest of these 'texts' within the text is this ironical response to the misnamed church of the 'title':

> REFORMED CHURCH
>
> my company was
> founded on dirty money
>   (*TS2000*, p. 140)

The purpose of such interruption is to prolong the saying, the avoidance of single thematization. This 'writing' gathers its thematics *in* its interruptive process. This does not mean that the poem is silent or complacently aesthetic. There are sardonic speculations about contemporary America:

> north americans smile
> because their lips
> can't meet
> over their teeth,
>   (*TS2000*, p. 171)

or about the role of the computer ('who will program program/ when program programs you?') (*TS2000*, p. 163). But acts of inscription and interpretation, even of gesture, are never far from the poem:

> for now
> she listens
> 'have you a headache?'
> 'no i'm looking
> out of my right eye'

with such
limited information
many connective gestures
remain unseen
both beginning
and end
being necessary
to between
          (*TS2000*, p. 170)

As was hoped in 'Tracking', the connectives here work ironically because they are interruptions, ruptures of their own saying. Everything gestures towards writing as process, through its invented verb: 'to between'.

Catacoustics is the most disparate and extreme of the longer texts. Building on the final parts of *Writing* (one has the sense of these poems as continuous) it is almost completely digressive, as though it constantly interrupts a text that remains invisible to the reader. The metonymic chain is laid out and then subverted, by switches into imbedded short poems, or into prose, or in the most extreme cases, into doodles and drawings in Raworth's hand: sabotaged mathematical symbols, the impossible oxymoron of imaginary signs, which can have no currency.[14] No wonder the poem opens so reflexively: 'should i begin again/ almost with a capital', questioning the graphological convention it foregrounds, but drops.[15]

Catacoustics is the part of acoustics that studies echoes or reflected sounds. The poem contains numerous patterns of, and references to, echoes, mirrorings, reflections, inversions, reversals, refractions, distortions, peripheral visions and barely caught memories. There is a prevalence of found, or overheard, materials so that echoing becomes an entropic feature of the text:

their inflexions
dovetail
entropy capital
issue
reissue
search
research[16]

Everything is open to the reiterative prefix 're-'. And yet there is the need for escape from the echo chamber, the 'fun-house mirror'.[17] The poem is full of literary echoes and parodies; academic graffiti distorts and denigrates the ideas of poststructuralism: 'Lacanic Man' is printed in reverse, as though every man has to re-enact Lacan's mirror-stage in order to read it aright.[18] A limerick rhymes 'Barthes' with 'fart', fresh from the witless semiosis of a university lavatory wall.[19] We are not being required to follow these academic clues since they are ridiculed as comic echoes of themselves. There are absurdist mergings of several texts, a cut-up, a 'glut/ of fiction',[20] which yokes by violence the opening of Hammett's *The Maltese Falcon* with the opening of Chandler's *Farewell My Lovely*: 'i had just come out of a three-chair "v" where a mouth thought a relief nostrils named dimitrious aleidis might be working'.[21] Such merging satirizes the literary judgement that suggests a combination of these 'masters'' styles would produce the ultimate detective fiction, but it is also a parody of the divinatory illumination of the cut-up method, as promised in Burroughs' rhetoric. As Raworth comments sardonically:

> literacy
> is also
> a wheelbarrow
> of westerns[22]

In a sense this text takes the world (in its texts) and refracts it back at itself, in a grand fun-house defamiliarization; artifice swallows itself:

> jeremy had been cutting 78s (for three labels, one unbreakable) which had 10% of the italian market. this one, called 'short cut', was, then spiralled into the hole in right-angled ar)cs (*sic*).[23]

Reading this poem is rather like listening to Jeremy's 78s, an echo of something miraculous disappearing before it may be grasped, leaving a wake of humour. As Keith Tuma says:

> Meeting each new line in the present of our act of reading the poem, we are forced to revise our sense of the last one. Our desire to stop, to settle in the grammar of a proposition, exclamation, or question is constantly frustrated; our memories of the immediate past suddenly become memories of something seen incompletely, words which have turned out to be other than what we imagined by virtue of our turning to the next line, moving down the page to set them in yet another combination.[24]

This can been seen in the parallel lines which, while describing refraction, deliberately echo, and enact, the central cultural obsession of the poem.

> reflecting on
> clear skin
> in which the letters   **in which hang**

```
hang                    letters
refracting through      refracting
visual emphasis         through visual emphasis
that gasp
of cheap mind
in the library of the blind[25]
```

Both of these long poems are here summarized – thematized – in ways the poems themselves refute: the discussion of paradigmatic links at a thematic level omits the *effects* and contents of the digressions, as described by Tuma. The sense that the grasping of a totality is futile, partial, the attempt to reduce experience to the said in what is emphatically saying, militates against a final naturalization of the text. Yet even *Catacoustics* offers a conclusion, another reflection upon refraction. It mysteriously suggests that surveillance prevents thought, in a sinister version of Heisenberg's uncertainty principle.

```
the twisted lens
diffuses senses of direction
'i won't think
while i'm being watched'
he sulks[26]
```

It points towards the darker social world of 'West Wind'.

Handbag

'West Wind', the shortest of these poems, takes a specific British social and political turn, quite consonant with the work of linguistically innovative writers in the early 1980s, such as Allen Fisher and Barry MacSweeney, and in younger writers, such as Ken Edwards, who remarked of the poem in 1986:

> It would be fatuous to say that living in America has politicized Raworth's poetry; as Jeff Nuttall has pointed out, such writing as his *is* political – in the strategies it chooses to adopt ... in the standpoint it *assumes* for itself ... Yet this explicit comment is new. It is not a boring didacticism, though ... it is crucial information that tilts the plane of the projective field ... Tom Raworth is back in England.[27]

The political turn is felt in a number of his poems of this period. The early years of Thatcher's long premiership were seen by those on the right as a re-assertion of Britain's leading militaristic role in the cold war world, and as inaugurating an ironic state-directed withering away of the state, in terms of reduced welfare and social spending. With the hegemony of the Conservatives' individualistic culture of enterprise, Britain was in danger of becoming a society bewitched by its leader's belief that there is no such thing as society. To those on the left it appeared that there was no light at the end of the tunnel, or worse, in the bleak title of one of Raworth's political texts of this time; 'No Light No Tunnel'.[28] A more teasing short poem is 'The West', which stands as an unofficial introduction to 'West Wind'; it appears in all editions of *Tottering State* on the page preceding the longer work.

> inhuman luxury
> writing this
> hidden labour
> around the world
> capital
> ends in electricity
> the north american skull
> is being restructured
> around perfect teeth
> although a quarter
> of the world's teeth
> are chinese
>   (*TS2000*, p. 208)

In 12 lines Raworth encapsulates the exploitation of the non-West, and the luxury enjoyed by some of the West's citizens, the result of invisible labour elsewhere. Another joke about the American obsession with orthodontic cosmetics leads to a shift of perspective in which China, othered by the West, is a threat to dental civilization with its overwhelming cold war display of alien teeth! What gives the poem its ethical charge is the recognition that even this 'protest poem' is complicit with global inhumanity.

Thatcher appears in the poem as 'handbag' (a Lady Bracknellesque synecdoche suggesting Thatcher's symbolic hitting of foreign leaders around the head, but, also, more sinisterly, hinting at the nuclear 'button' contained within her bag). Raworth presents a panorama of the British state in the 1980s:

> colourless nation
> sucking on grief

a handbag
strutting between uniforms
such slow false tears
sunlight tattoos
each cheek
with three brown dots
the state as
the status
quo
sitting in the path
of a high intensity beam
as war
advertises arms
we are pieces
of percentages
through that eye
for credit
is as far
as machines
can trust
what you own
and what you'll earn
while the homeless stare
at nightlong lights
in empty offices
    (*TS2000*, pp. 216–17)

The filmic flow of this poem, unlike its predecessors, draws together pieces
of information and suggests pertinent connections between them: the
Falklands War and its fortuitous opportunities for arms sales; the homeless
and jobless looking at new but empty offices (the results of property specu-
lation); questions about what humanity is in this administered world. Far
from being an accidental by-product, Raworth suggests, the underclass was
a structural component of Thatcher's society-which-is-not-one:

the poor
said handbag
are lucky to be alive
breathing my air
contributing nothing
to profit

> but without them
> how would we be
> off the bottom?
>> (*TS2000*, p. 229)

The joke about the proprietorship of air is an hyperbolic reference to the policy of privatization (the Conservatives privatised water utilities), as is the subtle remark about the deleterious effects of private health care on the National Health Service: 'the doctor/ is at the other hospital' (*TS2000*, p. 226).

In its combative gloom, and with its pageant of evil and social repression, the poem is akin to Shelley's *The Mask of Anarchy*. However, the title of Raworth's poem alludes to the utopian poem Shelley wrote immediately after his populist *Mask*: 'Ode to the West Wind' (1819). The revolutionary breeze, figured as 'The trumpet of a prophecy! O Wind,/ If winter comes, can Spring be far behind', is central to Shelley's study in political obliquity and utopian aspiration.[29] It would be wrong to call Raworth's politically outspoken anecdotes digressions, but they are necessarily embedded in the characteristic digressive flow of a Raworth poem (which I have underplayed in this reading). That poetic flow itself could be his own 'west wind', his 'Spirit fierce,/ My spirit!'[30]

Peter Brooker comments, slightly apologetically, on this very combination of anecdote and vectoral dispersion, which he reads as evidence of 'West Wind''s postmodernity:

> Wordly reference and narrative are obvious ... Lyotard's argument is that a leading feature of the postmodern era will be the supersession of the delegitimatized 'grand narratives' of bourgeois society by 'petit narratives', and that these will be local, fragile, temporary and unsure of their ground. Raworth's longer poems not only bear this out but show how such mini-narratives may be montaged together, in a reversible rather than linear sequence, in the same gesture that time's disjunctures and uncertainties are inscribed rather than smoothed away.[31]

Indeed, 'West Wind' contains more resistant little narratives than the other long poems. There are even personal vignettes about the hospitalization of Raworth's mother (she died in 1983), or a number of anecdotes about the 1983 general election, which use deadpan wit to show the reduction of the complex arguments of politics to binary choices and euphemism:

> 'are you
> the other side?'

asks
our conservative canvasser
without argument
the advertisement
of how happy they are
showed
'a west indian or asian'
   (*TS2000* , pp. 226–27)

This is an example of what Peter Brooker calls 'the wit and jaunty quips
Raworth draws ... from generational and class styles of English speech', [32]
here the unmasking of 'the conscience of a conservative' (to quote an earlier
title by Raworth) which sees ethnic difference itself in terms of two groups,
the indigenous and the amorphously other.

   In the face of illness and death, social decay and the technological control of an administered world, the question remains what it means to be
human. Raworth's concern with the nature of knowledge and its relationship to being (a theme from his earliest work) leads here to a meditation on
the non-human and amoral 'thinking' of the computer, which 'operates'

on limited knowledge
anaesthetised
by not knowing
more
it is
what it knows
we cannot
but conclusions
despatch us
to affect our what?
co-humans?
   (*TS2000*, p. 211)

The words 'thought' and 'thinking' resound throughout the poem. Human
intelligence, however detached from deeper processes,

thinking
the noise
of mind,
(*TS2000*, p. 219)

has to deal with the realities it faces. 'Nothing to feel with/ but the chemicals of thought' (*TS2000* p. 214) situates intellection within the fragile human organism, but this cerebral affectivity is constantly buffeted against questions of political control. 'Whose lives/ does the government affect?' the poem asks insistently, so much so that the (unanswered) question is posed in the text twice (*TS2000*, at both pp. 230 and 231).

Moving Them Around on the Page

Around 1986 Tom Raworth began working on the 14-line poems that were to occupy him for a number of years. The first 42 of these unusually formalist poems were published as 'Sentenced to Death' in *Visible Shivers* in 1987. The continuing and concluding 111, written between 1988 and 1990 were published in 1993 as *Eternal Sections*, the title I shall use to refer to all 153 poems. After the political anger of 'West Wind', they signal a return to obliquity but, as their titles suggest, humour is less common.[33]

In January 1991- that is, after 'Eternal Sections' was completed – Raworth, in a letter published in *Joe Soap's Canoe* magazine, explained his method of producing one such poem, noting, with a matter of factness that pervades this description of the 'context of the last poem' of the moment, that 'fourteen was the length I've been happy with for a while'.[34]

The commentary amounts to a narrative of Raworth's flâneur-like perambulations around Marseilles and his accumulation of jottings. The details of the town only obliquely enter the fragments he collects. The notes read like earlier poems by Raworth, which notate perceptually 'what was to one side or not real'.[35] A stop at a Tunisian's café, during which he hears a newsflash announcing the outbreak of the Gulf War, produces not quite social detail, nor the anti-West sentiment one might expect of the author of 'The West', but perceptual intensity.

> sitting there watching
> air decay
> between the levels
> of white tiles[36]

he scribbles on a scrap of blue graph paper. A while later he receives a letter telling him the Italian poet Patrizia Vicinelli has died and, although he searches his memory for actual details of her life and illness (which he relates in the commentary), he notes on the letter's envelope instead a single 'image of falling': 'tangles of wire/ toppling her to the ground', which seems appropriate to the occasion.[37] Later, on a walk around the docks, he collects the following rather jumbled set of data on the envelope:

> by the side of the numbers
> polished petrol tank
> unlike what he saw
> leaned down and picked up
> hoardings jutted out[38]

Finally the following lines are produced back at his room, as he listens to more Gulf War broadcasts and observes street cleaners outside.

> ejected from the real
> far away breathing
> to hold on to
> gloved fingers meshing
>   appeared.[39]

The commentary concedes that his new techniques are 'more juggling than attaching', suggesting that the linearity of the long poems of the 1970s and early 1980s has been replaced by a collage and juxtaposition within the constraint imposed by the 14 lines.[40] In this case Raworth rearranged the lines in such a way that few traces of the 'context' remain. He has made a poem, not attempted to reconstruct an experience.

In the resultant text (below) Raworth retains the first four lines, which position a possible observer 'sitting' and 'watching' the decaying air. The lines about Vicinelli, who becomes the dedicatee of the finished poem, are separated. The most expressive are therefore deliberately torn from their occasion. 'He saw' is detached from the third fragment to provide a subject and verb for the sitting and watching; it becomes a separate, pivotal, line. Poetic line operates as both articulation and interruption, since its integrity in the original notes is preserved, even as the lines in both of the last two fragments are radically reordered; none remains in its original order. (Very few words are omitted, though such economy may not be assumed of any other poem.) This creates what is often found in 'Eternal Sections', a discourse (here descriptive, but it could equally be some other) that has a recognizable semantic field, but its syntactical connections remain elusive.

> sitting there watching
> air decay

between the levels
of white tiles
he saw
tangles of wire
a polished petrol tank
hoardings jutted out
by the side of numbers
to hold on to
far away breathing
ejected from the real
gloved fingers meshing
toppling her to the ground

(*in memoriam Patrizia Vicinelli*)[41]

'Sitting there ... he saw' introduces a list of threatening sense data: indeterminate objects with their jutting angles and ejections, and a 'her' being savagely pushed to the ground. Gloved fingers, no longer those of the street cleaners, become sinister by implication, as they might in a Roy Fisher 'Interior'. 'He' breathes decaying air, suffocating.[42] The 'meshing' recalls the 'tangles of wire' and is indeed related to the second half of the original 'image of falling': 'toppling her to the ground'.

As Raworth transforms his materials he sabotages his intentionality. There is no paraphrasable content that may be excavated by the reader, no way of reconstructing the narrative that Raworth offers in his prose account of the genesis of the poem. More generally the poems in 'Eternal Sections' rupture various discourses in a textual way, creating the problem of how the units link together to create the 14 lines. If they are 'sonnets', as some commentators say, then they exhibit a volta – a turn – in nearly every line. Beyond that, there is the question of how the 153 poems connect, which raises similar questions about connection and interruption, on a larger scale.[43] At times there appear to be continuities between poems, at others, disarming interruptions.

Poetics and Ethics

'Eternal Sections' militates against excerption. To analyse one poem is not pertinent to its purpose, its ace in the game of the sequence's eternality. For the critic this poses a radical problem, one that it is partly the intention of these poems to refuse to solve. The desire for typicality inflicts a reductive fixity that the critic will call exemplification, but which might also be identified with the impositional violence of the said.

Raworth's poems attempt, by their technical devices and by their challenges to ordinary and critical reading, to hold the poetry open as a saying, precisely to avoid thematization in the said. The reader is offered structures that are at once over-determined and empty, proximate and yet distant, recognisable and disguised. In such a situation, the critical task can seem like betrayal, yet, as I have shown, Levinas reminds his reader always that the saying cannot remain eternally open. Eternity resides, an all too obviously temporary and temporal guest, in sections that are finite, in the saidness of text.

The variety of procedures and techniques of interruption can be best demonstrated by analysing three contiguous sections from the 1993 book *Eternal Sections.*

competing with the others
who treat and prevent ulcers
of personality if you like
a judgement system in voodoo
unless you've seen them
foremost in their memories
you start to notice things
grow up, make mistakes
look the same
in a parody of a stagger
to the point of paranoia
but profound nonetheless
an open invitation
over the pounding gaelic back-beat

even though the jazz feeling
the collaborative aspects
make a significant statement
until we're all happy
the artificial sound of tape
from one block to another
edits real fast
individual moments
layering and moulding

approaches to their instruments
where he could burn
wandering across
type time dimension
keys, tempos, etc.

such division into subjects
consequences of a failure
defined by humanist criticism
must be understood always
with the same concern in mind
a different style of beauty
may appear to be a contradiction
of generic character
capable of moving freely
in a diachronic process
over the motions and expressions
of beauty proper
the difficulty of this position
is not at all troublesome[44]

The second poem is the easiest to approach, partly because its found and treated materials are drawn from one identifiable source: an account of playing, recording and editing jazz. The ghost of an argument about the relative merits of the spontaneity of 'jazz feeling' against 'the artificial sound of tape' is hinted at, but it is never articulated, partly because of the way that the lines are themselves articulated, in the precise sense of *hinged*. The disarming 'even though' of its opening suggests that a doubt has been raised, but the syntax dissolves as the poem progresses before we can identify the object of these doubts. The possibility that, in the significant short seventh line, 'edits' may operate as a noun and not a verb, finally disintegrates the syntax. We will never recognize the argument, partly because the poem 'edits real fast' or its 'edits' are 'real fast/ individual moments' and consciousness is too fleeting to fix as ideation; Raworth still valorises intuition over intelligence. Indeed the 'he' of the poem who might 'burn' (which I read as an equivalent of the jazz musician's 'blow'), wanders intuitively across the merely technical 'etcs' of music, as some free musicians might.[45]

At times, the third poem stays close to denotative language, at least if we consider the lines as fragments of a discourse; the text, like *Catacoustics*, parodies or ironizes academic language. The poem divides into a number of possible articulatory units (for example, there could be a full stop after lines 5 and 12; or only after 8). Yet even the narrower disruption this brings serves to upset the causal as well as the clausal. As Andrew Duncan has said, 'The lack of causal relations in Raworth's poetry points to a universe, not one where causality does not operate, but where the causes and symptoms of things are not obvious.'[46] It articulates the problems of articulation, the 'division into subjects' which is a 'consequence of a failure/ defined by humanist criticism'. This fragment of post-structuralist summary which 'must be understood always' betrays the very divisions it subverts by its imperative to comprehend once and for all (although 'always' could be read deconstructively against itself as 'in all ways' of course). The concluding ironic ease of a 'difficulty' that causes no 'trouble' exposes the 'position' as yet another 'failure'. Likewise the poem seems to define several versions of 'beauty', one a 'contradiction/ of generic character' of the 'division' mentioned earlier, and one which would be 'beauty proper', over which the new beauty will move 'freely/ in a diachronic process'. Temporally, it will not be for 'always', therefore. Propositionally speaking, the poem's declaration is meaningless; it offers the counters of an argument, and a number of suggested moves, which the reader must negotiate. Performatively, the poem can be justified; it impels collaboration, because the familiarities of its content still invite the reader (few of the poems utilize obtuse or arcane materials). The difficulty of this poem is precisely troublesome, and is the more troublesome the more precise our attempted readings become.

Many of the 'Eternal Sections' poems are marked by narrativity in their careful recurrence of personal pronouns. In the first poem, the second person is employed, against which the actions of 'they/m' may be contrasted. Syntactic articulation is more hinged here. 'If you like' can be a dismissive ending to line 3, or a part of the statement in line 4. Likewise 'foremost in their memories' can be hinged with the line before or the line after to belong to either the 'voodoo' or the 'you'. 'Grow up,' with its rare comma, could be an imperative or an example of what 'you' begins to take 'notice' of in the previous line. Woven through this indeterminacy are repeated recognisable elements: terms like personality, paranoia, memories, from the lexis of psychology; and judgement, mistake-making and profound, from moral philosophy. The evocative figure of the 'ulcers of personality' may be a result of the stressful competitiveness that opens the poem, as looking the same, living in conformity, leads to paranoia.

The two incommensurables of the text both lie in references to culture. A 'judgement system in voodoo' is a rather startling index of difference, one markedly other than the competitiveness and conformity of advanced capitalism, hinted at elsewhere. It can be identified syntactically with the corrosive ulcers as yet another corruption, this time moral. Voodoo would not respect death – death haunts 'Eternal Sections' – to which, the sequence asserts, via one of its published titles and one of its puns, we are sentenced.

The second cultural oddity, 'the pounding gaelic back-beat' suggests musical hybridity, since backbeats are the insistent patterns in 4/4 time on beats 2 and 4 of certain jazz and rock grooves rather than the patterns of traditional Celtic music. But such a possibility operates, the poem says, as invitation.

These materials, these different discourses, interrupt one another; in 'Eternal Sections' the interruptions resound more strongly than the continuities. Interruption is both a form and a content. However, for the poem to work there must be the conviction for the reader that it will cohere or articulate: that its elements belong to one world, as Duncan argued. To know that they are fragments, even of Raworth's own notations, does not lessen the will to coherence and cohesion of the active reader in dialogue with these texts. In essence their dialogic invitation emanates from this strange power (or powerlessness) before the words, as the reader feels both proximate to, and distant from, the text.

What a poem says, here, is not to the point, in the sense of Levinas' central contention that 'Language as *saying* is an ethical openness to the other; as that which is *said* – reduced to a fixed identity or synchronized presence – it is an ontological closure of the other.'[47] The first poem above is not more open because its content may be made to echo Levinasian language in its thirteenth line: 'an open invitation'. The poetry is 'open' within the closed formal arrangement that constitutes its poetic artifice. It is this engagement with form in all the texts that is important. Ultimately they are concerned with what Levinas calls

Not the communication of a said, which would immediately cover over and extinguish or absorb the said, but saying holding open its openness, without excuses, evasions or alibis, delivering itself without saying anything said. Saying saying saying itself, without thematizing it, but exposing it again. Saying is thus to make signs of this very signifyingness of the exposure; it is to expose the exposure instead of remaining in it as an act of exposing.[48]

This sequence exposes its own openness, by foregrounding its artifice.

There is one commonsense question that blatantly recurs in even the most theoretical reading of these poems, one which Levinas articulates:

> But one can go back to this signification of the saying, this responsibility and substitution, only from the said and from the question: 'What is it about ... ?', a question already within the said in which everything shows itself.[49]

Raworth's poems will this anxiety into being, court it, play with it, occasionally deny or cancel this will to fixity in that very question, this critical necessity and impossibility. The poems cohere more by a reading of their formal means than by attempting to chart the semantics of a supposed context, even as readers are drawn into dialogue. The discourses are powerfully questioned and defamiliarized; indeed, the poems may never read the same way twice.

Later Raworth poems are an orchestration of interruptions of semantic fields, whose rhythm within and between the sections amounts to a percussive and hinged punctuation of themselves.[50] They are both empty and full. They turn content to form, and turn form into the content that is read. They offer as much resistance as is possible to the propositional function of language, however much they are forced to use it. Through this technical means, they turn the saidness of text – the materiality of the said – towards the eternality of saying.

Their openness to the textural other (making discourses say what they had not previously said) and their openness to the readerly other (the actual readers who must be exposed to this dialogic performance) marks clearly the site of ethics – of the 'Ethics of Ethics' – described by Levinas.[51]

They do not have designs on us. We must make designs with them.

Notes

1   'The Big Green Day: Tom Raworth talks to Don Watson about British poetry's tottering state', *City Limits*, February 16–February 23 1989, p. 57.
2   Marjorie Perloff, *The Dance of the Intellect* (Evanston: Northwestern University Press, 1996), p. 234.
3   There have been three editions of *Tottering State*, Raworth's selected poems. Each has a slightly different selection of his work. All three will be necessarily quoted in this chapter, but two will be marked by citations in the text. Tom Raworth (second edition) *Tottering State; Selected Poems 1963–1987* (London: Paladin, 1988) will be cited as *TS88*; Tom Raworth

(third edition) *Tottering State; Selected Early Poems 1963–1983* (Oakland: O Books, 2000 will be cited as *TS2000*. This quotation is *TS88*, p. 90.

4 Ezra Pound, *ABC of Reading* (London: Faber 1951), p. 81.

5 Geoffrey Ward, 'On Tom Raworth', *Perfect Bound*, (unnumbered first issue) (1976), pp. 14–19, at p. 17.

6 *Ace*, with *Bolivia: Another End of Ace* may be found in *Ace* (London: Cape Goliard, 1974) and *Bolivia: Another End of Ace* (London: Secret Books, 1974) and are both reprinted in *Tottering State Selected and New Poems 1963–1983* (first edition), (Great Barrington: The Figures, 1984) and in *Ace* (Washington: Edge Books, 2000); *Writing* may be found in *Writing* (Berkeley: The Figures, 1982) and in *TS2000*; *Catacoustics* may be found in *Catacoustics* (Cambridge: Street Editions, 1991); and 'West Wind' in all three selected poems.

7 Perloff suggests the older analogy of 'tickertapes' in her *The Dance of the Intellect*, p. 235.

8 Wallace Stevens, 'Selections from *Adagia*' in James Scully, ed., *Modern Poets on Modern Poetry* (London and Glasgow: Fontana/Collins, 1966), pp. 153–8, at p. 157.

9 Ken Edwards, 'Tom Raworth: *Tottering State*', *Reality Studios*, 8 (1986), pp. 78–83, at p. 78.

10 *Ibid.*, p. 78.

11 Tom Raworth *Tottering State* (first edition, 1984), p. 158. See footnotes 3 and 6 for details of the editions.

12 Perloff, *Dance of the Intellect*, p. 235.

13 The dedication and the sonogram are not reprinted in *TS2000* and may be found in Raworth, *Writing*.

14 At one mid-1980s Sub Voicive reading of *Catacoustics* and of 'West Wind', which contains a few of these, Raworth held up these strange symbols on A3 sheets. They include an exclamation mark with a comma instead of a point, raised to the power of one. See Tom Raworth, Catacoustics, p. 7.

15 Raworth, *Catacoustics*, p. 1. A small excerpt from the text may be found in Raworth, *Tottering State* (first edition, 1984) and *TS88* and *TS2000*.

16 Raworth, Catacoustics, p. 4.

17 *Ibid.*, p. 35.

18 *Ibid.*, p. 11: 'the mirror badge/ upon her breast/ that reads' precedes the graphic.

19 *Ibid.*, p. 11–12. This again makes play with orality and inscription. The word 'barthes' and its rhyme with 'farthes' has to be seen to be appreciated.

20 *Ibid.*, p. 3.

21 *Ibid.*, p. 8. I am grateful to Nate Dorward for this identification. See *The Gig* 3 (July 1999) p. 64.

22 Raworth, *Catacoustics*, pp. 8–9.

23 *Ibid.*, p. 10.

24 Keith Tuma *Fishing by Obstinate Isles* (Evanston: Northwestern University Press, 1998), pp. 234–35.

25 Raworth, *Catacoustics*, p. 13. On the taped reading of part of 'Catacoustics' on *Big Slippers On* (Solo KO – 01 (1993)) Raworth reads the columns horizontally, to make them sound like echoes or tape-spliced repetitions.

26 Raworth, Catacoustics, p. 41. The uncertainty principle states that observation of a phenomenon changes the phenomenon.

27   Ken Edwards, 'Tom Raworth: *Tottering State*', pp. 82–83.

28   Tom Raworth, (second edition), *Tottering State*, p. 232. Other directly political poems from this time include the animal rights poem 'Remember When People Were Tortured?' (p. 232), and the anti-nuclear 'Living Under the Divine Rights of Sherrifs' (p. 231) or the anti-royalist 'The Scent of Cars', *Visible Shivers* (Oakland: O Books, 1987) n.p.

29   Percy Bysshe Shelley, *The Poetical Works* (London: Frederick Warne, no date), p. 454.

30   *Ibid.*, p. 454.

31   Peter Brooker, 'Postmodern postpoetry: Tom Raworth's "tottering state"'in Anthony Easthope and John O' Thompson, eds., *Contemporary Poetry Meets Modern Theory* (New York: Harvester Wheatsheaf, 1991, pp. 153–65, at p. 164. The theme of reversibility would seem more relevant to *Catacoustics*, although Brooker may have in mind such performance traits as Raworth reportedly reading *Writing*, line by line, backwards.

32   *Ibid.*, p. 162.

33   *TS88* contains the beginning of the sequence, under the title 'From *Sentenced to Death*', pp. 237–47. Apart from the poem dealt with in this section, there are two further sequences of 14-line poems in *Clean & Well Lit: Selected Poems 1987–1995* (New York: Roof Books, 1996): the 28 poem sequence 'Survival' (pp. 36–49) and the 9 poem 'Name Unknown' (pp. 88–92).

34   Tom Raworth, 'Dear Martin', *Joe Soap's Canoe* 14 (1991), n.p.

35   *Ibid.*, n.p.

36   *Ibid.*, n.p.

37   *Ibid.*, n.p.

38   *Ibid.*, n.p.

39   *Ibid.*, n.p.

40   *Ibid.*, n.p.

41   *Ibid.*, n.p.

42   It could also suggest that the breathing is ejected from real, rather than unreal, gloved, fingers.

43   A private recording made by Ken Edwards of Raworth's 1988 Battersea Arts Centre reading reveals the three texts I consider here in a different order, suggesting some juggling between poems.

44   Tom Raworth, *Eternal Sections* (Los Angeles: Sun and Moon Press, 1993), pp. 30–31. As I have quoted the poems in full there are no further citations to them in the following five paragraphs of analysis.

45   Such as the quotations from Evan Parker in Chapter 3.

46   Andrew Duncan, 'Kicking Shit with Arvel Watson and C. Day Lewis', *Angel Exhaust* 16 (January 1999), pp. 94–118 at p. 101.

47   Emmanuel Levinas, 'Ethics of the Infinite', interview with the editor in *Dialogues with Contemporary Continental Thinkers*, ed. Richard Kearney (Manchester: Manchester University Press, 1984), pp. 47–69, at p. 65.

48   Emmanuel Levinas, *Otherwise than Being, or Beyond Essence*, (The Hague: Martinus Nijhoff, 1981), p. 143.

49   *Ibid.*, p. 44.

50   Apart from the abandonment of the 14 line structures, later work, in *Clean & Well Lit* and

Meadow (Sausilito: The Post-Apollo Press, 1999) seems to be constructed on the same hinging principle.

51   Jacques Derrida, 'Violence and Metaphysics', in *Writing and Difference* (London and Henley: Routledge and Kegan Paul, 1978), pp. 79–153, at p. 111.

8

Creative Linkage in the Work of Allen Fisher, Adrian Clarke and Ulli Freer during the 1980s and 1990s

Linking the Unlinkable: Technique into Ethics

Since modernism, linkage – what Raworth calls 'connectives' – has been an essential issue for any art which achieves formal defamiliarization and deautomatization through effects of fragmentation. Indeterminacy and discontinuity have long provided descriptions of radical art, as in Umberto Eco's poetics of the open work.[1] However, Gilbert Adair, in the short document which furnished the term Linguistically Innovative Poetry, points out that because, for example, 'advertisements are ample in "discontinuities"', the term is not neutral and can only be used of British Poetry if it expresses 'positivities'.[2] He says, usefully, 'Cutting across formations categorized as discrete, "discontinuity" is so only if it makes other relations; or else it is mimesis of actual informational chaos.'[3] In other words, to use terms appropriated from Lyotard's lecture 'Discussions, or phrasing "after Auschwitz"', disjoining, to be efficacious, must simultaneously link. In literary experimentation, this is demonstrated most obviously in forms of collage, as long as it is remembered, obversely, that 'to link is to disjoin'.[4]

Indeed in this context it is interesting to see two major late twentieth-century thinkers, both of them students of Levinas, Derrida as well as Lyotard, consider the term linkage in its ethical dimensions, ones which I believe, ultimately lead us back to the heart of what is most effective and affective in British poetry of the 1980s and 1990s, and which are related to the ethical poetics I have offered so far in this study, particularly with regard to the paradoxically interruptive linkages throughout Raworth's work.[5]

In 'Discussions, or phrasing "after Auschwitz"', a lecture that introduces the terms of his major philosophical work *The Differend; Phrases in Dispute*, Lyotard considers the name that, for Adorno, risked overstamping all human endeavour, including famously, and relevantly to my current purpose, poetry, that is: Auschwitz.[6] For Lyotard, 'Auschwitz' is 'a model' but not an example for 'the incommensurability between the universe of prescriptive phrase (request) and the universes of the descriptive phrases which take it as their referent'.[7] The essential difference lies in the Nazi's use of the prescription 'Die' which is utterly different from other commands, since to obey is to concede to 'this immobilization clause in the game (i.e. death)'; it is the limit case for a philosophy of linkage, what Lyotard calls a 'differend'.[8] In less extreme situations – such as the writing of poetry – the 'agon of phrases is perpetual'.[9] The just action can only be to effect 'the linkage "that suits" in a particular case, without there being known what the rule of suitability is'.[10] One can only '"invent" rules for the linkings of phrases'.[11]

Derrida responds to Lyotard's lecture but reveals himself less interested in the philosophy of the phrase, to which we shall return in discussion of Adrian Clarke, than in the processes of necessary linkage, in the implications of the attitude rather than the technique. We have, Derrida says, again referring to Lyotard's limit case, 'to make links, historically, politically, and ethically with the name, with that which absolutely refuses linkage'.[12] He continues, naming the name: 'If there is today an ethical or political question and if there is somewhere a *One must* it must link up with a *one must make links with Auschwitz.*'[13] But this necessity could be broadened, both ethically and technically; it suggests a writing practice that must link the components of the daily catastrophe, along with all its ecstasies. Against Lyotard, Derrida wonders: 'Perhaps Auschwitz prescribes – and the other proper names of analogous tragedies (in their irreducible dispersion) prescribe – that we make links.'[14] To extend the implications of this ethics into discussions of literary practice, one in which linkage is central, would be to necessitate a rigorous practice without pre-determining the nature of that practice: 'It does not prescribe that we overcome the un-linkable, but rather: because it is unlinkable, we are enjoined to make links.'[15] Indeed, linkage is the technical, socio-political and ethical issue that links the three poets I will now consider, and it links them to others discussed in this book.[16]

Necessary Business: The Poetics of Allen Fisher

A writer's poetics may be defined as the product of the process of reflection upon writings, and upon the act of writing, gathering from the past and

from others, and casting into the future, speculatively. It exists for the writer
and for others in a hoped for poetic community, to produce, to quote Rachel
Blau DuPlessis, a 'permission to continue'.[17] It involves a theory of practice;
a practice of theory – its answers are provisional, its trajectory nomadic, its
positions temporary. In the United States the formal development of this
discourse has been strong, from the Imagists to the language poets, but in
the poetries of the British discontents this has not been the case.

Allen Fisher's *Necessary Business* is a notable exception. Composed between 1980 and 1985, and published in the year of its completion, by Spanner, Fisher's own press, Fisher attempts to manufacture poetic community
in the very text-making of his 'considerably small room' during the years
following 1978 (as examined in Chapter 6).[18] As poetics, I have already offered this text as a pivot between the British Poetry Revival and Linguistically Innovative Poetry; it is clearly a dividing line between Fisher's two
long sequences *Place* (1971–80) and *Gravity as a Consequence of Shape*
(1982–2005). Despite the fact that it is the most considerable working out
of a useable linguistically innovative poetics there has been little study of
Fisher's piece, although it lies behind some important work of the 1980s
such as Adrian Clarke's, to which I shall return.

Fisher's formally innovative essay is not merely accompanied or appended
by interviews, since they 'interrupt' each other and the flow of the first half
of the essay.[19] Fisher's poetics, like his creative work, here is process-showing, and in dialogue with itself. As I shall demonstrate, his concern with
jumps and multi-voiced presentation, and various spacetimes, is encoded
in his poetics.

Necessary Business comprises largely of a detailed reading of works physi-
cally present on Fisher's desk: J.H. Prynne's *Down where changed* (1979),
Eric Mottram's *1980 Mediate* (1980), and cris cheek's *A Present* (1980).[20] As
already outlined, Prynne has been characterized as the chief exponent of a
supposed Cambridge poetry; Mottram, as a poet, theorist, and collector of
poetics, has been thought the principal figure in a London poetry. However, their shared attachment to the poetry and poetics of Charles Olson
points to commonalities, even though Prynne took Olsonian concerns with
knowledge into an increasingly impacted textual density, as I have shown,
while Mottram took the use of 'resources' and quotation in the poetic text
towards open field presentation and collage, an attitude which influenced
Allen Fisher's *Place* and suggested the creative linkage of *Gravity as a*

Consequence of Shape. Indeed these characteristics might be thought of as determining factors of the two respective poetries.

Cris cheek may be considered a London poet, as could Allen Fisher himself, but is most usefully thought of as coming from the experimental and performance context of Bob Cobbing and his Writers Forum workshops of the 1970s; cheek was also associated with some American language poets (and later with performance writing in the 1990s). Significantly, he is a younger poet than Fisher and was probably selected as an example of the current (or even future) state of poetry. In short, the three represented a considerable range of poets across the British Poetry Revival, each offering a contrasting area of strength. The purpose of the contextualizing interviews between which the main argument is collaged, seems to be to discover points of comparison and contrast. I wish to dwell primarily upon the essay's function as poetics rather than as literary criticism, because that is more important to my argument here concerning how Linguistically Innovative Poetry came into being.[21]

Fisher characterizes an 'impertinent' poetry as one that merely affirms the values of existing society; it shows a flattering mirror to its audience but is ultimately an ideological mirage. Its corrective opposite is the poetry of 'the new pertinence'.[22] Fisher borrows the term 'pertinence' from Ricoeur's characterization of the fresh significatory effects of 'live', as opposed to 'dead', metaphor. Such poetry similarly, though not necessarily with metaphorical useage, creates fresh significations, not in itself, but when engaged by an active reader. Fisher acknowledges several reader response theorists such as Fish, Iser and Jauss, but he avoids the hypostacization of an ideal reader, as had Lee Harwood when he less theoretically expounded his poetics of the open work. Not having to provide an encompassing theory of reading has its advantages from the point of view of poetics: Fisher remains faithful to acts of reading as productivities of particular readers grounded in historical and social processes.

Such engagement can be seen as assisting in the subversion of dominant and impertinent social values. A text is judged on its ability to escape the writer and invigorate the reader's continuous engagement, an engagement that is the site of an utopianism. His or her very participation in text-realization is the 'necessary business' of Fisher's title, a productive use of the strictly rationed leisure time granted under capitalism's providence. While not denying the importance of text-construction the theoretical emphasis is on this vital reader-engagement.

Fisher briefly considers (only to reject) the idea that the text might describe or outline a revolutionary programme. Such a text, he argues, could be assimilated by the audience in an impertinent, unengaged reading, which is the equivalent of a thematizing reading. This would only have the effect of pacifying the politicization that is being theorized, which needs to be embodied in textual structuring made with the eventual act of reading in mind. It would be self-defeating, unchallenging, and thus not provocative of the kind of active engagement privileged in Fisher's model of reading.

Fisher does not articulate these issues in terms he might have derived from North American language poetry nor does he ever refer explicitly to Levinasian terms; indeed he prefers to found his own poetics upon Mukarovský's concept of the aesthetic function, as outlined in the Prague School linguist's 1936 essay *Aesthetic Function, Norm and Value as Social Facts*.[23] This work attempts to distinguish the 'aesthetic', while managing to make it a socio-historical process, a subsisting though changeable feature among the variations of fashion or change. 'Aesthetic function,' writes Mukarovský, 'is one of the most important agencies in human affairs, and every object can manifest it'.[24] This flexible concept is best thought of in relation to the function of valuable everyday objects. The antique clock on the mantlepiece that stops working one day can thenceforth only have an aesthetic function, becomes essentially art, where once it had a use function. Yet as Fisher argues, echoing Mukarovský, in art it must be the dominant function (though it may have other, less constitutive, functions). Political art whose function seems predominantly political is not (paradoxically) art at all, because, in Mukarovský's words, 'the aesthetic function is facultative and subordinate' and the propagandist or informational function predominates.[25] Indeed, he states, 'The aesthetic function, by dominating over the informational function, has changed the very nature of the information.'[26] The importance of Mukarovský's essay, which is used quite selectively in Fisher's poetics, lies in its preservation of the arena of the aesthetic as the centre of literary experimentation. It is a bulwark against conceptual art theories that tend to collapse the distinction between art and life, such as the thinking of the Fluxus movement, a British offshoot of which, Fluxshoe, Fisher had been once aligned to.[27] Life can only be admitted as the necessary 'challenge which can be met by overcoming the contradictions encountered during the complex process of perceiving and evaluating the work', the necessity of the engagement of an active readership.[28]

Fisher summarizes this position:

> The new pertinence is a poetics that undertakes its aesthetic function from the ground
> – from its activity …. Poetry does not collaborate with society, but with life; its field
> of collaboration is predominantly aesthetic, that is its main function. Whatever else
> I may get from a work of art, because its dominant function is aesthetic it requires
> my engagement to create it, to produce it. The significance I most warmly value
> derives from this production, its affirmation of life.[29]

The various entries of the various readers into the actual text constitute its
affirmative moments, actualizing activities that emphasize the text's saying.
However small the community Fisher was addressing in the early 1980s, he
avoids the illusion of the ideal reader, which could function only as a principle of theoretical reading.

One such active reader is Fisher himself, in his approaches to Prynne,
Mottram and cheek in *Necessary Business*. The reading of one poetic text
by each is the central activity of Fisher's essay. Thus he mimes his poetics'
essential point in the process-showing of his poetics presentation.[30] His ex-
trapolations of a poetics of textual construction derive from his 'readings',
which are not the focus of this chapter. Transformative power for the reader
derives from a demanding and also unpredictable poetry that doesn't predi-
cate society as it is. It is openly habit-breaking; indeed, poetry breaks its
own rules and paradigms to create discontinuities and leaps.[31]

New Memories: *Gravity as a Consequence of Shape* as Poetics and Poetry

Most pertinently, for Fisher, his three poets create structures that 'deconstruct
consistent and chreodic memory'.[32] The term 'chreod' – also spelt 'chreode'
– comes from Waddington, in whose 'biological terminology', Fisher tells
us, it means a '"necessary path", whose charge is canalized once started in a
certain direction'.[33] Fisher both describes and enacts this process in the text
Philly Dog, part of *Gravity as a Consequence of Shape*, published in 1995:

> I am a homeorhetic system
> of attractor surfaces of chreods, necessary pathways,
> located in multi-dimensional spacetimes
> in which crossovers correspond to catatrophes
> Folds on the surface that suspend descriptive

referential functions and any temporal character
of my experience and lead into a world unfolded
by every narrative[34]

Through techniques of textual rupture and jumps, Fisher's texts 'intuitively
invent new memories'; reading is seen as a revolutionary act to divert consciousness along these new canals.[35] Memory becomes a reinvigorated in-
vention of perception. The techniques of creative linkage involve the reader
in constructing otherness, from the different times and places of the text,
along with a resultant polyphony of voices, or 'plurivocity' as Fisher puts
it.[36] Both of these things disturb the impertinent desire for consistency or
a single referent in a discourse. The pathways of chroedic memory are
disturbed by catastrophic crossovers. The world Fisher constructs for his
reader in his own poetry is clearly modelled upon this poetics, as can be
experienced in the discourses, times and places collaged in 'Around the
World':

This gravitational song meted against displacement
The slow movement of holding you
By the lake, deep amid fir and silver poplar
Dream sleep's energetic function
During meditation each finger rayed in cactus spikes
Blake crossed out sweet desire, wrote iron wire
It was the discovery of human electromagnetism
made a sign, opened curtains, revealed the garden
Mouth perpendicular to mouth energized desire[37]

In this poetry intertextuality becomes an image of experiential multidi-
mensionality and plurivocity (as in Blake's deleted 'desire' which hints at
contemporary usages of that concept, such as Kristeva's). As another of
Fisher's poems says, though in ironically painless lines:

The quantum leap
between some lines
so wide
it hurts.[38]

The effect of the disruptive flow of many poems in *Gravity as a Consequence of Shape* is to foreground textual 'cleavage' as both the division and
holding together of materials in the very metaphor of Fisher's title: gravity.
Without this textural energy or dynamic, everything flies apart. The speed

of the shifts determines the pace. He calls Mottram's technique of breaking syntax to produce rhythm in 'phrasic positioning' a 'quantum-jump methodology'; in Prynne's work, 'the aesthetic of his selection tensioned in collisions of the same set (or line)' in *Down Where Changed*, has a similar effect.[39] These are precisely analogous to the flickering aces, the hinged lines, of Raworth's characteristic practice.

In a note on poetics, written in 1995, Fisher is particularly candid about his method of text-construction in *Gravity as a Consequence of Shape*. He describes the three overlapping stages of composition as 'research, selection, and presentation'.[40] I shall examine a short part of a particularly effective poem, 'Birdland', from the first, 1985, showing of the project, *Brixton Fractals*. The volume's title is almost an index of creative linkage. On the one hand, it denotes the troubled London borough that has furnished Fisher with much of his poetry of place. On the other hand, a fractal is an irregular action or shape, such as a cloud or a coastline, which is complex, though not now impossible to measure mathematically, and to establish the laws which govern its shaping. Fisher's point is that the place in London where he lived through its years of deprivation and riots is traceable only by his irregular technique, particularly in 'Birdland', where he tries to connect the place in its sexual, ideological and linguistic shapings:

> Endless destruction
> makes Brixton
> Call it coexistence of prohibitions and
> their transgression
> Call it carnival and spell out jouissance and horror,
> a nexus of life and description, the child's
> game and dream plus discourse and spectacle.
> On the edge
> of death High Road, the Busker
> starts up a reel, it begins as dance interlaced
> with anger. I guess at the ridiculous partners
> that perform. The busker dances with
> her saxophone
> 'Ideas of Good and Evil' are subsumed into this nexus,
> production knots and
> unknots paranoia
> Blake stands his ground
> on the Common asks, Are

> Her knees and elbows only
>   glewed together.[41]

Shadowy traces of selected 'research' are perceptible: quotations from Kristeva
as Fisher's Mottram-like 'resources' confirm, and also the remark of William Blake, a notebook jest about marriage and sex.[42] But the quotations are
not isolated, as in the spatial collage of *The Cantos* or even of Fisher's earlier open field *Place*. Indeed, 'research is adumbrated and imbricated with
personal research from an accumulation of notes from living experiences' –
in other words, the two kinds of discourse, the found and the 'autobiographical', overshadow and overlap one another.[43] This mode of creative
linkage is visible in the opening four lines, where notes on Brixton catch the
faint echo of the choral lines 'Call it ... Call it', with their unannounced
capitals and their authoritative academic identification of contradiction.
The reader's impulse towards syntactical cohesion allows the imbrication to
occur, although this is only slenderly satisfied. Fisher is careful, in this creation of 'new memories' by creative linkage, to hold off the gratifications of
seamlessly conventional syntax. In the best of these poems the linkage holds
traces of its disjoining, the illusion complete enough for the creation of
'new memories' but never descending into the illusory; they are precisely
the 'jumps from tensioned collisions' Fisher found in Prynne.[44]

The Busker (one of the many 'characters' that haunt this almost-narra-
tive) takes Blake into her strangely ambivalent performance, is questioned
cheekily by him, even, and is positioned precariously 'On the edge/ of death
High Road', where the line-break (one of the decisions of the presentation
stage) minimizes the obvious disjoining link whilst preserving its visibility.[45]
The edge of death is a moment not a place; on the edge of the High Road is
geographically locatable. Time collapses into space. Throughout the poem
contradictory actions, or contraries, such as Blake's Good and Evil, 'discourse and spectacle', dancing and anger, all 'ridiculous partners', are situated, through creative linkage, in their ethical relations, in the paranoiac
productivity that is Brixton. Busking itself is semi-legal, a literal 'coexist-
ence of prohibitions/ and their transgression'.[46] The 'disruption of autobiographical voice through the use of many voices, aspiration to multiple and
collage form through the pasting of many sources', is clearly visible, to create new, but artificial, memories of 'many spacetimes'.[47]

The reader witnesses a constantly interrupted narrative, yet sees text as
textual, and sees the links which are simultaneously joining and disjoining,

'process-showing' as Fisher had earlier called it.[48] Indeed, the whole process of the project *Gravity as a Consequence of Shape* has been shown to the reader. William Blake also provides one of the project's structural homologies. *Gravity as a Consequence of Shape* is modelled on Blake's *Notebooks*, which are mapped across the project; quotations from it (as in 'Around the World' and 'Birdland') are sometimes juxtaposed at the selection stage with other materials. The titles of the poems (and the order of the project) derive from an alphabetical list of 188 dances, drawn up in 1982, when Fisher was writing *Necessary Business*. First published in *Ideas on the Culture Dreamed Of*, the list of titles runs from 'Accretion' and 'Acuity' to 'Zeitgeist', 'Zig Zag' and 'Zip'.[49] Across this necessary path the project dances its variations, the results of which fill many hundreds of pages.

And a Phrase: Creative linkage in the work of Adrian Clarke and Ulli Freer

Adrian Clarke is one British writer to have acknowledged both Fisher and Lyotard in the poetics of his creative linkage, particularly with regards to the books that constitute 'The Ghost Trio': *Ghost Measures* (1987), *Spectral Investments* (1991), and *Obscure Disasters* (1993). In his homage to Fisher he precisely re-functions Fisher's lines into an appreciation of his linking and disjoining method, where creation matches breakage:

> unclassified signals glow from
> the walkway creates what
> happens next by spins
> where the culture breaks[50]

Lyotard's thinking, as we have seen in his sense of the postmodern condition as one in which metanarratives are resisted by the petit narratives, suggests a method of fragmentary resistance to the totalising tendencies of modern society. The discourse of the State (one might almost say statement) is rejected in favour of ceaseless phrasing. Lyotard's work, in *The Differend; Phrases in Dispute*, if one misreads the translated term 'phrase' literally – Lyotard never intended to contrast a complete sentence with the incomplete phrase – nevertheless offers a near description of the central technique of Clarke's work: the creative linking of indeterminate phrases.[51] In his 1991 Sub Voicive Colloquium talk, *Listening to the Differences*, Clarke adapts Lyotard's material to his own use.

> The way in which Lyotard attempts to subvert … totalizing concepts is by resort to
> the phrase … a linguistic instance that cuts across genres and categories as it evades
> closure. With phrases we are set adrift from narrative and logic to struggle with what
> they present without hope of return to safe ground: 'for a phrase to be the last
> phrase, another phrase is necessary to declare this, and thus it is not the last one'.[52]

This is precisely the movement of Clarke's work: phrase leads to phrase, not
to the cohesion of a narrative, grand or small, but to catachresis. '*And a
phrase* is necessary. It is necessary to link.'[53] The rigid anti-metric of word
count, a highly determined but arbitrary form, means, in Robert Hampson's
words, that 'the compression of the short lines encourages the floating phrases
to form new links'.[54] As Lyotard says in a passage not quoted by Clarke: 'A
genre of discourse inspires a mode of linking phrases together, and these
phrases can be from different regimens'.[55] If poetry is this genre of discourse,
states Clarke, then it results in

> a subversive plurality that many of the rules available to link phrases may also be
> used to sustain, short-circuiting the connections that might combine to pronounce
> a sentence, but not necessarily those constitutive of a critical judgement whose force
> is less than absolute.[56]

Indeed, 'short-circuiting', as Clarke puts it, is an interesting analogy for his
wholly unexpected and deregulated linkage. 'Lyotard's approach attempts
at once to undermine all totalizing political philosophies and a radical extension of politics into the smallest linguistic transactions.'[57] A pertinent
but, perhaps, more importantly, suggestive, quotation from Lyotard appears both in Clarke's talk and as the epigraph to his 'Obscure Disasters 15':
'The linkage of one phrase with another is problematic, and this problem is
politics.'[58] The poem's opening section begins self-referentially, like Raworth's
Catacoustics, with a metalingual doubt about poetry's fragmentation:

> something unusual about this
> for a first draft
> language in pieces grasps
> particulars as spectral hues[59]

The fragments here seem not to focus 'contemporary particulars' as Clarke
puts it in his homage to, and quotation from, Objectivist poet Louis
Zukofsky.[60] The desperation of writing grasping for its meaning, diffuses

into spectral hyperreality. (The metaphor of the spectre haunts 'The Ghost Trio'.) But the phrasal method yields different results if we read on. Clarke has appropriated his linking techniques partly from the work of Rosmarie Waldrop, particularly her *The Road is Everywhere or Stop this Body* (1978) in which lines (rather than phrases) often only cohere with contiguous lines, linking and disjoining at once in the performance of the whole poem.[61] As Clarke puts it in his homage to Waldrop: 'barriers/ and obstacles of sense' are produced by the active reader's 'effort towards syntax'.[62] Note how the above lines re-align themselves as the poem proceeds.

> language in pieces grasps
> particulars as spectral hues
> stake out a fundamental
> site diminishing traffic suburbanised[63]

'Spectral hues' is now a pivotal noun phrase, turning on 'as'. Read this way, language can now grasp particulars, because the spectral, like the hyperreality it suggests, has (also) become a property of the dullest of realities, the suburban. The traffic that is diminished is that political space between the grasping language and the staking out of the particulars it attempts to grasp.

The celerity of Tom Raworth's long sequences has clearly been important to Clarke. 'The race of thoughts spins' Clarke writes in his homage in *Ghost Measures* to Raworth, yet this phrase describes equally the effects of Waldrop's experiment, *and* recalls the 'spinning' and 'swerving' Clarke praises in the fractal progression of Fisher's sequences.[64] The energetic creative linkage of these three writers, taken to authorize a phrasal linkage, arguably harnessed in the greater tension of a strict numerical form, produces the unique power of Clarke's work, a discourse that is political in its refusal to settle on fixed meanings, and is as ethical as Raworth's work in its refusal to *say* anything definitive; it dwells in its conditional saying.

In section two of *Spectral Investments* metafictionality abounds, recalling Raworth's texts within texts: 'begins CHAPTER 1 with/ a pattern of flowers' is neither a description of flowers nor is it at the beginning.[65] It provides a relentless foregrounding of commentary on a fiction that has 'a content to be/ described' but which is not: 'named characters elaborately set up to/ conclude in words'.[66] The resulting partial details seem indexical but empty, as in the recurrently noirish images: 'a cigarette denotes/ an agony of choice' and 'a damp cigarette indicative of the expository code'.[67] This evokes a world 'begging/ to be described in total',[68] which is what the grand narratives were for, of course, but it remains incomprehensible and impoverished, 'beggaring/ description' as 'the words fragment themselves a constellation fictional or/ parasyntactic in the turn of events'.[69] The turns of phrase will not cohere into sentences or formal statements yet neither will they relinquish meaning.

Both fiction and grammar contain 'subjects' and the text opens with what could have been its title: 'in which the subject gets lost'; characters and sentences break down under the pressure of the indeterminacies which structure the text, 'in a double meaning where the subject gets lost'.[70] To take one example only from this complex text, the slogan 'NO REPRESENTATION/ WITHOUT REPRESENTATION addressing her image' asserts a double meaning that articulates the problem of, and the interdependence of, the politics of mediation and the mediation of politics.[71]

The reader (another subject) is lost, left 'to struggle … without hope of return to (the) safe ground' of familiar narrative.[72] The reader's loss is continual; but so is his or her discovery. The text offers both 'a duplicate reality' and 'an alternative universe'.[73] Language, in the last phrase of the section, proliferates its narratives, 'imitations that go forth and multiply'.[74] This is both a prophecy of the spread of totality *and* of its breaking down into resistant double and multiple meanings. The text resists itself almost successfully.

Techniques of textual transformation can be observed if we take Clarke's address in 'Obscure Disasters 7', to Lawrence Upton, reminding him, as poet to poet, of

> the common
> sense utopia where we
> all swop notes[75]

and trace how this is transformed in the ending of a poem upon which I wish to concentrate, 'Obscure Disaster 12', for Salman Rushdie:

> the enemy of images
> faded a little picture
> from the catastrophe where
> we put our hats[76]

The title of *Obscure Disasters* derives from Mallarmé's 'Calme bloc ici-bas chu du'un désastre obscur' in his 'tombeau' for Poe.[77] Tributes and addresses to fellow writers who write of disasters (the opening Gulf War 'epinicion' reminds them of one such contemporary disaster) abound. The 'common/ sense utopia' has transformed into Mallarmé's 'catastrophe' (out of which appropriate 'noirs vols du Blasphème' will blow).[78] The verbal transformation suggests the interdependence of the concepts with which it plays language-games. The place 'we put our hats' is proverbially 'home,' a dangerous place for Rushdie during the years of the *fatwah*; the phrase also has an affirmative note, an echo, perhaps, of putting our money where our mouths are. For all the techniques of indeterminacy, the poem is a statement of solidarity with Rushdie. The 'enemy of images' who is responsible for the death threats is, of course, the Islamic cleric Khomeni (whose own image, ironically, was a national icon in Iran), but the phrase is Rushdie's own to describe the homeless exiled paranoiac Imam of *The Satanic Verses*.[79] 'The Fellow Upstairs/ skims phantasmal scripts';[80] the Iman enacts a partial reading of the *Koran* which amounts to an 'authorized grand narrative' (and one which clearly operates to endanger Lyotard's petit narratives and its phrases).[81] One example of this 'implicit cultural script' is Clarke's view of the absurd lengths of authoritarian rule:

> bullet
> proofed delectibubbles the sacred
> frames in an inflated
> era[82]

of inflated claims, of inflated 'currency recycled', in a world haunted by the 'commerce wraith' of global capital.[83]

The epigraph from George Herbert may seem out of place, but Herbert's Christian version of plain fashion balances the text, which might otherwise be seen as solely an attack on the Islamic fundamentalist *fatwa*. Herbert's rhetorical questions, 'Who says that fictions only and false hair/ Become a verse? Is there in truth no beauty?' are refunctioned in the text.[84] The second becomes the poem's epigraph (where the 'in truth' becomes ambiguous). The first is woven into the poem's opening phrase: 'houses that fictions only/ wigged become averse to circulate' – the houses being possibly the publishing houses which refused to circulate *The Satanic Verses*, except in mutual disguise as The Consortium.[85]

The rules of this subversive linkage, Clarke's work teaches, have to be invented continually to counter absoluteness with plurality. The disruption of the authority of the sentence by what might be thought of almost as the micro-judgements of the phrase is one way of achieving this. The apparent arbitrariness of a certain number of words per line, an isoverbalist mode of measure all the more contentious and combative for largely lacking the kinds of antecedents free verse and open field poetry claim for themselves, is another. Constraints such as those used by the Oulipo writers (particularly Jacques Roubaud, who calculates his measures and words with increasing complexity); and Zukofsky, who mathematically uses and abuses the sonnet, are obvious precedents.

However, there are many complementary techniques, as linguistically innovative writers momently create new 'rules' for linkage, to suit the particular 'case' of each work: the disparate materials in need of procedural linkage. Lyotard describes the paradox of this process in *The Postmodern Condition*: 'The artist and the writer ... are working without rules in order to formulate the rules of what *will have been done*.'[86] As Lyotard declares, 'To link is necessary, but how to link is not.'[87]

Many of the writers to whom Clarke dedicates 'catastrophes', including Fisher, are also British practitioners of creative linkage: Lawrence Upton, Gilbert Adair, Maggie O'Sullivan, Robert Hampson and myself.[88] Clarke also addresses Ulli Freer, in whose long work, *TM*, the technique of juxtaposition amounts to an *indissoluble* compound of diction and discourses.

The texts in *Blvd.s*, an excerpt from the larger project, published by Equipage, are printed large, centred on the page, carry the thingness of monumental abstract canvases. 'Blvd.' and its unlikely plural are odd abbreviations for an English eye, but a resonant word, politically. The 'blvd.s' of Paris were designed by Haussmann to minimize the opportunities for insurrection, yet they have been the scenes of uprisings, in the insurrections of 1968, which signal so much, socially and intellectually, for Fisher, Clarke and Freer.

> baited sidewalks blockades
> ugh hugs tediously
> wordless police cordoned off
> enkindle hope from
> alleviation sneers vaguely
> dubbed to be free
> elaborately stranded
> dressed in spidery gabardines
> rumble pulses[89]

This is a passage of contrasts and of identity in difference, carried by the syntax of creative linkage. The 'ugh' of a comic book punch eye-rhymes

with the 'hugs' that are emotionally its opposite, however 'tedious'. 'Baited
... blockades ... cordoned off ... stranded' suggest alienation and entrap-
ment, rather than the object of the linkage, 'alleviation' and 'hope'. 'Wordless police' are 'dubbed', both speechless and spoken for, at once. 'Dubbed
to be free' sounds suspiciously like somebody else is rhetorically doing our
talking for us, despite the subject matter. The 'spidery gabardines' connote
surveillance and traps, again by the police. The concluding 'rumble pulses'
combination is oxymoronic: a rumble is a constant, a pulse is an interval,
pulses a series of them. Like the histories of the blvd.s of Paris (along which
traffic both rumbles and pulses) the text links external control with the
desire for liberation, the pulse of purposeful 'praxis' juxtaposed with purposeless interference. As the text puts it elsewhere

praxis
strong as a pulse embedded in random
noise[90]

The isolated 'praxis' holds its own against 'noise'. Pulses, as poetic rhythms,
are links in a chain, not of communication, but of creation.

Notes

1   Umberto Eco, 'The Poetics of the Open Work', in *The Role of the Reader* (London:
    Hutchinson, 1981), pp. 47–66, to which I have referred in the Introduction and Chapter 4.
2   'Dear Robert, "Linguistically innovative poetry" for which we haven't yet a satisfactory
    name', *Pages* 65–72 (March 1988) p. 68.
3   *Ibid.*, p. 68.
4   Jean-François Lyotard, 'Discussions, or phrasing "after Auschwitz"', in *The Lyotard Reader*,
    ed. Andrew Benjamin (Oxford: Blackwell, 1989), pp. 360–92, at p. 385; this lecture is re-
    vised and incorporated as the chapter entitled 'Result', pp. 86–106, in Jean-François Lyotard,
    The Differend: Phrases in Dispute (Minneapolis: University of Minnesota, 1988).
5   See Lyotard's chapter in 'Obligation', *The Differend*, particularly the pages 'Levinas', pp.
    110–15. See Derrida's 'Violence and Metaphysics: An Essay on the Thought of Emmanuel
    Levinas' in *Writing and Difference* (London and Henley: Routledge and Kegan Paul, 1978),
    pp. 79–153. This essay may well have prompted the linguistic turn of Levinas' later philoso-
    phy. See also Jacques Derrida, *Adieu to Emmanuel Levinas* (Stanford: Stanford University
    Press, 1999).
6   The famous pronouncement of 1967 'To write poetry after Auschwitz is barbaric' that lyric
    poetry was no longer possible after Auschwitz – hence Lyotard's title – was later retracted by
    Adorno; Theodor W. Adorno, 'Cultural Criticism and Society' in *Prisms* (Cambridge, MA:
    MIT Press, 1981), p. 34.

7 Lyotard, 'Discussions, or phrasing "after Auschwitz"', p. 385.

8 *Ibid.*, p. 374. A differend is an impasse between pleas at a tribunal, where the sense of wrong and damage, of right and responsibility, is not shared, is precisely incommensurable. One example might be the demands of workers and employees: there can be no reference to higher justice to determine rights. The case of the Jews under Nazism is that there was not even a differend because there was no tribunal; there was just the 'phrase', 'Die'.

9 *Ibid.*, p. 386.

10 *Ibid.*, p. 386.

11 *Ibid.*, p. 386. Rules, of course, are what the postmodern artist creates in process of his or her creating.

12 Responding, and quoted in, Lyotard, 'Discussions, or phrasing "after Auschwitz"', p. 387.

13 *Ibid.*, p. 387.

14 *Ibid.*, p. 387.

15 *Ibid.*, p. 387.

16 It is also in accord with the poetics developed for my own creative writing. This first section recasts my poetics essay, 'Linking the Unlinkable' (collected in my *Far Language; Poetics and Linguistically Innovative Poetry, 1978–1997* (Exeter: Stride Publications, 1999), pp. 54–55.)

17 Rachel Blau du Plessis, *The Pink Guitar* (New York and London: Routledge, 1990), p. 156. For my discussion of poetics as a discourse see 'The Poetics of Poetics: Charles Bernstein, Allen Fisher and "the poetic thinking that results"', in *Symbiosis*, vol. 3, no. 1 (April 1999), pp. 77–92. My "The Poetics of Writing: The Writing of Poetics", published in the *Proceedings of the 1998 Conference on Creative Writing in Higher Education*, Sheffield Hallam University, pp. 99–109 is a more pedagogic piece for teachers of creative writers.

18 Allen Fisher, *Necessary Business* (London: Spanner, 1985), p. 163. The text (though without the interleaved interviews) is reprinted in *The Topological Shovel: Four Essays* (Willowdale: The Gig Editions, 1999).

19 *Ibid.*, p. 183.

20 J.H. Prynne, *Down where changed* (Lewes: Ferry Press, 1979), Eric Mottram's *1980 Mediate* (Maidstone: Zunne Heft, 1980), and cris cheek's *A Present* (London: Bluff Books, 1980).

21 Fisher's essay also charts the aesthetic changes stimulated by the haitus between the British Poetry Revival and the beginnings of Linguistically Innovative Poetry.

22 Fisher, *Necessary Business*, p. 163.

23 Jan Mukarovský, *Aesthetic Function, Norm and Value as Social Facts* (Ann Arbor, MI: Slavic Contributions, 1979).

24 *Ibid.*, p. 95.

25 *Ibid.*, p. 87.

26 *Ibid.*, p. 72. This is strictly in accordance with Forrest-Thomson's Wittgensteinian insistence that information in poetry is changed by its aesthetic context. See Veronica Forrest-Thompson, *Poetic Artifice* (Manchester: Manchester University Press, 1978), p. x.

27 See 'Instruction sheet for a boring participatory poem in apathy & fear & fatigue; conceived by Allen Fisher for FLUXSHOE Croydon 1973' in *Prosyncel* (New York: Strange Faeces Press, 1975), p. 42 which lists the equipment and procedure necessary for this performance.

28 Mukarovský, *Aesthetic Function, Norm and Value as Social Facts*, p. 85.

29　Fisher, *Necessary Business*, p. 164–65.

30　It is often one of the distinguishing features of poetics as a discourse that it mimes the procedures of the creative work to which it belongs, or to which it will give form.

31　Fisher finds an instructive moment of criticism, or of outer limit, in one of his examples. His reservations about the 'float perceptions' of cris cheek's *A Present* lies in the perceived danger of homogenous disorder which would have the impertinent effect of stability, (Fisher, *Necessary Business*, p. 184), but he concludes: 'His risk is the balance of noise and music and to hell with the balance' (p. 231).

32　*Ibid.*, p. 196.

33　*Ibid.*, p. 196.

34　Allen Fisher, *Philly Dog* (Hereford: Spanner, 1995), n.p.

35　Fisher, *Necessary Business*, p. 211.

36　*Ibid.*, p. 237.

37　Allen Fisher, *Brixton Fractals* (London: Aloes Books, 1985), p. 13.

38　*Ibid.*, p. 4.

39　Fisher, *Necessary Business*, p. 225.

40　Allen Fisher, 'A Statement of Poetics', *West Coast Line*, number seventeen, vol. 29, no. 2 (1995), pp. 109–10, at p. 109.

41　Fisher, *Brixton Fractals*, p. 73.

42　William Blake, *The Complete Poems*, ed. W.H. Stevenson (London: Longman, 1972), p. 484.

43　Fisher, 'A Statement of Poetics', p. 109.

44　Fisher, *Necessary Business*, p. 225.

45　Fisher, *Brixton Fractals*, p. 73.

46　*Ibid.*, p. 73.

47　Fisher, *Necessary Business*, p. 110.

48　Fisher, *Prosyncel*, p. 36.

49　Allen Fisher, *Ideas on the Culture Dreamed Of* (London: Spanner Editions, 1982), pp. 4, 9, 15, 20, 24, 26, 29, 35, 37, 42, 46, 48, 50, 59, 63, 74, 85, 89, 91, 94, 95. A more informative account of the actual writing of Fisher's poems is to be found in Scott Thurston's thesis 'Rescale: Method and Technique in Contemporary Poetry and Poetics', PhD thesis, University of Lancaster, 2001, especially Chapter 6: 'Allen Fisher'.

50　Adrian Clarke, *Ghost Measures* (London: Actual Size, 1987), p. 29. 'Where the culture breaks' is the apposite second line of the first poem in the first showing from *Gravity*. 'Banda', Fisher, *Brixton Fractals*, p. 1. Clarke (and I) paid prose homage to Fisher in the Afterword in Adrian Clarke and Robert Sheppard, eds., *Floating Capital: new poets from London*, (Elmwood: Potes and Poets Press, 1991), pp. 121–25.

51　The translators' glossary to Lyotard, *The Differend* defines 'phrase' thus: 'the English cognate has been used throughout rather than the semantically more correct *sentence* for a number of reasons. The term, as Lyotard develops it here, is *not* a grammatical – or even linguistic – entity (it is not the expression of one complete thought nor the minimal unit of signification, but a *pragmatic* one, the concern being with the possibility (or impossibility) of what can (or cannot) be 'phrased', of what can (or cannot) be 'put into phrases' (p.194).

52　Adrian Clarke, *Listening to the Differences* (Carshalton: RWC Extra, 1991) reprinted in

Millennial Shades & Three Papers (London: Writers Forum, 1998), to which subsequent reference will be made, n.p. A similar Lyotard quotation can be found in Lyotard, *The Differend*, p. 11.

53   Clarke, *Millennial Shades & Three Papers*, n.p. A similar Lyotard quotation can be found in Lyotard, *The Differend*, p. 66.

54   Robert Hampson, 'Producing the unknown: language and ideology in contemporary poetry', in *The New British Poetries*, eds., Robert Hampson and Peter Barry (Manchester: Manchester University Press, 1993), pp. 134–55, at p. 151.

55   Lyotard, *The Differend*, p. 128.

56   Clarke, *Millennial Shades & Three Papers*, n.p.

57   *Ibid.*, n.p.

58   *Ibid.*, n.p.; also in *Obscure Disasters* (London: Writers Forum, 1993). I have not found the exact quotation in Lyotard, but he does write less epigrammatically, 'Politics … is the threat of the differend. It is not a genre, it is the multiplicity of genres, the diversity of ends, and par excellence the question of linkage'. (Lyotard, *The Differend: Phrases in Dispute*, p. 138).

59   Clarke, *Obscure Disasters* (London: Writers Forum, 1993), n.p.

60   *Ibid.*, n.p. See also Louis Zukofsky, 'An Objective' (1930, 1931), in *Prepositions: The Collected Critical Essays of Louis Zukofsky* (California: The University of California Press, 1981), pp. 12–18, at p. 12.

61   Rosmarie Waldrop, *The Road is Everywhere or Stop this Body* (Columbia, MO: Open Places, 1978).

62   Clarke, *Ghost Measures*, p. 64.

63   Clarke, *Obscure Disasters*, n.p.

64   Clarke, *Ghost Measures*, p. 68.

65   Adrian Clarke, *Spectral Investments* (London: Writers Forum, 1991), n.p.

66   *Ibid.*, n.p.

67   *Ibid.*, n.p.

68   *Ibid.*, n.p.

69   *Ibid.*, n.p.

70   *Ibid.*, n.p.

71   *Ibid.*, n.p.

72   *Ibid.*, n.p.

73   *Ibid.*, n.p.

74   *Ibid.*, n.p. A demotic use of the phrase is as an euphemism for 'fuck off'.

75   Clarke, *Obscure Disasters*, n.p.

76   *Ibid.*, n.p. This use of verbal transformation Allen Fisher calls rhyme and uses extensively in his work as a principle of the processual. (See Thurston, 'Rescale', Chapter 6.) It is another form of going forth and multiplying (see note 74). I have already, in Chapter 6, traced similar patterns in the work of cris cheek.

77   Stephane Mallarmé, *The Poems*, trans. Keith Bosley (Harmondsworth: Penguin, 1977), pp. 174–75.

78   *Ibid.*, p. 174.

79   Salman Rushdie, *The Satanic Verses* (Dover, DE: The Consortium Inc, 1992), pp. 205–9.

80   Clarke, *Obscure Disasters*, n.p.

81 *Ibid.*, n.p.

82 *Ibid.*, n.p.

83 *Ibid.*, n.p.

84 *Ibid.*, n.p. George Herbert, 'Jordan' in *The Metaphysical Poets* ed. Helen Gardner (Harmondsworth: Penguin, 1957, p. 125).

85 Clarke, *Obscure Disasters*, np

86 Lyotard, *The Postmodern Condition*, p. 81.

87 Clarke, *Millennial Shades & Three Papers*, n.p. Taken from Lyotard, *The Differend*, p. 66.

88 For Lawrence Upton, see, for example, *Wire Sculptures* (London: Reality Street Editions, 2003), as well as his collaborations with Bob Cobbing treated in the next chapter; see also Adrian Clarke, 'An A–U of Upton's Assent', *Angel Exhaust* 8 (Autumn 1992), pp. 107–10. For Gilbert Adair's work later than *Hot Licks* (London: Sub-Voicive Books, 1987), analysed in Chapter 6, see, for example, *Jizz Rim*, 1st outtake (London: Writers Forum, 1993), and *Jizz Rim* 5th outtake (London: Writers Forum, 1997). Maggie O'Sullivan is the subject of Chapter 10. Robert Hampson's co-editing of *New British Poetries*, and his contribution to it, have already been mentioned; his poetry is collected in *Assembled Fugitives: Selected Poems* (Exeter: Stride Publications, 2001). My creative work from the project *Twentieth Century Blues* may be found in *The Flashlight Sonata* (Exeter: Stride Publications, 1993) and *Tin Pan Arcadia* (Cambridge: Salt Publishing, 2004).

89 Ulli Freer, *Blvd.s.* (Cambridge: Equipage, 1994), n.p. See also *Speakbright Leap Passwood* (Cambridge: Salt Publishing, 2003).

90 *Ibid.*, n.p.

9

The Ballet of the Speech Organs:
The Poetry of Bob Cobbing 1965–2000

VERBIVISIVOCO

Bob Cobbing, who died in 2002, was a senior and major exponent of the international concrete poetry movement, but he was a visual artist before he was a poet. His earliest duplicator print of 1942 presages his later work and his interest in the mechanics and accidents of office, rather than fine art, printing.[1] However it was not until 1964, after some years of involvement in the literary underground, as recorded in Chapter 2, that Cobbing came to maturity with the alliterative sequence *ABC in Sound*. By this time the awareness he had gained of the international concrete poetry movement and the various forms of 1960s interart, meant he gave himself to such experimentation with great energy.[2]

The basic orientation that unites most forms of concrete poetry – in its recent century of experiment – is that it foregrounds, by emphasis or distortion, one or more of the conventional elements of poetic artifice (such as lineation or rhyme and alliteration, or even simply letters and their appearance in books), or their attendant sounds, and concentrates upon the resulting materiality of language. Appropriately, at one time the term 'abstract' was as popular as 'concrete' to describe this work. The link between the physical signifier and the conceptual signified of other kinds of language is problematized, a particular kind of the suspension of the naturalizing processes that Forrest-Thomson describes, another way of literally emphasizing the saying of language as against its said.

This poetry has been conventionally divided into two types: visual poetry and sound poetry, both of which were practised by Cobbing.[3]

In visual poetry the physical signs of print on paper assume prominence. At its simplest there are the pattern poems of George Herbert or Dylan Thomas.[4] The more experimental 'calligrammes' of Apollinaire prefigured modernist experiments in words arranged in patterns upon the page,[5] whether it be the characteristic typographical violence of Futurist 'words in freedom' ('ScrAbrrRrraaNNG!') or the comparative stasis of Gomringer's word 'constellations' (itself a term borrowed from Mallarmé's influential *Un Coup de dés* of 1897), such as his 'silencio' (the word repeated in rows, though with a 'silent' gap in the middle).[6] The Brazilian Noigandes group of the 1950s, the Lettrism of Heidesieck, and the spatialism of Pierre Garnier suggest the range of visual experiment.[7] There were brief vogues for signalist and semiotic poems (which used signs), and for op, pop and kinetic poems, which textually mimed the procedures of the visual artists who adopted those terms in the 1960s.[8] The huge overprinted panels of Steve McCaffery's work of the 1970s, *Carnival* (a text which had to be partly destroyed to be unfolded for assemblage) contrast with the recent clean typographical devices of Johanna Drucker.[9] The stone and architectural fantasies of Ian Hamilton Finlay, particularly the site-specific works in his temple garden at Stonypath, contrast with the earlier printed word-towers of Furnival's 'Temples'.[10] The bookmaking projects of artist Tom Phillips, particularly his *Humument: A Treated Victorian Novel*, involving the systematic overpainting and isolation of found texts from his original, is analogous to several kinds of concrete poetry.[11] At its most abstract, visual poetry can present fractured signs that barely resemble orthographies, such as dom sylvester houdédard's 1960s metaphysical and sometimes wordless typewriter designs that Edwin Morgan called 'typescracts'.[12] Cobbing's use in the 1970s, by himself and by some of those he has influenced, such as Clive Fencott, Lawrence Upton and cris cheek, of the misuses of printing equipment in which ink, rather than print, becomes the medium, points towards the total integration of text and event in performance writing.[13]

Sound poetry has been divided into *poesie phonetique* and *poesie sonore*, in France at least. Phonetic poetry originated, in modern times, with the primitivism of the Russian 'zaum' poets and with Kurt Schwitters' *Ur-Sonate* (1923–28).[14] This permitted later work such as Ernst Jandl's 'niaga/ra fëlle',[15] or Edwin Morgan's poems of the 1960s, which work by making sound structures of syllables and words, meaningful or not.[16]

Poesie sonore, such as the work of Frenchman Henri Chopin, resident in Britain during the 1960s and 1970s, uses the voice and electronic superimpositions and speed variations to create sound textures, from whispers to bellows.[17] François Dufrêne's cri-rhythms take this essentially wordless technique one stage further.[18] Some poets use unaided voice; others use electronics, particularly the Swedish 'text-sound' poets, such as Sten Hanson.[19]

Language experiments which do not distend either the visual or the aural might be called, after the work of Polish emigré Stefan Themerson, 'semantic poetry'.[20] Themerson's work, such as the semantic poetry translations in his 1949 novel *Bayamus*, utilizes dictionary definitions of every word to rewrite a selected text, for example a folk song. Found texts, such as those of Cobbing himself, work by framing an utterance and isolating it. A treated text is not necessarily the opposite of a found text, because both are methods of disrupting already existent texts. A treated text of Cobbing's in the 1990s, which I quote here to complicate the narrative of his 'development' that this chapter might otherwise suggest, the incomplete sequence *Life the Universe and Everything*, is a hilarious collage taken from various popular science sources which perfectly preserves the dead-pan absurdity of the originals:

> Predicting the weather
> is one thing
> predicting it correctly
> is another ...
> elephants   fleas
> have a natural length-scale
> coastlines don't.[21]

Cut-up, an analogous technique used, more occasionally than supposed, by William Burroughs, himself British-based for a while in the 1960s, was practised by Cobbing as far back as the 1950s. The procedural and permutational works of the Oulipo movement, founded in 1960, and still active, suggests another relationship, one seen in Cobbing's sideswipe at the inane figurative play of the 1993 *New Poetry* when he generates lines such as 'rock 'n' roll makes me feel like rolypoly/ a little lechery makes me feel like spotted dick' from Liz Lochhead's 'a good fuck makes me feel like custard'.[22]

While the exemplary internationalism of the concrete poetry movement must be acknowledged, the rigid distinctions of the French have not appealed to British artists and performers. Dufrêne and Chopin are, according to Cobbing,

> very suspicious of using the word so importantly. Whenever I turn to non-verbal sounds, Chopin welcomes me with open arms! ... But I go back to the word again, and they tell me the word is finished.[23]

It is not simply Cobbing's achievement that he has taken the rare route of practising all the forms of concrete and semantic poetry, but it is crucial to his work that his (freestanding) visual poems are always scores for performance. Cobbing has done more than most concrete poets since Zurich Dada to liberate the text from the page into performance contexts – to use all manner of marks as a notation for vocal (and other) performance – yet the page is also a visual text. One of Cobbing's titles, *Sonic Icons,* exemplifies the interdependence of the two sides of his work through its appropriate anagram. As mentioned in Chapter 6, Cobbing performed in various ensembles, sometimes with improvising musicians such as David Toop and Lol Coxhill, or dancers, such as Jennifer Pike or Sally Silvers, but often with other poets, such as Bill Griffiths or Lawrence Upton. A group can develop techniques and procedures, possibly even establish provisional conventions of translating marks on the page into sound – even when the 'text' is apparently non-linguistic. As Eric Mottram writes, in the introduction to Cobbing's thirteenth volume of Collected Poems, *Voice Prints*: 'The issue of what images instigate what sounds, and the lengths and tones and volumes of the performance are left to the combined sense of a particular occasion.'[24] The scores are indeterminate invitations, as in some of the 'open work' scores Umberto Eco examines, such as those of John Cage,[25] or, more contemporary to Cobbing himself, the composer Cornelius Cardew.

Cobbing's division of labour between performance and self-publishing ensured the unity of his creative project, although the emphasis upon the performative element has sometimes obscured his work as a maker of publications and as a publisher. Eric Mottram clearly summarizes the ethos of Cobbing's little press, Writers Forum: it 'stood for high standards of innovative work, inexpensive material production and rapid distribution to a reading public who wished to buy poetry but had restricted budgets'.[26] Indeed it is the most generous and exemplary little press of our time, as outlined in Chapter 2 – and this 'cheap and neat' attitude sets it apart from the exclusivity and rarity of most of the art book market.[27] (The work of the press is best illustrated by its anthology, *Verbi Visi Voco*; a note in it declares that all of its publications remain in print. Writers Forum had by 2000 produced over 1000 booklets or pamphlets; *Verbi Visi Voco* gives some idea of the scope of the press and its associated workshops.)[28]

The ownership of the means of production (at first an office duplicator and then a photocopier) also had implications for Cobbing's own work since, as he put it in 1974, 'With a visual poem, the printing stage is a vital part of the creative process.'[29] In later work the printing stage *becomes* the creative process, since his misuse of machinery matches his 'misuse' of language: 'I do things with the duplicator that Gestetner really get horrified over,' he said in 1973.[30] Printing is, in effect, performance. The making of books, both in terms of conceptualising them and in terms of producing them, is the making of poetry. For Cobbing it was a source of creative self-renewal.

A B C

'The *ABC in Sound* (1964) led me to believe I could become professional,' Cobbing explained.[31] This 26-page alphabetical suite was first performed at Better Books, where Cobbing was manager, and published as a record and booklet in 1965 by Writers Forum. Originally entitled *Sound Poems*, the revised title balances the visuality of an ABC with its realization in sound; it celebrates the release of language from its referential function, through a variety of techniques. It also belongs to the ancient tradition of alphabet poems. Peter Mayer's anthology *Alphabetical Poems* reprints Anglo-Saxon riddles alongside works by Pope and Coleridge, houédard and Chopin, as well as Cobbing's *ABC in Sound.*[32]

The text was originally printed with no typographical deviation and primarily existed as an unpunctuated score for recitation;[33] the 1965 BBC Radiophonic Workshop version makes full use of tape speed changes, echoes and overdubs.

'J' presents an alliterative counterpointing of the forces of law and of desire; the indentation was translated into speed changes in the studio version:

> Juridiquement
> Jugeur jugeur jugeur
Jouer jouissance
Joyeusement joyeuseté[34]

There is the mock deathliness of the whispered 'G':

grin
grim
gay green
grey green
gangrene[35]

'S' is a sardonic commentary upon the jargon of sociolinguistics:

Semanticdifferential
Supportingredundancy
Sociallyinstitutionalized
Systematicwholeofspeechsounds

each line getting longer (and typed to emphasize this in the first edition)
until the short final line, after a stanza break: 'Shit'.[36] As another
Franchophone text reminds us, ironically, 'Langage/Est mort'.[37] More abstract is the found text 'M', an alphabetic list of 35 Scottish and Irish sur-
names, performed at double speed over a bagpipe-like voice drone:

Macbean
MacBrayne
MacBryde[38]

'N' and 'O' use letters as structuring devices, the former as though they
were prefixes,

N
Ndue
Ndemic[39]

O is again a list, from a dictionary, of official initials that becomes a 'quick,
fairly high pitched' rhythmic recitation in performance, according to
Cobbing's 1964 performance notes.[40] It subtly rhymes and alliterates:

OD
OE
OED
OEEC
OES
OF[41]

In 'R' there are the beginnings of individual performance routes around a
text, from 'Rebus' to 'Repeat'; a performer may choose any direction along
or across the four columns of seven words, all them titles of paintings by
Rauschenberg, to whom the piece is dedicated.[42]

The most complex texts are those that enable a virtuosic oral performance, although some still use recognizable words. The use of Japanese for
non-speakers of that language tends towards pure sound:

Da dageki daha dai dai daido
    Daigo-tettei dai-itchakushu
Daija daijobu Daijoe daikyu[43]

Similar effects are present in 'P', which rapidly alternates the music of the consonant with the various articulations of the vowel 'o':

| oll/ollapodrida oll | oberammergau | oll/oll/potpourri |
| poc/pocahontas | poc/popocatapetl | poc/poc/opossum[44] |

More complex still is 'W', an alliterative palindrome that demands a slow reading (which it receives on the BBC recording, over low sounds derived from the text):

wordrow worn row
wombat tab mow
womb mow wort row
weser re-sew
wolf flow
wolf-dog god flow
won't now
wonder red now
wordrow[45]

The finest piece is probably 'T', a re-arrangement of a six-word Veda song, which was described by dom silvester houédard as 'the most elegantly complex and sophisticated pure-sound-poem bob cobbing has written':[46]

The first of its six verses runs (in 'light quick rhythms' according to Cobbing's notes):[47]

tan tandinanan tandinane
tanan tandina tandinane
tanare tandita tandinane
tantarata tandina tandita[48]

Its organising of '9 basic syllables' dictate the chant heard in the early recordings and later performances.[49] However, the text as now reprinted was the work of film maker Stephen Dwoskin, Cobbing explains, 'after he had heard me perform the poem in 1966. He has very successfully attempted to match the shape of the sound performance'.[50] Cobbing had started softly, risen to a crescendo; and then the sound faded. This simple modification of his text (a centred arrangement with variable type sizes) may well have been the impulse for Cobbing's gradual movement towards what had become the unique distinction of his work by the early 1970s: to match the visual and the sonic, to see shape as sound, to shape text and non-text in terms of the eye and the ear, and to allow for versions of a text. As Cobbing warns of Dwoskin's typography: 'Performances of this poem varied exceedingly, especially in later years, so Steve's version is an equivalent only'; it has itself become the text for later improvisations.[51] On the three 1968 'Variations' recording (which segues out of the original recording, sounding much as Cobbing describes it above, the larger type of Dwoskin's visualization indicating increased studio echo) the dense, multivoiced interplay of several performers (including François Dufrêne and the two poets' wives) preserves the poem's rhythm, through paralinguistics, as whispering and coughs begin to take over the rhythm of the chant.[52] What distinguishes it from the versions by vocal singing groups is the eschewal of harmony in favour of the grain of the voice as an articulatory mechanism, not as a musical instrument. As Cobbing remarked the same year, 'Material is now unimportant, treatment is all.'[53]

A E I O U

The Five Vowels of 1974 contrasts with the phonetic austerity of the *ABC* of a decade before. The work (in its 1986 second edition) consists of duplicated coloured ink on coloured card (one colour for each vowel, alluding to Rimbaud's sonnet 'Voyelle') taped into double or triple folded A4, collected with an introductory sheet in an envelope with a printed cover, as Writers Forum Folder No 16.[54] In this work the page has become a field, the text arranged visually around it, yet the 'text' here is limited to repetitions of a single vowel shape. Whether it is the brown print of lower-case 'i's, building up on the yellow folio into loose blocks, or the separate 'O' pages where a tight constellation of irregular reddish ovals on gold paper contrasts with the more solid page where the Os form holes in an unevenly inked rectangle, the 'Five Vowels can be the basis for a wide range of vocal exploration', as Sten Hanson puts it, partly because of its suggestive non-linearity, a feature of many music texts of the era.[55] The performers move freely around the field of the text with momently-made variations of direction and sound. The shaping in its own right is there for sounding in its own right. The technique of overprinting resembles, or suggests, the technique of audio overdubbing, and this is nowhere clearer than in 'E' where an e, which is itself constructed of tiny lower case letters, is overprinted and reversed into 12 different clusters of blue-green ink on blue paper; on the recorded version of 1973, *e colony*, the single vowel is alternately used to create long droning diphthongs, and jerkily stressed articulations, with swirling overdubs and chatters of repeated E sounds in various pronunciations resembling, but not imitating, the sound of bees, as the title suggests.[56] The most radical poem is the brown on pink 'U'. Whereas the others use lettraset (Cobbing was quick to grasp any new innovation), this text is built up from the imprint of lips on a page, the physical impressions of the sound being made. Yet this impression is graphologically close enough (with some editing and cutting, as well as overprinting) to constitute the letter shape, and can be used as a score for further performance – in a self-generating process.

'It is a small step,' Cobbing declares disingenuously, 'from using the texture and shape of lips to using the imprint of bark or leaf (and) ... a further small step to composing marks that are not directly from nature.'[57] His contemporaries agree. Augusto de Campos' 'Poemas Popcretos', for example, uses pop-art media images (of eyes);[58] Steve McCaffery's 'Defence of Rhyme', 'rhymes' images of a mascara eyelash and an earwig.[59] But Cobbing's work, in the late 1970s and early 1980s, in which non-linguistic marks (both natural and manmade) may be regarded as sonic signifiers, leaves the barest of referential functions and only a residual convention of the alphabetic principle: that shapes have sounds. This open system of notation, in which 'conventions' have to be momently and provisionally established during undirected improvisation, meant that some who had followed Cobbing thus far were repulsed around the late 1970s. Given this commitment to indeterminacy, Cobbing also seems to have largely abandoned claims for the ritualistic nature of this incantatory work in performance in preference for exploratory experiment and the processual. In performance these inky maps became scores for the various groups he formed.

XEROX

In a series of 17 pamphlets and sheets entitled 'Processual' made between 1982 and 1985 (and issued as a boxed set as *Processual: collected poems 10* in 1987), Cobbing used his photocopier as both a new poetic tool and as the latest mode of production of Writers Forum.[60] 'Processual' refers directly to the serial photocopied processing of materials, which was a major development in Cobbing's work. This led to transformational, almost impersonal, series of texts. Most of the booklets were generated from 5 pages of '(almost) random snippets' – fragments of adverts, Muybridge images selected for contrasts of light and dark, scientific language, rubbish.[61] The systematic magnification and reduction of images suggest both microscopic and cosmic forms, but in fact are often produced by mundane objects, such as a wine glass on the copyboard. Cobbing's earlier propensity towards making versions is given a renewed and exhaustive necessity. Its linearity of method enabled the magnifications of the texts, with their unpredictable breaking up of patches of ink, to be reprocessed. The work signals Cobbing's wider commitment to a machinic sense of the production of productivity, as Deleuze and Guattari would put it. The work is a homage to, and demonstration of, the power of process over product, although the boxed product is a substantial 'process-showing', to use a phrase of Allen Fisher (from whose vocabulary the title was also drawn).[62]

One of the boxed booklets, *A Processual Nonny-Nonny*, exemplifies the method: '18 variations on the design finally selected for No 9 in the series'.[63] From this complex image come simpler but similar variations, a kind of visual rhyming that lends the book a unity, and which were created during the changes and chances of the photocopying processes. Printing is writing, in this work, despite the absence of words and letters. The performance of this part of the project by the then Bird Yak line up of Cobbing, Clive Fencott and Hugh Metcalfe in 1985 placed Cobbing's live art at the free anarchic edge of British improvised music and performance. Phonetics had given way to frenetics, as alphabet had given way to imprint.

Cobbing continued to produce many smaller items, and developed his techniques; in the pieces of the early 1990s, a vectoral trace, a swift movement traversing the stillness of a page is produced by what might be called action printing: moving material on the copyboard as the print is made. This is followed by arrangement, cutting, collage, enlargement, reduction, or re-printing with changed contrast settings: processing the already processed. The title *Congruence of Speed and Stall* (1990) describes this process accurately.[64] The first photocopy texts of the 1980s appear static by comparison.

Between 1994 and 2000, working with Lawrence Upton resulted in an astounding collaboration of both texts and performances that dwarfed

Processual. Entitled *Domestic Ambient Noise*, the completed project consists of 300 booklets; each processes a single theme drawn from the other poet's work to produce 6 page-length variations. Partly because it is a collaboration with the younger poet Upton, who brought his experience of cartoons, clip art, posters, computer art and more conventional forms of Linguistically Innovative Poetry to the project (as well as his experiences of performing with cheek, Fencott, and Cobbing, in the 1970s) it is an eclectic exploration using various techniques. The two poets drew (and dared) each other into new areas as one created 'variations' from the 'theme' produced by the other, any of which may, in turn, have become the 'theme' for the next stage.

From the point of view of Cobbing's development it is fascinating to see that he had a superb eye for selecting and imaginatively processing any Upton theme into a distinct set of 'original' Cobbing variations: icons and computer graphics are crumpled into innovation; images are abstracted; handwriting becomes ideogram; a banal smiley face suggests a new set of surreal portraits; a negative review of *Verbi Visi Voco* is magnified into a visual poem. In the text Cobbing produced on his 75th birthday, *Domestic Ambient Moise*, Upton's cut up handwriting is transformed into six beautiful suggestive calligraphic visuals, some of them demonstrating Cobbing's experimentation with speed, movement and arrest.[65] The risky dialogue between the two writers ensured the injection of unpoetic materials, even by Cobbing's standards: packaging, clipart, Marmite smears as well as calligraphy, found texts and even semantic texts. Cobbing and his latest photocopier could process any materials he was challenged with, and transformed them into surprising and beautiful texts.

Cobbing's contention that he remained a poet, although the page was covered with no signs which would be recognisable under socially agreed conventions of reading, is reinforced by his insistence upon the book format and his work as a maker of books. Even as other conventions are broken, there is a particular and limited visual field that we associate with reading, and that is the space of most of Cobbing's work. Mainly black and white, obstinately inky, upon the page and folio, the texts he produces assert their 'bookness', reject the possibility of the gallery wall. To watch Cobbing's eyes moving across the page as he performed was to witness a reading not a looking. In early human history, reading was conducted out loud, however private and quiet. It is one of the aims of Cobbing's work to

regain that somatic response to text, not to close the gap between the signifier and the signified (in which he has little interest), but to put into a new
relation with one another the graphic signifier and the sonic signifier. It
represents an outer limit of maintaining the radical openness of saying, as
the text's ontological status (is it a text? it asks) is disrupted. Nevertheless,
the book format concretizes the potentialities of its various performances (a
literal set of sayings) as a said.

X Y Z

The *Third ABC in Sound*, a work of Cobbing's 80th year, 2000, revisits the
alphabet poem, but whereas the first *ABC* demands oral, but still relatively
conventional, performance, the reader of the new poem would have to be
familiar with Cobbing's performance methods outlined above. Despite its
title and despite the presence on each page of a letter (sometimes minimally, sometimes as the entirety of the visual component), its suggestive
visuality is what is most immediately striking.

The letters of the alphabet become elements of play in the visual field, as
in the *Five Vowels*, not dominant structural alliterations as in the first *ABC*.[66]
Variable font styles almost symbolize the intrusion of the arbitrary into the
apparent orderliness of the alphabet. On the opening page, we see a bloated
bubble 'a', backed by a ghost of its shape, and some vague intimations of
text, even a roughly cut fragment of a word at the bottom of the page. The
whole rises above a textured, but cracked background, with the arc of a
curve slashing through to the left. 'G' (or 'g') is dominated by a lower case
letter, the bottom oval forming not the 'grin' of the 1964 alphabet, but a
glowering, menacing, empty mouth shape. Other texts show a pull towards
angularity and clarity. 'L' is lost against a latticework of girders, one of the
few visually mimetic traces in the texts. The letter M looks disassembled, its
almost sculptural components rest angled against a sloped background of
the night sky. 'O' consists of beautifully arranged white arcs against a pure
black background. None is complete, yet each suggests the circle that forms
the oldest letter shape in the world. On the other hand, 'K' looks like a
powdery tornado, and only if one knows the page is alphabetic, is one likely
to notice the K at the base of the twister. Turn it 45 degrees and the viewer
realizes the image is a shadowy depiction of a pair of lips, as though Dali's

Mae West Lips had met the 'U' of the *Five Vowels*. 'S' resembles a negative of one of Duchamp's nudes, and has the stately beauty of an art lithograph. 'V', on the other hand resembles (perhaps even derives from) a mysterious scientific photograph of jumping particles (in v-shaped trajectories). As in *Processual*, the apparently microscopic is tensioned against the cosmic, and there is a vertiginous loss of scale in these texts.

Cobbing clearly utilizes the full possible articulations of the mechanical devices available (photocopying, overprinting, cutting, juxtaposing, enlarging, cracking images, dispersal through magnification, mis-inking, etc.) yet it is difficult to determine how he has produced many of these texts, possibly because techniques are mixed. After the exploratory to and fro and deliberate hit and miss of the *Domestic Ambient Noise* collaboration, the care over each page – and the stylistic individuality of each – is evident. In 'X' the letter is half obscured and wedged by other shapes. This points to a late development in Cobbing's work; there is often *in* (rather than *on*) these pages a clear sense of figure operating against ground, with the letter often, but not exclusively, acting as the figure. The combination of the earliest form of concrete poem, designing with the basic alphabetic graphemes of the language, and concrete poetry's outer point of development, the use of the print-sound-scape which Cobbing has made his own on the page and off it, is the work's impressive novelty.

The play of letter against abstraction, the play of one symbolic system against another – the slightest of temporalities that the letter form as sound poses against the spatiality of the visual field, for example – are probably what create the heightened sense of foregrounding and three-dimensionality noted above. This, along with the indeterminacies of scale, also mentioned above, presents a complex of (new) signs for performers; even the most familiar of these, perhaps even Cobbing himself, would have needed to invent new strategies, perhaps moment by moment as they performed these texts.

Apparent in all of Cobbing's work is a concentration upon the usually unutilized potentialities of language, upon a supplementarity that gestures, literally and metaphorically, towards the saying over the said. It is also an exploration of the limits of the medium of poetry, in terms of intermedia and cross-art performance, and is both a precursor, and potential extension, of performance writing. Indeed, one of its lessons is to make readers see the potentialities of this supplementarity breaking into conventional poetry, of interrupting the saidness of text with a saying that both threatens and liberates it. The international Writers Forum anthology *Word Score Utterance Choreography in verbal and visual poetry*, edited by Upton and Cobbing in 1998,[67] demonstrated an appreciation of the graphic and aural dimensions of other poetries.

One American contributor was Johanna Drucker. In her study *The Visible Word, Experimental Typography and Modern Art 1909–1923*, she presents the typographical experiments of modernism (which she continues in her own work) as a material practice with two orders of materiality. The first is the 'stuff of apparency',[68] the 'sheer concrete thingness of printer's type', as another contributor to *Word Score*, Edwin Morgan, puts it.[69] Such an order may not exclude questions of historical and cultural value; the same text on paper, brass or gold surely is validated differently.

The second order, Drucker reminds us, following Saussure, is that the text is bound also by the relational signifying system we call language. There is no necessary connection between these material codes; whereas the linguistic system is rule-bound (in terms of grammar, syntax, etc.), the realm of the visual is less encoded, although historical conventions are not absent.

Yet this double-headed materiality is ever present in language, and in all physical inscription of language. Writing is not on paper, like a flat projection upon a screen, but is *in* the paper, as it were. 'Materiality of language,' as McCaffery says,

> is that aspect which remains resistant to an absolute subsumption into the ideality of meaning … To see the letter not as phoneme but as ink, and to further insist on that materiality, inevitably contests the status of language as a bearer of uncontaminated meaning.[70]

As some contributors to Cobbing and Upton's anthology say, such 'contamination' of Drucker's two systems is present in the physical appearance on the page of 'verbal' texts too. This is not simply a question of design, layout, presentation, but of a visual syntax. There are no non-meaningful elements of a poem; Forrest-Thomson was right about artifice but not about limiting its provenance. The spatial orientation of language on the page, for example, affects the reader's active engagement, and can be manipulated deliberately.

The spatial field of the page has often suggested notation for reading performance, whether it is in the precise spacing of a text like Jackson Mac Low's 'Forties' in which pauses are determined by space,[71] or the openness of

Cobbing's visual sound-scapes or page-fields. Both imply eye-movement as text-realization, but again are more coded in the case of language (left to right, top to bottom, for example) than in the image (though conventions of perspective, centre and frame may dictate starting points, as I have suggested of Cobbing's third *ABC*).

Some work collected in Cobbing and Upton's anthology almost magically holds the two 'systems' in a separate and parallel state. Drucker's cool spatiality matches the semantic with a rare poise and assurance, whereas McCaffery (to compare these two again) writes of presenting a number of writing systems on one plane, something that invades the collaborations of *Domestic Ambient Noise*. In some of the more hybrid texts the system of language and the field of the visible collapse into one another, beyond the typographical doubleness described and enacted by Drucker. Each begins to take on aspects of the other. Letter forms or what might be letters, lose their relation to the system, as in Cobbing's *Five Vowels*. Yet shape and image begin to take on the look of letter shapes, symbols in an alien script, something that it forced upon the performer of such texts (for that is what a reader has become).

The irruption of thingness in language (effected through the whole raft of techniques examined in this, and previous, chapters) is the irruption of material historical occasion, of making, validation, and performance of the text, which will unsettle the linguistic system. It declares its rooted but excessive presence, a saying crying out from the said, but is ever drawn back to its material occasion, to its suspended, but inevitable, thematization.

Notes

1 See *Bill Jubobe: Selected Poems 1942–1975* (Toronto: Coach House Press, 1976), p. 102 for the 1942 'first duplicatorprint'. Cobbing had a tendency to refunction his early visual pieces as sound poems.

2 See *Art without Boundaries 1950–1970*, ed. Gerald Woods, Philip Thompson and John Williams (London: Thames and Hudson, 1972) for an account, and examples of, crossovers between design and art, performance and art, etc, including Cobbing on pp. 88–89. Of artists treated in this chapter it also features Robert Rauschenberg, Stefan (and Franciszka) Themerson and dom sylvester houédard.

3 Major concrete poetry anthologies are: *An Anthology of Concrete Poetry* ed. Emmett Williams (New York: Something Else Press, 1967); *Concrete Poetry: An international anthology*, ed. Stephen Bann (London: London Magazine Editions, 1967) Cobbing himself was

involved with five anthologies, the first exclusively concerned with the subject: *Concerning Concrete Poetry* eds. Bob Cobbing and Peter Mayer (London: Writers Forum, 1978); *GLOUP AND WOUP*, ed. Cobbing (Gillingham: Arc Publications, 1974); *Changing Forms in English Visual Poetry – the influence of tools and machines* (London: Writers Forum, 1988); *Verbi Visi Voco*, eds. Bob Cobbing and Bill Griffiths (London: Writers Forum, 1992); *Word Score Utterance Choreography in verbal and visual poetry*, edited by Lawrence Upton and Bob Cobbing (London: Writers Forum, 1998). Anthologies including concrete poetry are the two volumes of *Poems for the Millennium: The University of California Book of Modern and Postmodern Poetry*, eds. Jerome Rothenberg and Pierre Joris, (Berkeley: The University of California, 1995/1998). Concrete poetry of various kinds may also be found in *Imagining Language: An Anthology*, eds. Jed Rasula and Steve McCaffery, (Cambridge, MA: The MIT Press, 1998).

4   See Dick Higgins, *Pattern Poetry: Guide to an Unknown Literature* (Albany: State University of New York Press, 1987) for the long history of this form of writing.

5   For Apollinaire's 'Horse Calligram' see *Poems for the Millennium* eds. Rothenberg and Joris, vol. 1, p. 119.

6   For Gomringer see *Concerning Concrete Poetry*, eds. Cobbing and Mayer, p. 31, and *An Anthology of Concrete Poetry*, ed. Williams, n.p. Also Marjorie Perloff, *Radical Artifice: Writing in the Age of the Media* (Chicago and London: University of Chicago Press, 1991), pp. 115–16. Mallarmé's *Un Coup de dés* may be found in Stephane Mallarmé, *The Poems*, trans. Keith Bosley (Harmondsworth: Penguin, 1977), pp. 253–97.

7   All three are exemplified in *An Anthology of Concrete Poetry*, ed. Williams. For letteriste statements see Cobbing and Mayer, *Concerning Concrete Poetry*, p. 18. Noigandres are discussed in Perloff, *Radical Artifice*, pp. 116–17. See also Cobbing and Mayer, eds., *Concerning Concrete Poetry*, p. 19. There is a spatialist statement by Garnier in *Concerning Concrete Poetry*, p. 23 and p. 34.

8   These are exemplified in *An Anthology of Concrete Poetry*, ed. Williams. For signalist poetry see *Concerning Concrete Poetry*, eds. Cobbing and Mayer, p. 52. There are two signalist poems in Steve McCaffery, *Modern Reading, Poems 1969–1990* (London: Writers Forum, 1992), n.p.

9   Both are discussed in Perloff, *Radical Artifice*, Drucker at pp. 120–29, and McCaffery's *Carnival* at pp. 111–14. There are reproductions of the poems in the text (and on the cover).

10   For early Finlay see *An Anthology of Concrete Poetry*, ed. Williams, n.p. He is discussed by Perloff in *Radical Artifice* on p. 114, and in Alan Young, 'Three "neo-moderns": Ian Hamilton Finlay, Edwin Morgan, Christopher Middleton' in *British Poetry since 1970*, eds. Peter Jones and Michael Schmidt (Manchester: Carcanet, 1990), pp. 112–24, at pp. 114–119. Furnival's work may be found *An Anthology of Concrete Poetry*, ed. Williams, n.p. and in *GLOUP AND WOUP*, ed. Cobbing, loose cards in folder.

11   Tom Phillips, *A Humument: A Treated Victorian Novel* (London: Thames and Hudson, 1980). The title of his original was *A Human Document*. Even in its title its method of deletion, re-inscription, and design is evident.

12   The work of dom sylvester houdédard (dsh – the spelling of his first name is inconsistent in texts; the dom indicates that he was a Dominican friar) is found in most of the British anthologies listed in note 3. See also *In Memoriam dsh* ed. Cobbing (London: Writers

Forum, 1995) which is actually a collection of dsh's work. See *Concerning Concrete Poetry*, eds. Cobbing and Mayer, p. 53 for a statement by houdédard.

13   See Cobbing, *Changing Forms in English Visual Poetry* for aspects of misuse. See the three poets' work in *Verbi Visi Voco* eds. Bob Cobbing and Bill Griffiths for evidence of influence.

14   See *Poems for the Millennium* eds. Rothenberg and Joris, vol. 1, p. 224 for Khlebnikov's zaum poem; p. 323 for Schwitters. A recording of the complete *Ursonate* by Schwitters has been recently discovered, and is available on CD as Kurt Schwitters, *Ursonate, original performance by Kurt Schwitters*, WERGO 6304–2, (Mainz, Germany, 1993).

15   Jandl is in most of the major anthologies; there is a larger selection in *The Vienna Group: 6 Major Austrian Poets* ed. Rosmarie Waldrop (Barrytown: Station Hill Press, 1985), pp. 17–34. 'Niaga/ra fëlle' appears on p. 28 in translation and in Upton and Cobbing, eds., *Word Score Utterance Choreography*. Other works may be heard on the record *Sound Texts/ ?Concrete Poetry/Visual Texts* Stedelijk Museum, Amsterdam, 1970.

16   See Edwin Morgan, *Selected Poems* (Manchester: Carcanet, 1985), and *Concerning Concrete Poetry*, eds. Cobbing and Mayer, pp. 20–21. See also Morgan's 'Into the Constellation: Some Thoughts on the Origin and Nature of Concrete Poetry', in *Essays* (Manchester: Carcanet, 1974) pp. 20–34.

17   See (or rather hear) 'Espaces et gestes' on *Sound Texts/?Concrete Poetry/Visual Texts*, and Henri Chopin, *Audiopoems*, Tangent Records, TGS 106 (1971), LP record. See also 'Throat Power', *1983*, number 2, 1975. (cassette). Chopin's own print magazine *OU* often contained records. See *Concerning Concrete Poetry*, eds. Cobbing and Mayer, pp. 47, 56–57.

18   See *Concerning Concrete Poetry*, eds. Cobbing and Mayer, p. 49–50. He speaks of the 'CRIRYTHME, my desire to create a phonetic poem, beyond any concept of writing, directly on to the tape recorder' (p.50). Hear 'Crirythme pour Bob Cobbing' on *Sound Texts/?Concrete Poetry/Visual Texts*

19   Hear Sten Hanson's 'Subface' on *Sound Texts/?Concrete Poetry/Visual Texts*

20   See *On Semantic Poetry* (London: Gaberbocchus, 1975) and *Collected Poems* (Amsterdam: Gaberbocchus Press, 1997). See also *Concerning Concrete Poetry*, eds. Cobbing and Mayer, pp. 37–42.

21   Bob Cobbing, *Kob Bok: Selected Texts 1948–1999* (Buckfastleigh: Etruscan Books, 1999), p. 62; also found in Bob Cobbing, *Life the Universe and Everything* (London: Interim Books, 1992), n.p.

22   Cobbing, *Kob Bok*, p. 63.

23   Eric Mottram, *Composition and Performance in the Work of Bob Cobbing: a conversation* (1973) (London: Writers Forum, 2000), n.p.

24   Eric Mottram, 'Bob Cobbing's Voice Prints: Introductions', in Bob Cobbing, *Voice Prints* (Seaham: Amra Imprint, 1993), n.p.

25   Umberto Eco, 'The Poetics of the Open Work', in *The Role of the Reader* (London: Hutchinson, 1981), pp. 47–66. See, for Cage, John Cage, *Roaratorio: An Irish Circus on Finnegans Wake* ed. Klaus Schoening (Koeningstein: Atheneum Verlag, 1982) discussed by Perloff in *Radical Artifice*, pp. 200–16.

26   Eric Mottram, 'Writers Forum: A Successful Campaign', in *Bob Cobbing and Writers Forum*, ed. Peter Mayer (Sunderland: Ceolfrith Press, 1974), pp. 15–24, at pp. 17–19.

27   Compare Cobbing's mimeo and photocopied pamphlets with the lush productions item-
      ized in *Bookworks: A Partial History and Sourcebook*, eds. Jane Rolo and Ian Hunt, (Lon-
      don: Bookworks, 1996).
28   *Verbi Visi Voco* eds. Bob Cobbing and Bill Griffiths. The book charts the development of
      the press and workshop throughout its years. I have already detailed its work in Chapter 2
      (and in its note 18).
29   'An Interview with Bob Cobbing – Peter Mayer', in *Bob Cobbing and Writers Forum*, ed.
      Peter Mayer, pp. 55–60, at p. 57.
30   Eric Mottram, *Composition and Performance in the Work of Bob Cobbing: a conversa-
      tion*, n.p. The subsequent problems for the men and women from Canon were no less
      severe.
31   'An Interview with Bob Cobbing – Peter Mayer', p. 56.
32   *Alphabetical Poems and Letter Poems: A Chrestomathy*, ed. Peter Mayer (London: The
      Menard Press, 1978). It also contains Cobbing's 'An Alphabet of Fishes', an alphabet of
      Cornish names of fish; (e.g. 'Silliwhig'), p. 76.
33   *An ABC in Sound (recorded 1965)/Trilogy (recorded 1968)* (C60 cassette) Blasam Flex,
      circa 1980, is the tape I am referring to. For a detailed and fascinating account of a 1968
      Cobbing performance, see Jonathan Raban, *The Society of the Poem* (London: Harrap, 1971),
      pp. 88–9. See also 'Bob Cobbing: Sightings and Soundings', in Robert Sheppard, *Far Lan-
      guage: Poetics and Innovative Linguistic Poetry 1978–1997* (Exeter: Stride Research Docu-
      ments, 1999), pp. 61–67.
34   *ABC in Sound* (London: Writers Forum, fourth edition, 1986), n.p.
35   *Ibid.*, n.p.
36   *Ibid.*, n.p.
37   *Ibid.*, n.p.
38   *Ibid.*, n.p.
39   *Ibid.*, n.p.
40   *Ibid.*, n.p.
41   *Ibid.*, n.p.
42   *Ibid.*, n.p.
43   *Ibid.*, n.p.
44   *Ibid.*, n.p. The line here is altered from that originally printed, to a new version that Cobbing
      supplied in 2000, which he regards as more correctly permutating the letters. The word
      'oberammergau' is the correct replacement for the 'wrong' word 'omeramergau' in the 1965
      text, but as Cobbing pointed out, this means one loses the permutation 'om', with its
      Buddhist overtones and has to substitute 'ob'.
45   *Ibid.*, n.p.
46   dom silvester houédard, 'Bob Cobbing: Troubadour & Poet' in *Bob Cobbing and Writers
      Forum*, ed. Peter Mayer, p. 27.
47   Cobbing, *ABC in Sound*, n.p.
48   *Ibid.*, n.p.
49   houédard, 'Bob Cobbing: Troubadour & Poet', p. 27.
50   'An Approach to Notation; Bob Cobbing' in *Bob Cobbing and Writers Forum*, ed. Peter
      Mayer, pp. 32–42, at p. 32.

51   *Ibid.*, p. 32.
52   Hear 'Three Variations on a Theme of Tan' on *Sound Texts/?Concrete Poetry/Visual Texts.*
53   Nicholas Zurbrugg, 'Four Years After: fragments from "typographical problem" question-naire', *Second Aeon* 15, 1972, pp. 37–43, at p. 42.
54   *The Five Vowels* (London: Writers Forum, 1974). See Arthur Rimbaud, 'Voyelle', trans. F. Scott Fitzgerald, in *Poem into Poem*, ed. George Steiner (Harmondsworth: Penguin, 1970), p. 141, for a different colour scheme.
55   Sten Hanson, 'Bob Cobbing – The Sound Poet' in *Bob Cobbing and Writers Forum*, ed. Peter Mayer, pp. 43–45, at p. 45.
56   I am describing *E Colony* (made with Peter Finch in Cardiff in 1973) *Typewriter Magazine* No 4 (1973), single.
57   'An Approach to Notation; Bob Cobbing', p. 38.
58   *Concerning Concrete Poetry*, eds. Cobbing and Mayer, p. 37.
59   McCaffery, *Modern Reading, Poems 1969–1990* (London: Writers Forum, 1992), n.p.
60   *Processual: collected poems 10* (London: New River Project, 1987).
61   Separately first issued as *(Almost) Random Snippets from Works in Progress* (London: Writers Forum, 1982).
62   See Allen Fisher, *Prosyncel* (New York: Strange Faeces Press, 1975), p. 36.
63   *A Processual Nonny Nonny* (London: Writers Forum, 1985), n.p.
64   *Congruence of Speed and Stall* (London: Writers Forum, 1990)
65   Bob Cobbing and Lawrence Upton, *Domestic Ambient Moise* (London: Writers Forum, 1995).
66   *Third ABC in Sound* (London: Writers Forum, 2000)
67   Upton and Cobbing, eds., *Word Score Utterance* Choreography. The rest of this chapter is largely based upon my introduction to the book, entitled 'a Thing or Two upon the Page', n.p.
68   Johanna Drucker, *The Visible Word: Experimental typography and modern art 1909–1923* (Chicago: The University of Chicago Press, 1994), p. 45.
69   *Concerning Concrete Poetry*, eds. Cobbing and Mayer, p. 21.
70   Quoted in *Perloff, Radical Artifice*, p. 129. In many ways this describes the project of *Imagining Language: An Anthology*, eds. Jed Rasula and Steve McCaffery.
71   See his contribution and accompanying note in Upton and Cobbing, eds., *Word Score Utterance Choreography*, n.p. See also *Representative Works: 1938–1985* (New York, Roof Books, 1986).

10

Be come, Be spoke, Be eared:
The Poetics of Transformation and Embodied Utterance in the work of Maggie O'Sullivan during the 1980s and 1990s

Love Letters in the Sound

A poetry reading or performance by Maggie O'Sullivan can baffle or delight, baffle *and* delight. The steady stream of words, delivered with careful attention to their rhythmic weight, to their alliterative connections, seemingly at the expense of their meanings, can be a difficult experience to relate to, for those not used to it. In 'A Love Letter', Adrian Clarke becomes Roland Barthes' blissful reader, finding himself desired by a text from her 1993 Reality Street book, *In the House of the Shaman*. He explains:

> For those of us who have attended any of her readings, these pages summon Maggie – never one to function as the institution 'author', rather a figure 'lost in the midst of a text' – whose striking if not conventionally beautiful dark Irish features are transformed, transfused with beauty as she reads unhurriedly letting the measured syllables relate to establish rhythms in an appropriate time.[1]

This poetry demands a greater dialogue with, response from, its readers than most. The reader or listener has to be prepared for a structure that is largely organized by sound and has to pay attention to the particular and peculiar lineation, spacing and punctuation on the page. A connection between the powerful sonic features and a revitalized semantics is negotiated through her preference for the portmanteau word and the pun. Neologism is so complete that at times we are offered a controlled experiment in language change. O'Sullivan changes the endings of words and changes their case, something which takes centuries in 'natural' language: 'missingly'; 'yonderly'; 'gived'.[2] She invents new lexical items, some fairly simple, 'twindom' to suggest a doubled domain,[3] but others approach the polysemenous Joycean pun: 'superates'; 'reversionary'.[4] New compounds surprise: 'Sylla/ bled' takes a word apart, and emphasizes utterance as suffering, sliced on enjambement, uniquely connected to breathing.[5]

Derek Attridge writes in *Peculiar Language* that this particular form of linguistic inventiveness, the portmanteau word, 'refuses, by itself, any single meaning, and in reading we have to nudge it towards other signifiers whose meanings might prove appropriate'.[6] Thus sound, or soundings, the performative aspect of the poetry, opens the reader, through semantics (and the semantic suggestions of grammatical units, such as prefixes, and, by extension, through etymological roots), to conceptual richness. Attridge, writing of lexical onomatopoeia, deals with this single form of neologism in a way that is relevant to the devices and techniques of O'Sullivan's work.

> All speech involves muscular movements ... and the particular aspects of this complex physical process which function in a given example of onomatopoeia depend less on the specific configurations of the phonetic sequence in question than on the meaning of the passage. The result is a diversion of attention away from the referent in itself to the activity of referring carried out by language.[7]

The reader has to recognize a moment that resembles language being born rather than language being used to represent something, the moment saying exists without regard to the said which will finally capture it. It is not consciousness that the reader sees unfolding, as in the Joycean stream of consciousness technique. (Nor is the Joyce of *Finnegans Wake* the best guide to the poetics, whatever the surface resemblance.) It is almost as if an ideolect, a personal register of language, becomes a loose sociolect that the audience temporarily shares, nudging away at the lexical items, entering it in social dialogue. This is never more so than in the communal space of a public reading where the saying may be literally kept open (but, as I shall argue, may not always be open in a Levinasian sense).

The process of writing these poems might best be thought of as a series of transformations of descriptive language into exuberant and performative language, a transformation that is fully aware that the material of poetry is not perception –however important – but language. There is a strange tension in the literary influences – late Romantic and extreme Modernist – on Maggie O'Sullivan's work, which reflects the tensions within it. Like Hopkins, sound seems to function as onomatopoeic equivalence of 'all things hitting the sense with double but direct instress' as he put it, to match the perceptual imprint of 'great brilliancy and projection' of phenomenal nature, which strikes the eye before it is transformed into sound: 'the eye seemed to fall perpendicular from level to level along our trees, the nearer and further Park'.[8]

Yet Kurt Schwitters' use of detritus and mistakes in his visual collages, as well as pure sound in his poetry, such as the extended *Ur-Sonate*, as O'Sullivan puts it, 'showed the retrieval of potentials within materials',[9] pointed towards the medium itself, towards 'saying saying saying' as Levinas attempts to describe it.[10]

As this poetry passes from precision to exuberance, it attempts to link the verbal equivalence of Hopkins and the artistic autonomy of Schwitters, but with Schwitters' admission of error and mistake into the creative process, as the richness of pun: a kind of communal hallucinatory malapropism.

The Naming and the Named

O'Sullivan's 'Naming', comes from a section of *In The House of the Shaman*, called 'Kinship with Animals'. Its epigraph – and indeed, the title of the volume – is drawn from Joseph Beuys, the German installation and performance artist. O'Sullivan describes working on the BBC Arena programme on Beuys in the late 1980s, appropriately, as a 'transformative experience',[11] so much so that soon after she decided to resign as a researcher and become a full-time poet. It is no wonder that Beuys, who also grappled with these tensions between a fidelity to nature and the creation of cultural artefacts, should be such an ethical figure for O'Sullivan. The only way to make language shift like the lard that Beuys used as his 'sway substances' is to work with the instability within the linguistic sign,[12] 'underneath, behind, with language', as Maggie O'Sullivan says.[13] This materiality engenders a paradoxical freedom to transform, something evident in Beuys' lard sculptures. The epigraph provides the necessary philosophic stance for O'Sullivan's balancing and fusing, even confusing, of natural processes and cultural materialism: 'To stress the idea of transformation and of substance. This is precisely what the shaman does in order to bring about change and development: his nature is therapeutic.'[14]

'Naming',[15] whose emphatic last line is 'This is called fish', is certainly not pure music, but it does not offer the certainties of denotation that it might seem to promise. Mariannne Moore's delightful 'The Fish', which begins comfortably with the words 'The Fish' is almost its antitext; its title forms its first line.[16] O'Sullivan refuses such naturalizations as Moore's equation of mussel shells with broken fans in favour of neologism and conundrum. 'Water/ they unlidder' the poem begins, refusing yet to name, offering a half rhyme for 'water', the element upon which the poem focuses. To unlid something would be to remove its lid, to open; lidder would seem to be also a noun, but operates as a verb here, and makes the act of 'unliddering', through sound, through grammar, a very deliberate one: opening the receptive eyes, perhaps, as the lids part, though it seems more violent, to rip the lids away for permanent seeing, though it is the water's surface the unnamed 'they' peel away. (If they are fish, they have no lids themselves, of course.) The water's surface is also broken by the named and noisy 'scraping fowls'.

> shrieve hurtled
> folded,
> suffixes – Dots. Dashes. Scraping fowls
>   Unescourted, Blade Goes Them
>   from a far orange –

In the sound of the word 'shrieve' one can hear the 'hurtling' of the birds, as in Hopkins' onomatopoeic 'the whole landscape flushes on a sudden at a sound'.[17] But the Old English etymology of the word points to an act of confession, the Latin to the act of writing. Together they suggest a document as a testament. The bird's natural motion becomes a cultural inscription, or is seen in terms of one. Wings and pieces of paper can both be folded, both are possible concealments, of that which is confessed. The scraping on the water is an hieroglyphics of sorts, cut with a blade that could be a fowl's wing, hence the parts of words and dots and dashes, the disturbance on water. This act of descriptive precision is turning into a description of a Maggie O'Sullivan poem, into its own material saying, the abruptness of its own punctuation, its sudden suffixes; yet the strange headline quality of the last phrase recalls the Barry MacSweeney of *Odes*.[18]

> *DRAGON*,
>   plum-BURR
>   plum-BURR
>   plum-BURR

To name a dragon, italicized '*DRAGON*', is to evoke its presence, yet the 'plum-BURR/ plum-BURR' of its fiery breath or leathern wing (in which may be heard the punned the 'hum-WHIRR' of its lesser namesake, the dragonfly) is echoed in the triple, chant-like, charm-like, human chorus of

Be come.
Be spoke.
Be eared.

The interrupted prefixes (matching the suffixes earlier in the poem) emphasize the Be-ing of their imperatives: for existence, for speech (with perhaps a bespoke sense of quality) and – the third a characteristic O'Sullivan neologism – attentive listening (and attentive listening here will reveal the word 'beard', a name of certain wild flowers). As she asserts elsewhere, uniting the three aspects in the activities of an 'I': 'lip drove I eared' and 'Ear-Loads I Sing!'[19] Whether or not we are in the presence of a dragon's breath, there is an 'ear-Load' more of transformation in the phrase or word 'plum-BURR': plumage be-comes plum, cut down. Plum is a colour, BURR a sound, a choke in the throat. Plum is a fruit, also, and burr, through another definition, the seed case of the fruit; these connotations stress an interchangeable yet changing natural environment.

Even 'DRAGON' is an almost anagram of the distant 'ORANGE' (another colour and fruit noun, like plum) that could also serve as a description of plumage. Several facets of the natural world are semantically encoded, but not described, in the sounds of this super-natural beast (though if merely a dragonfly, it is still, in terms of nomenclature, a hybrid). Such cross-species malapropism mimes the evolutionary connection between lizards (the nearest actual creature to dragons) and fish (which the poem claims to name).

The first five letters of the mysterious 'plum-BURR' also spell 'plumb' in the sense of measuring the depth of water, whether lidded or not, which the poem enacts. Be eared, the poem seems to say, to the polysemantics of nature: colour and fruition; be kin to animals (because we are akin, as the title of the section reminds us). But the semantics are held off by the thick devicehood of the poem, its saying glorified in the act of being born in our reading, and dying only slowly into the thematized fixity of our interpretations, particularly as we follow words through their etymologies and connotations. As a reader follows such semantic trails he or she must retreat from the actual performance of the poem, a paradox to which I shall return.

The apparent return to denotation is abrupt: 'Teal.' Noun: fullstop. The duck is isolated on the surface of the river, although this too is brought to sonic life by its rhyme with the later 'squeal'.

Teal. Nor into
is drumming. Erred
bonnets alight: tattering grey Slackens.
Cause Doth
Middling shudder, squeal
Driven to Summit.

The ancient connection between wandering and error is asserted (though
'erred' also half-rhymes with 'eared'); yet the shuddering suggests both a
disturbance of water surface and of light as the migratory and brilliantly
plumed bird alights (a plume that is pre-echoed, as it were, in plum). The
assault on the water surface is a kind of drumming (another rhyme with
'plum') on the depth of the water as the squeal rises in tone (though it is also
possible to hear a Yorkshire dialect referring to 'summat' in that last line).

Bearings.
Oaths.
Mixed Pulses etched
Finningly

The play on the transitory momentary nature of mixture and pulsation, of
fish darting, against the permanence of etching, 'finningly' (which echoes
'fittingly') returns us to the notion of the delicacy and motion of the effect
of small independent fins in the larger movement, pulses mixed, the opposite of the drumming and squealing that operate like oaths and curses. (This
poem, like another in the book, is a charm.)[20] 'Finningly, brilliant corners
decapitate.' Light kills or at least wounds as the water stirs its reflections
and refractions, under which fish hide, perhaps from the teal, and which
suggests the cutting movement of fish through water. ('Brilliant Corners' is
also a composition by Thelonious Monk, a particularly angular and abra-
sive jazz pianist.) The violence of the river is suggested next in lines that
contain echoes of Anglo-Saxon linguistic collocations, the compound words,
the grouping of stressed syllables, that may owe a debt to Basil Bunting or
Bill Griffiths.[21]

          Beast's
coat Loading
battlegivens:

gifts that are accepted as burden without rancour, 'bearings'. (In 'plum-
BURR' one might also hear 'plunder'). It is a gift, a garment, a load to bear,

> wound
> Livery:
> laid into rivers, nails of
> similarly blood-fine hatching

A martial uniform is perhaps involved in a battle, as in the demotic usage 'laid into', though it simultaneously echoes 'loading' in Ear-Loads of pun. The word 'laid' is well chosen because eggs are laid, before 'hatching' as small fish: nails remind us of the drumming and the hammering earlier in the poem, as does the idea of etching, of forceful impression upon the body of the river which is not exactly a body. Similarly 'blood fine hatching' evokes the delicacy of the natural refining of fins, like small nails scratching into the material of the river, as 'laid into' evokes the delicacy of jewellery. 'Fine' – another notion of delicacy – echoes the small fry's 'fins' in a web of connotation.

The flat ending, complete with definitive fullstop is a shock after such associations and linguistic transformations:

> this is called/
>
> fish.

The noun is isolated on a line of its own like a fish itself, below the surface (note the oblique stroke) of the rest of the poem. The poem seems to move from 'Naming' as concept in its title, to plumbing the viscous but fluid body of the poem, to the fish, the aim of its closure, the very name itself.

Reading this ending is only *like* solving a riddle; the generic word 'fish', like 'fowl' earlier but unlike 'teal', is necessarily and deliberately imprecise and inadequate. The solution tells one nothing, because naming, rather than the named – in an analogy with the saying and the said – is what is enacted throughout the poem. The named 'fish' represents the thematized fixity that denies the semantic, syntactic and referential flux of the rest of the poem.[22] 'Fish' is not a Bakhtinian last word. We could now metaphorically read the poem backwards (and make it resemble the Moore poem so that 'Fish' becomes its title, its theme now, rather than the process of naming, but this has first to be earned).

The poem enacts the primacy of evocation over 'naming', of connotation over denotation, or of a radical re-orientation of denotation, and of the role of a linguistically transformative exuberance, of the preference for the pleasure of the riddle's processes to the comfort of its solution, for the saying over the said.

Yet it also asserts its 'kinship with animals' in its evanescent precision and etymological play. If this is description then the objects described are largely displaced. It is instructive to see how O'Sullivan herself deals with this dichotomy between linguistic autonomy and reference to the natural world, in her poetics essay 'riverruning (realisations' which itself is a collage of quotations from her own, and others', works, and from a number of intentional and autobiographical statements, in which she amplifies upon influences and tensions identified earlier. On the one hand she speaks of Kurt Schwitters' 'superb use of the UN – the NON and the LESS – the UNREGARDED, the found, the cast-offs, the dismembered materials of culture'.[23] Again, Hopkins provides the balance to Schwitters, since O'Sullivan speaks, in tones reminiscent of Hopkins' theory of instress, of her leaving London 'to the moorland impress of tongue'.[24] 'In celebration of this, I praised the trees & hugged & planted them – to make a mood – a spirit of the woods in Celtic imagination where the whole world was alive.'[25]

Again, only Beuys (who was similarly fascinated by the Celtic) could also have straddled this divide convincingly and it is interesting to see 'riverruning (realisations' failing to resolve the tension between the cultural and the natural. The force of the word 'Also' in this passage separates these concerns. (She embodies her poetics with the same transformative precision that is found in her poetry.)

> The works I make Celebrate ORigins/ENtrances – the
> Materiality of Language: its actual contractions &
> expansions, potentialities, prolongments, assemblages -
> the acoustic, visual, oral & sculptural qualities
> within the physical: intervals between; in & beside.
> Also, the jubilant seep   In So of Spirit – Entanglement
> with vegetations, thronged weathers, puppy-web we agreed
> animals.   Articulations of the Earth of Language   that is
> Minglement, Ceasura, Illumination.
> Heart.[26]

As the processes of the natural world lead to the evolutionary changes, in what we call natural history, the changes of language (either real in etymology in the history of the language, or novel in the neologistic play of the text), lead to changes in the poem's language. Her work embodies the 'Also' that connects the two. But it is embodiment itself that explains how Maggie O'Sullivan imagines the Also to be an And.

The link, of course, is in the materiality of the literary work and the physicality of nature: 'Articulations of the Earth of Language', 'a Mattering of Materials',[27] where 'mattering' hints at both material reality and signification; materials are no longer simply cultural. But there is more than just an equivalence here, and the roles of sound in language and language in the body need exploring with reference to performance itself.

If text in performance is a version of shamanistic therapy, how is it administered? The answer may lie in Adrian Clarke's assertion that it is O'Sullivan's person – her body – that is transformed as she reads the texts, and in Attridge's remarks about the muscular aspects of signification.

The Word Made Flesh

Bakhtin's early essay 'Content, Material, and Form in Verbal Art', focuses, rarely for him, upon poetry, and argues that the transformation of material into architectonics, of technique into aesthetic object, and the making of the poem, 'allows the author-creator to become a constitutive moment of form.'[28] 'The feeling of verbal activeness, the feeling of the active generation of signifying *sound* is the governing moment of poetry, a moment that could happen on the page (the irruption of thingness, as I called it in the last chapter), but I believe is particularly re-created and fulfilled in performance;[29] it is 'a moment into which both the organism and meaning-directed activity are drawn, because both the flesh and the spirit [the signifier and the signified I take Bakhtin to mean] are generated together in this concrete unity'.[30]

Theory may have recently seen the re-birth of the author, but not yet, I think, as performer, but Bakhtin points towards ways of achieving that: 'The movement that generates acoustical sound, and is most active in the articulatory organs, although it takes hold of the whole organism ... is incommensurably more important than what is *heard*', not in a retreat from meaning, but because the poem has 'taken possession of the whole active human being'.[31] This literal incarnation, at the moment that poetic language comes into being, is what O'Sullivan achieves when she turns ideolect to a kind of dialect. Her 'Earloads' are becoming *physical* burdens, for the performer-poet, as in Bakhtin's formulation of the lyric, 'when the body, generating the sound from within itself and feeling the unity of its own productive exertion, is drawn into form.'[32] This birth of language (a meta-phor which unites nature and culture) is indeed a glorification of produc-tive exertion in the body: the word made flesh. It is also the most poignant example of a saying that pre-empts the power of the said.

I believe that what the exuberance of O'Sullivan's work – particularly its sonic performance – is trying to do is to discover a further productive unity: one between culture and nature – to replicate the productive exertion of the natural forces she celebrates. Kinship with animals implies making the poem a part of organic nature, which is only possible *through* sound, articulated *through* the living body of the poet, in writing, but more publicly, in the dialect become sociolect of performance. The performance of poetry is the 'Be-coming' of the text. One of O'Sullivan's statements of poetics confirms this: 'For me, poetry is a process, an exploration of breath-word-making that allows the beauty and power of words to find ways of meaning through me: in this sense the poems are always beyond/ahead of me.'[33]

The hallucinatory ideolect of the O'Sullivan performance may engender temporary modalities of being, of creating, in its own way, what Felix Guattari called 'mutant subjectivities' for the audience, that constitute a 'preliminary deconstruction of the structures and codes in use and a chaosmic plunge into the materials of sensation. Out of them a recomposition becomes pos-sible', says Guattari.[34]

How can the ideolect-cum-dialect of any poetry performance become a shared sociolect? I believe that Guattari's reading – re-writing – of the Bakhtin essay provides one theoretical answer. Now transformed into the general chapter 'On the production of subjectivity' in *Chaosmosis*, an earlier ver-sion was published as 'Language, Consciousness and Society', and spoke more particularly of poetry while simultaneously developing a theory of polyphonic subjectivity, and promoting a view of subjectivity as a produc-tive process of subjectivation.[35] He identifies Bakhtin's sense of the performative verbal activity which gives autonomy to content and engen-ders activity in the author and audience with his own notion of the 'ritornello' or 'refrain'.

A refrain is a detached existential motif which orders chaos and assists the process of subjectivation. His examples of the refrain range from en-abling and territorial birdsong through to the condition of an individual watching the TV, where his or her subjectivity is polyphonized by existing at the intersections of disparate experiences on and off the screen. The refrain 'acts upon that which surrounds it, sound or light, extracting from its various vibrations or decompositions, projections, transformations'.[36] It ruptures the dominant redundancies and catalyses their re-combination in a sort of multidimensional epiphany. The refrain function in Maggie O'Sullivan's text and performance is this exuberant creation of temporary dialect, or even sociolect, the sensation of linguistic activity of which Bakhtin speaks, the catalyzing of what feels like meaning being created, doubly, through sound, through the specialized semantics of neologism. Indeed, Guattari says that performance art engenders a process of existential detachment and disordering which is then supplemented by existential *recomposition* of the fragments for the audience.

Poetry in performance, whatever its tensions, can be argued to be the production of a productivity: always of machinic combinations of different elements of poetic language and performance events.[37] Catalyzing changes in both authors and readers could potentially assist, in a new aesthetic paradigm of experience, the individual and collective means of producing healthily polyphonic subjectivities, capable of achieving autonomy or 'autopoesis', as Guattari would say. 'Thus it is not only in the context of music and poetry that we see the work of such fragments detatched from content ... the polyphony of modes of subjectivation actually corresponds to a multiplicity of ways of "keeping time". Other rhythmics are thus led to crystallize existential assemblages.'[38]

Yet one could argue that performance which includes poetry, particularly in an expanded context like an environment or an installation piece, such as that discussed by Bergvall, or cris cheek's recordings, is a machinic productivity *out from* text, *alongside* texts, *into* texts, in a flexible multisystemic activity, and its aims are, as Guattari would say, indeed did say, of performance art: 'a forward flight into machinations and deterritorialized machinic paths capable of engendering mutant subjectivities ... a proliferation not just of forms but of modalities of being'.[39] In such a formulation, tensions and contradictions are not problems but productive complexities with a role that is not exclusively literary.

To theorize performance in terms of machinic productivity suggests an irreversible, unpredictable activity, but it also avoids certain ways of thinking that might prioritize combined media in a live art context, or relationships between elements, or impose models of unity, such as metaphors of fusion, synthesis, organic wholeness, or counterpoint. To think of the elements as machines allows for the development of simultaneous, asymmetric processes, of finding the work in performance, of finding un-prescribed relationships or even lacks of relationship. Finally this suggests both the transformation of all the possible elements and their potential breakdown as performance develops.

Perhaps once this stage has been reached it is no longer possible to speak of poetry as an autonomous art-form. On one's attachment to the particularities of the art-form – its linguistic complexity, its etymological richness, which are so important in O'Sullivan's texts, for example – will depend on one's response to such hybrid productivity.

The Reading and the Read

Performance has been a valorised term, and a recurrent theme, in this study. The liberation of text from the page, and ever widening definitions put it squarely at the heart of Linguistically Innovative Poetry. For so long it has been assumed, particularly in the Pound-Olson tradition that the supposed connection between verse and music (and dance) subsisted until the Renaissance and was undone by the rise of 'print-bred poetry' as Olson put it, with its practice of silent solitary reading: 'What we have suffered from, is manuscript, press, the removal of verse from its producer and its reproducer, the voice, a removal ... from its place of origin *and* its destination.'[40]

Until recently less attention has been directed towards what may have been gained rather than lost in such developments, particularly in the ways trained readers respond to the page. To use the term 'audience' (rather than reader) might be thought a neutral term, but to privilege the auditory to is underplay other aspects of poetic artifice. For one, we need to consider, to use the deceptively simple title of a pertinent book, 'the look of it'.[41] Olson, of course, sang the praises of the typewriter, though chiefly as a scoring device for breath performance. O'Sullivan's texts use space meticulously, not just as a score for performance – that would render such meaningful artifice secondary, less meaningful – but as a primary field for the play of devices. Her work is an example of what Marjorie Perloff calls 'the new nonlinear poetries' that have extended the range of so-called free verse, which she has also argued is itself primarily a visual, rather than rhythmical, ordering.[42]

'Naming' is a conservative, linear, poem, by O'Sullivan's standards, though even here, where the materiality of language is emphasized (those dots, dashes and suffixes) the lines are indented. The 'plum-BURR' repeated thrice, is indented, visually isolated (as is the last line, as I have shown). It is as though, in order to consider the range of connotations this lexical item contains, in order to open up the realm of the saying it inaugurates, we must stop, or pause, the different temporal saying of performance. The reader needs to hold dialogue, to mentally scribble in the white space, to allow the semantics of neologism, its avenues of connotation, to unfold.

Indeed, there may be aspects of sound in poetry that operate in a non-performative way, or in a way that re-defines performance. This is partly the strategy of Bergvall's theorizing, outlined in Chapter 6, although her delineations of performance writing usually emerge from a text, though the problem remains: what is *not* performance writing? One problem of my theoretical use of the concepts of the saying and the said is that saying suggests oral performance while the said suggests a page-based reception of text.

Christopher Middleton has theorized a discrimination of 'voices' in the poetic text that is relevant here, which suggests another way of theorizing Bakhtin's sense of the author's autopoesis, one which questions the equation between performance and the performative. There exists 'an imaginary voice, a voice that was launched by [the poet's], but one that has a distinct imprint. That imaginary and unmistakeable voice is a kind of *endophone*.'[43] This is not to be confused with 'the exophones or voices with which we speak and to which we listen under ordinary conditions'.[44] More importantly, while the endophone is 'time-traversing', the time of performance imposes limitations, supplies simplifications, along with its undoubted permissions.[45]

> Performances can raise such sound-sequences into profile. Actual vocalizing, unless it is vitiated by histrionics, can nourish the inner ear's competence to pick up and assemble sequences. Yet the inner ear is capable of an auditory complexity which exceeds almost any audible vocalizing: the latter tends to be reductive, if not falsifying, also it may straighten out shocks and distortions which, to the inner ear, are part of the real thing that is the voice in the text and the delight of the text.[46]

Middleton offers a counterbalance to the author-centred reading, or any verbal performance, which again places dialogue with the reader at the centre of aesthetic exchange, the reading acting as the 'other' of the read.

> It could be argued that it is the act of silent, or at most murmured reading ... which can realize the vocal qualities of a text, the sequences of sounds, the timbres, the tonal colourings. That kind of act, reading from a page ... can also *dwell* on patterns of sound, as they exfoliate and intertwine, so as to arrive at a fullbodied perception of the relations (phonic, semantic, syntagmatic) which are being voiced here and now in the text.[47]

Performance may feel ontologically represssive if the condition of saying inherent in a text may only fully be realized by a reader in dialogue with the text, unfolding its sounds in the variable temporalities that reading and memory allow, a virtual performance of an endophone separate from the actualities (however well performed) of the author's (or other performers') exophones. It is when the to and fro of this virtual reading, this arrest of temporal sequencing, is lost that performance might be thought to remove a vital empowerment of the reader. Whatever other machinic senses of catalytic change performance and live art may engender, it will be a different empowerment, one that might leave the potentialities of poetic artifice behind. My insistence upon a poetry that foregrounds its saying as against its said may be more fully present in the kinds of endophonic reading proposed by Middleton, during which the visual and the aural, the performative and the semantic, work together in the reader-controlled temporality of reception. Indeed, is this not another site for experiencing the Guattarian refrain? It is the challenge for those working in performance with text – and Cobbing and O'Sullivan have been highlighted here as two notable successes, along with the work of Williamson, cheek and Bergvall, dealt with earlier – to keep that dialogic aspect of poetry alive, even if it no longer calls itself poetry.

However much we attend to Maggie O'Sullivan reading, transforming her self, and potentially transforming her audience, however much we valorize public performance of the text more generally, we need to acknowledge the private performance of the silent reader, or near silent reader murmuring, opening the book to its spectral saying on the saidness of the material page.

The page, of course, is becoming increasingly metaphorical, as literal machines are used to produce what has been called 'cyberpoetics'. John Cayley for one, in *Indra's Net*, utilizes 'generative algorithms and semi-aleatory processes ... to set up a feedback loop' so that a text on the computer screen is generated in unpredictable ways.[48] Later versions of the CD Rom text allow the reader a performative intervention into the process to irreversibly change the text. Michael Joyce argues, 'The book is slow, the network is quick; the book is many of one, the network is many ones multiplied; the book is dialogic, the network polylogic.'[49]

Whether or not the dialogue of the book will be superseded it is clear that *Indra's Net* allows for an openness of eternal saying, with never more than a screen's space of temporary saidness and thematization for a few moments. However, Levinas' insistence upon the inevitability of the saying being materialized in the said may give pause for thought. Whether the cyberpoetics of the future can accommodate the ethical poetics that underpins this study is an open question.

Notes

1   Adrian Clarke, 'A Love Letter', *Responses* 6, n.d. (circa 1991), n.p.

2   Maggie O'Sullivan, *In the House of the Shaman* (London and Cambridge: Reality Street Editions, 1993), pp. 59, 41, 61.

3   *Ibid.*, p. 55.

4   *Ibid.*, pp. 54, 55.

5   *Ibid.*, p. 61.

6   Derek Attridge, *Peculiar Language: Literature as Difference from the Renaissance to James Joyce* (London: Methuen, 1988), p. 201.

7   *Ibid.*, pp. 153–54.

8   *Gerald Manley Hopkins: A Selection of his Poems and Prose*, ed. W.H. Gardner (Harmondsworth: Penguin, 1953), p. 122.

9   Maggie O'Sullivan, 'riverrunning (realisations' in *West Coast Line*, number seventeen, vol. 29, no. 2 (1995), pp. 62–71, at p. 68. This poetics essay has now been reprinted in her *Palace of Reptiles* (Willowdale: The Gig, 2003).

10   Emmanuel Levinas, *Otherwise than Being, or Beyond Essence* (The Hague: Martinus Nijhoff, 1981), p. 143.

11   O'Sullivan, 'riverrunning (realisations', p. 68.

12   *Ibid.*, p. 69.

13   'A Talk Concerning Edges of Her Work (with Adrian Clarke)' *Angel Exhaust*, 6 (Winter 1986), p. 13.

14   O'Sullivan, *In the House of the Shaman*, p. 28.

15   'Naming' may be found in O'Sullivan, *In the House of the Shaman*, p. 32. Because I quote the entire poem in my reading here, there are no further citations in the text. (The text is presented sequentially.)

16   Marianne Moore, 'The Fish', in *The Complete Poems of Marianne Moore* (London: Faber, 1958).

17   *Gerald Manley Hopkins*, p. 80.

18   See, for example, 'Ode Stem Hair', in Barry MacSweeney, *Odes* (London: Trigram Press,

1978), p. 29.

19   O'Sullivan, 'riverrunning (realisations', p. 65.

20   See 'Narrative Charm for Ibbotroyd' in O'Sullivan, *In the House of the Shaman*, p. 44.

21   See, for example, certain passages in the second part of 'Briggflatts' in Basil Bunting, *The Collected Poems* (London: Fulcrum, 1968), pp. 55–60; and part VII of 'Mantras' in Bill Griffiths, *Nomad Sense* (London: Talus Editons, 1998) pp. 14–15.

22   The importance of naming itself should not be forgotten; it is one of the basic functions of language. A naming stage in the acquisition of language provides a conceptual leap forward, as Jean Aitchison writes. 'The sudden realization that things have names appears to lead to a surge of "labelling" everyday objects.' (Jean Aitchison, *The Articulate Mammal*, second edition (London: Hutchinson, 1983), p. 119.

23   O'Sullivan, 'riverrunning (realisations', p. 68.

24   *Ibid.*, p. 68.

25   *Ibid.*, p. 68.

26   *Ibid.*, p. 66.

27   *Ibid.*, p. 67.

28   M.M. Bakhtin, 'Supplement: The Problem of Content, Material, and Form in Verbal Art' in Bakhtin, *Art and Answerability*, eds. Michael Holquist and Vadim Liapunov (Austin: The University of Texas Press, 1990) pp. 257–325, at p. 308.

29   *Ibid.*, p. 309.

30   *Ibid.*, p. 309.

31   *Ibid.*, p. 318.

32   *Ibid.*, p. 314.

33   Quoted in Cliff Yates, *Jumpstart: Poetry in the Secondary School* (London: The Poetry Society, 1999), p. 58. This book reprints 'Naming', pp. 56–57.

34   Félix Guattari, *Chaosmosis: an ethico-aesthetic paradigm* (Sydney: Power Publications, 1995), p. 90.

35   Félix Guattari, 'Language, Consciousness and Society' in *Poetics Journal* 9 (1991), pp. 106–17.

36   See Gilles Deleuze and Félix Guattari, *A Thousand Plateaus* (London: The Athlone Press, 1988), p. 348.

37   My own experience of performing with the dancer and choreographer Jo Blowers informs my sense of the meaning of performance. See my 'A Note on Performance', *And* 10, 1998.

38   Guattari, *Chaosmosis*, p. 15.

39   *Ibid.*, p. 90. Gilbert Adair in his 'Taking the Side of Poetry', *Angelaki*, Volume 5 number 1 (April 2000), pp. 9–19, also makes use of Guattari's readings from Bakhtin, to argue for 'mimetic-alteric' poetry, which seizes 'fragments of content from multiple domains' (p. 11).

40   Charles Olson, 'Projective Verse' in Donald Allen and Warren Tallman, eds., *The Poetics of the New American Poetry* (New York: Grove Press, 1973), pp. 147–158, at p. 153.

41   See Richard Bradford, *The Look of It: a theory of visual form in English Poetry* (Cork: Cork University Press, 1993).

42   Marjorie Perloff, 'After Free Verse: The New Nonlinear Poetries' in *Poetry On & Off the Page* (Evanston: Northwestern University Press, 1998) pp. 141–167. O'Sullivan is discussed at pp. 164–65.

43 Christopher Middleton, 'Ideas About Voice in Poetry', in *Jackdaw Jiving*, (Manchester: Carcanet, 1998) pp. 88–101, at p. 91.
44 *Ibid.*, p. 91.
45 *Ibid.*, p. 91.
46 *Ibid.*, p. 92.
47 *Ibid.*, p. 92.
48 *Poems for the Millennium: The University of California Book of Modern and Postmodern Poetry, Volume Two: From Post War to Millennium* eds. Jerome Rothenberg and Pierre Joris, (Berkeley: The University of California, 1998), p. 828.
49 *Ibid.*, p. 829.

Bibliography

Ackroyd, P., *Notes for a New Culture* (London: Vision Press, 1976).

Ackroyd, P., *The Diversions of Purley* (London: Abacus, 1987).

Adair, G., 'Bruce Andrews: Give Em Enough Rope', *Reality Studios,* 10, pp. 101–10.

Adair, G., 'Dear Robert, "Linguistically innovative poetry" for which we haven't yet a satisfactory name', *Pages* 65–72 (March 1988).

Adair, G., 'Taking the Side of Poetry', *Angelaki,* vol. 5, no. 1 (April 2000), pp. 9–19.

Adair, G., *Hot Licks* (London: Sub-Voicive, 1987).

Adair, G., *Jizz Rim,* 5th outtake (London: Writers Forum, 1997).

Adair, G., *Jizz Rim,* 1st outtake (London: Writers Forum, 1993).

Adorno, T.W., 'Cultural Criticism and Society' in *Prisms* (Cambridge, MA: MIT Press, 1981).

Aitchison, J., *The Articulate Mammal,* second edition (London: Hutchinson, 1983).

Allen, D. and Tallman, W., eds., *The Poetics of the New American Poetry* (New York: Grove Press, 1973).

Allen, D., *The New American Poetry 1945–1960* (New York: Grove Press, 1960).

Allnutt, G., D'Aguiar, F., Edwards, K. and Mottram, E., eds., *The New British Poetry* (London: Paladin, 1988).

ALP Newsletter (July 1977).

Alvarez, A., ed., *The New Poetry,* second edition (Harmondsworth: Penguin, 1966).

Andrews, B., 'Transatlantic', in Clarke, A. and Sheppard, R., eds., *Floating Capital; new poets from London* (Elmwood: Poets and Poets Press, 1991), pp. i–v.

Andrews, B., *Paradise and Method: Poetics and Praxis* (Evanston: Northwestern University Press, 1996).

Angel Exhaust, 'The Bloodsoaked Royston Perimeter', 8 (1992).

Anon., 'Little Magazine Index: *Migrant*', *Poetry Information,* 17 (1977), pp. 95–98.

Anon, 'Poetry Review', *Poetry Information,* 20/21 (1979–80), pp. 142–54.

Armitage, S. and Crawford, R., eds., *The Penguin Book of Poetry from Britain and Ireland since 1945* (Harmondsworth: Penguin, 1998).

Armitage, S., *Zoom* (Newcastle upon Tyne: Bloodaxe, 1989).

Ashbery, J., *The Mooring of Starting Out: The First Five Books of Poetry* (Manchester:

Carcanet, 1997).

Attridge, D., 'Innovation, Literature, Ethics: Relating to the Other', *PMLA* (January 1999), pp. 20–31.

Attridge, D., *Peculiar Language: Literature as Difference from the Renaissance to James Joyce* (London: Methuen, 1988).

Bailey, D., *Improvisation* (Derbyshire: Moorland Publishing, 1980).

Bakhtin M.M., 'From M.M. Bakhtin and P.N. Medvedev, "The Formal Method in Literary Scholarship", 1928' in Morris, P., ed., *The Bahktin Reader* (London: Arnold, 1994), pp. 136–60.

Bakhtin, M.M., 'Supplement: The Problem of Content, Material, and Form in Verbal Art' in Holquist, M. and Liapunov, V., eds., *Art and Answerability* (Austin: The University of Texas Press, 1990).

Bann, S., ed., *Concrete Poetry: An international anthology* (London: London Magazine Editions, 1967).

Barry, P., 'Allen Fisher and "content-specific" poetry' in Hampson, R. and Barry, P., eds., *New British Poetries* (Manchester: Manchester University Press, 1993), pp. 198–215.

Barry, P., '"Birmingham's what I think with", Roy Fisher's Composite-Epic', *The Yale Review of Criticism,* vol. 13, no. 1 (2000), pp. 234–68.

Barthes, R., 'The Death of the Author', in *Image – Music – Text,* ed. Heath, S. (London: Fontana, 1977).

Bell, I.F.A., and Lland, M., 'Osmotic Investigations and Mutant Poems: An Americanist Poetic' in Kerrigan, J. and Robinson, P., eds., *The Thing About Roy Fisher* (Liverpool: Liverpool University Press, 2000).

Bergvall, C., 'What do we mean by Performance Writing?' *www.dartington.ac.uk/ Performance_Writing/keynote.html,* 23 October 2000.

Bernstein, C., 'Leaking Truth: British Poetry in the '90s', *Sulfur,* 35 (Fall 1994), pp. 204–12.

Bernstein, C., 'Semblance', *Reality Studios,* vol. 2, no. 4 (May–June 1980), pp. 66–68.

Bernstein, C., *A Poetics* (Cambridge, MA: Harvard University Press, 1992).

Berry, J., ed., *News for Babylon* (London: Chatto, 1984).

Blake, W., *The Complete Poems,* ed. Stevenson, W.H. (London: Longman, 1972).

Bockris, V., 'Extracts from a Conversation with Lee Harwood', *Pennsylvania Review* (1971), pp. 7–14.

Bradbury, M., 'The Cities of Modernism' in *Modernism,* Bradbury, Malcolm and McFarlane, J., eds. (Harmondsworth: Penguin, 1976), pp. 96–104.

Bradford, R., *The Look of It: a theory of visual form in English Poetry* (Cork: Cork University Press, 1993).

Brooker, P., 'Postmodern postpoetry: Tom Raworth's "tottering state"'in Easthope, A. and Thompson, J.O., eds., *Contemporary Poetry Meets Modern Theory* (New York:

Harvester Wheatsheaf, 1991), pp. 153–165.

Buck, C., 'Poetry and the Women's Movement in Postwar Britain' in Acheson, J. and Huk, R., *Contemporary British Poetry* (Albany: State University of New York Press, 1996), pp. 81–111.

Bunting, B., *The Collected Poems* (London: Fulcrum, 1968).

Burroughs, W., *The Job* (London: John Calder, 1984).

Bush, C., *Out of Dissent* (London: Talus Editions, 1997).

Caddell, R. and Quartermain, P., eds., *Other; British and Irish Poetry since 1970* (Hanover: Wesleyan University Press, 1999).

Cage, J., *Roaratorio: An Irish Circus on Finnegans Wake*, ed., Schoening, K. (Koeningstein: Atheneum Verlag, 1982).

Celan, P., *Selected Poems*, trans. Hamburger, Michael (Harmondsworth: Penguin, 1990).

Champion, M., Kidd, H., Tarlo, H. and Thurston, S., *Sleight of Foot* (London: Reality Street Editions, 1996).

cheek, c. (sic), *A Present* (London: Bluff Books, 1980).

cheek, c. (sic), '*Hybridising Writings and Writing Technologies*: To research, examine and contextualize key influences, of emergent technologies and those additional convergent agencies cogent to poetic writing practices, in England between 1994–2001, that hybridize writings', PhD thesis, University of Lancaster, 2004.

cheek, c (sic), *Skin upon Skin* (Lowestoft: Sound and Language Publishing, 1996), CD.

Chopin, H., 'Throat Power', *1983*, number 2, 1975, Cassette.

Chopin, H., *Audiopoems*, Tangent Records, TGS 106 (1971), LP.

Clarke, A. and Sheppard, R., 'Afterword' in Clarke, A. and Sheppard, R., eds., in *Floating Capital; new poets from London* (Elmwood: Poets and Poets Press, 1991), pp. 122–23.

Clarke, A. and Sheppard, R., eds., *Floating Capital; new poets from London* (Elmwood: Poets and Poets Press, 1991).

Clarke, A., 'A Love Letter', *Responses* 6, n.d. (circa 1991), n.p.

Clarke, A., 'An A–U of Upton's Assent', *Angel Exhaust*, no. 8 (Autumn 1992), pp. 107–10.

Clarke, A., 'For Bob Cobbing's 75th birthday', *And*, 9 (1995), n.p.

Clarke A., 'Underground Terminal', *Angel Exhaust*, no. 8 (1992), pp. 15–17.

Clarke, A., *Ghost Measures* (London: Actual Size, 1987).

Clarke, A., *Listening to the Differences* (Carshalton: RWC Extra, 1991).

Clarke, A., *Millennial Shades & Three Papers* (London: Writers Forum, 1998).

Clarke, A., *Obscure Disasters* (London: Writers Forum, 1993).

Clarke, A., *Spectral Investments* (London: Writers Forum, 1991).

Cobbing, B. 'ALP – The First Fifteen Years', *Poetry and Little Press Information* 5 (1981), pp. 3–32.

Cobbing, B. and Griffiths, B., eds., *Verbi Visi Voco* (London: Writers Forum, 1992).

Cobbing, B. and Mayer, P., eds., *Concerning Concrete Poetry* (London: Writers Forum, 1978).

Cobbing, B. and Upton, L., *Domestic Ambient Moise* (London: Writers Forum, 1995).

Cobbing, B., 'An Approach to Notation' in Mayer, P., ed., *Bob Cobbing and Writers Forum* (Sunderland: Ceolfrith, 1974), pp. 32–42.

Cobbing, B., 'An Interview with Bob Cobbing – Peter Mayer', in Mayer, P., ed., *Bob Cobbing and Writers Forum* (Sunderland: Ceolfrith, 1974).

Cobbing, B., *ABC in Sound*, fourth edition (London: Writers Forum, 1986).

Cobbing, B., *(Almost) Random Snippets from Works in Progress* (London: Writers Forum, 1982).

Cobbing, B., *An ABC in Sound (recorded 1965)/Trilogy (recorded 1968)* (London: Balsam Flex, circa 1980, Cassette.

Cobbing, B., *Bill Jubobe: Selected Poems 1942–1975* (Toronto: Coach House Press, 1976).

Cobbing, B., *Changing Forms in English Visual Poetry – the influence of tools and machines* (London: Writers Forum, 1988).

Cobbing, B., *Congruence of Speed and Stall* (London: Writers Forum, 1990).

Cobbing, B., ed., *GLOUP AND WOUP* (Gillingham: Arc Publications, 1974).

Cobbing, B., ed., *In Memoriam dsh* (London: Writers Forum, 1995).

Cobbing, B., *Kob Bok: Selected Texts 1948–1999* (Buckfastleigh: Etruscan Books, 1999).

Cobbing, B., *Life the Universe and Everything* (London: Interim Books, 1992).

Cobbing, B., *Processual: Collected poems 10* (London: New River Project, 1987).

Cobbing, B., *The Five Vowels* (London: Writers Forum, 1974).

Cobbing, B., *A Processual Nonny Nonny* (London: Writers Forum, 1985).

Cobbing, B., *Third ABC in Sound* (London: Writers Forum, 2000).

Cobbing, B., *Voice Prints* (Seaham: Amra Imprint, 1993).

Cobbing, B., *E Colony* (with Peter Finch) *Typewriter Magazine* No 4 (1973), 45 rpm record.

Cockburn A. and Blackburn, R., eds., *Student Power* (Harmondsworth: Penguin, 1969).

Conquest, R., ed., *New Lines* (London: Macmillan, 1956).

Couglan, P. and Davis, A., *Modernism and Ireland: The Poetry of the 1930s* (Cork: Cork University Press, 1995).

Creeley, R., *The Finger* (London: Marion Boyars, 1970).

Critchley, S., *The Ethics of Deconstruction* (Oxford: Blackwell, 1992).

Crozier, A. and Longville, T., eds., *A Various Art* (Manchester: Carcanet, 1987; second edition, London: Paladin 1990).

Crozier, A., 'Thrills and Frills: poetry as figures of empirical lyricism' in Sinfield, A., ed., *Society and Literature 1945–1970* (London: Methuen, 1983).

Crozier, A., *The Veil Poem* (Providence, RI: Burning Deck, 1974).

Culler, J., *Structuralist Poetics* (London: Routledge, 1975).

D'Aguiar, F., 'Have you been here long? Black poetry in Britain' in Hampson R. and Barry, P., eds., *New British Poetries* (Manchester: Manchester University Press, 1993), pp. 51–71.

Davie, D., *Articulate Energy* (New York: Harcourt, Brace and Company, 1958).

Davie, D., *Purity of Diction in English Verse* (London: Routledge and Kegan Paul, 1952; second edition, with postscript, 1974).

Davie, D., *The Poet in the Imaginary Museum* (Manchester: Carcanet, 1977).

Davis, A., 'Deferred Action: Irish Neo-Avant Garde Poetry', *Angelaki*, vol. 5, no. 1 (April 2000), pp. 81–93; also in *The Journal*, Issue, 1999, n.p.

Deleuze, G. and Guattari, F., *A Thousand Plateaus* (London: The Athlone Press, 1988).

De Muth, S., 'Aural anarchy from the sound of silence', *The Independent*, Wednesday 1 March 1995, p. 23.

Derrida, J., 'Violence and Metaphysics', in *Writing and Difference* (London and Henley: Routledge and Kegan Paul, 1978), pp. 79–153.

Derrida, J., *Adieu to Emmanuel Levinas* (Stanford: Stanford University Press, 1999).

Dorn, E., *The Collected Poems, 1956–1974* (Bolinas: Four Seasons Fountain, 1975).

Dorward, N., 'Notes and Queries', *The Gig*, 3 (July 1999) p. 64.

Dorward, N., ed., *The Poetry of Peter Riley*, *The Gig* 4/5 (November 1999/March 2000).

Drucker, J., *The Visible Word, Experimental Typography and Modern Art 1909–1923* (Chicago: The University of Chicago Press, 1994).

Duncan, A., 'Kicking Shit with Arvel Watson and C. Day Lewis', *Angel Exhaust*, 16 (January 1999), pp. 94–118.

Duncan, A., 'The Cambridge Leisure Centre: Traits', *Angel Exhaust*, 8 (1992), pp. 5–14.

Du Plessis, R.B., *The Pink Guitar* (New York and London: Routledge, 1990).

Eaglestone, R., *Ethical Criticism, Reading After Levinas* (Edinburgh: Edinburgh University Press, 1997).

Eagleton, T., 'A Permanent Casualty', *Socialist Review* (May 1993), pp. 22–23.

Easthope, A. and Thompson, J.O., eds., *Contemporary Poetry Meets Modern Theory* (New York: Harvester Wheatsheaf, 1991).

Easthope, A., *Poetry as Discourse* (London and New York: Methuen, 1983).

Eco, U., 'The Poetics of the Open Work', in *The Role of the Reader* (London: Hutchinson, 1981), pp. 47–66.

Edwards, K., '*L=A=N=G=U=A=G=E* / "language" / language: three attempts at an introduction,' *Reality Studios*, vol. 2, no. 4 (May–June 1980), pp. 63–65.

Edwards, K., 'Reviews' (of Mottram, Pryor, Halsey and Reed), *Reality Studios*, vol. 2, no. 1 (1979), p. 9.

Edwards, K., 'The Two Poetries', *Angelaki*, vol. 5, no. 1 (April 2000).

Edwards, K., 'Tom Raworth: *Tottering State*', *Reality Studios*, 8 (1986), pp. 78–83.

Edwards, K., 'Writing and Commodities', *Association of Little Presses Catalogue 1985* (London: ALP, 1985), n.p.

Edwards, K., *Drumming and Poems* (Newcastle upon Tyne: Galloping Dog Press, 1982).

Ellis, R.J., 'Mapping the UK Little Magazine Field', in Hampson, R. and Barry, P., eds., *New British Poetries* (Manchester: Manchester University Press, 1993), pp. 72–103

Eskin, M., *Ethics and Dialogue in the Works of Levinas, Bakhtin, Mandel'shtam, and Celan* (Oxford: Oxford University Press, 2000).

Feyerabend, P., *Against Method* (London: Verso, 1978).

Fisher, A., 'A Confluence of Energies', *Poetry Information*, 15 (1976) pp. 3–6.

Fisher, A., 'A Statement of Poetics', *West Coast Line*, 17, vol. 29, no. 2 (1995), pp. 109–10.

Fisher, A., *Becoming* (London: Aloes Books, 1978).

Fisher, A., *Brixton Fractals* (London: Aloes Books, 1985).

Fisher, A., *Ideas on the Culture Dreamed Of* (London: Spanner Editions, 1982).

Fisher, A., *Necessary Business* (London: Spanner, 1985).

Fisher, A., *Philly Dog* (Hereford: Spanner, 1995), n.p.

Fisher, A., *Place* (Carrrboro: Truck Press, 1976).

Fisher, A., *Prosyncel* (New York: Strange Faeces Press, 1975).

Fisher, A., *Stane* (London: Aloes Books, 1977).

Fisher, A., *The Topological Shovel: Four Essays* (Willowdale: The Gig Editions, 1999).

Fisher, A., *Unpolished Mirrors* (London: Reality Studios, 1985).

Fisher, R. and Frazer, T., ed., *Interviews Through Time, and Selected Prose* (Kentisbeare: Shearsman Books, 2000).

Fisher, R., 'Seven Attempted Moves', *Cambridge Opinion*, 41 (October 1965), p. 24.

Fisher, R., *Birmingham River* (Oxford: Oxford University Press, 1994).

Fisher, R., *City* (Worcester: Migrant Press, 1961).

Fisher, R., *Nineteen Poems and an Interview* (Pensnett: Grosseteste Press, 1975).

Fisher, R., *Poems 1955–1987* (Oxford: Oxford University Press, 1988).

Fisher, R., *Birmingham River* (Oxford: Oxford University Press, 1994).

Fisher, R., *City* (Worcester: Migrant Press, 1961).

Fisher, R., *The Cut Pages* (London: Oasis Books/Shearsman Books, 1986).

Fisher, R., *The Dow Low Drop: New and Selected Poems* (Newcastle upon Tyne, 1996).

Fisher, R., *Three Early Poems* (London: Trangravity Press, 1971).

Fisher, R., *Turning the Prism: An Interview with Roy Fisher by Robert Sheppard* (London: Toads Damp Press, 1986).

Forrest-Thomson, V., *Collected Poems and Translations* (Lewes: Allardyce, Barnett, 1990).

Forrest-Thomson, V., *Poetic Artifice* (Manchester: Manchester University Press, 1978).

Fredman, S., *Poet's Prose: The Crisis in American Verse* (Cambridge: Cambridge University Press, 1983).

Freer, U., *Blvd.s.* (Cambridge: Equipage, 1994).

Freer, U., *Speakbright Leap Passwood* (Cambridge: Salt Publishing, 2003).

Gardner, H., ed., *The Metaphysical Poets* (Harmondsworth: Penguin, 1957).

Gilonis, H., ed., *For the Birds: Proceedings of the First Cork Conference on New and Experimental Irish Poetry (26 April 1997)* (Sutton and Dublin: Mainstream/ hardPressed Poetry, 1998).

Ginsberg, A., *Howl* (San Francisco: City Lights, 1956).

Glob, P.V., *The Bog People* (London: Paladin, 1971).

Goodby, J., *Irish Poetry Since 1950* (Manchester: Manchester University Press, 2000).

Gortschacher, W., *Little Magazine Profiles* (Saltzburg: University of Saltzburg, 1993).

Gregson, I., *Contemporary Poetry and Postmodernism: Dialogue and Estrangement* (Basingstoke: Macmillan, 1996).

Griffiths, B. and Cobbing, B., *ALP: The First 22½ Years* (London: The Association of Little Presses, 1988).

Griffiths, B., *Cycles* (London: Pirate Press and Writers Forum, 1976).

Griffiths, B., *Nomad Sense* (London: Talus Editons, 1998).

Griffiths, B., *Rousseau and the Wicked* (London: Invisible Books, 1996).

Guattari, F., 'Language, Consciousness and Society', *Poetics Journal*, 9 (1991), pp. 106–17.

Guattari, F., *Chaosmosis: an ethico-aesthetic paradigm* (Sydney: Power Publications, 1995).

Haffenden, J., ed., *Viewpoints: Poets in Conversation* (London: Faber, 1982).

Hamilton, I., 'The Making of the Movement' in *A Poetry Chronicle* (London: Faber, 1973).

Hampson, R. and Barry, P., 'The scope of the possible' in Hampson, R. and Barry, P., eds., *New British Poetries* (Manchester: Manchester University Press, 1993), pp. 1–11.

Hampson, R. and Barry, P., eds., *New British Poetries*, (Manchester: Manchester University Press, 1993).

Hampson, R., 'Producing the Unknown: language and ideology in contemporary poetry', in Hampson, R. and Barry, P., eds., *New British Poetries* (Manchester: Manchester University Press, 1993), pp. 134–55.

Hampson, R., *Assembled Fugitives: Selected Poems* (Exeter: Stride Publications, 2001).

Hand, S., ed., *The Levinas Reader* (Oxford: Blackwell Publishers, 1989).

Hanson, S., 'Bob Cobbing – The Sound Poet' in Mayer, P., ed., *Bob Cobbing and Writers Forum* (Sunderland: Ceolfrith, 1974), pp. 43–45.

Harrison, T., *Selected Poems* (Harmondsworth: Penguin, 1984).

Harrison, T., *V* (Newcastle upon Tyne: Bloodaxe, 1985).

Harwood, L., 'At the "New Departures" Reading 1975, Not 65', *Great Works*, 5 (1975), p. 15.

Harwood, L., 'Surrealist Poetry Today', *Alembic*, 3 (1975), p. 50.

Harwood, L., *Crossing the Frozen River: Selected Poems* (London: Paladin, 1988).

Harwood, L., *HMS Little Fox* (London: Oasis Books, 1975).

Harwood, L., *Morning Light* (London: Slow Dancer Press, 1998).

Harwood, L., *The Sinking Colony* (London: Fulcrum Press, 1970).

Harwood, L., *The White Room* (London: Fulcrum Press, 1968).

Harwood, L., trans., *Chanson Dada, Tristan Tzara, Selected Poems* (Toronto: Coach House Press/Underwhich Editions, 1987).

Harwood, L., trans., *Tristan Tzara, Selected Poems* (London: Trigram Press, 1975).

Heaney, S., *Field Work* (London: Faber, 1979).

Heaney, S., *The Death of a Naturalist* (London: Faber, 1966).

Hewison, R., *Future Tense: A New Art for the Nineties* (London: Methuen, 1990).

Higgins, D., *Pattern Poetry: Guide to an Unknown Literature* (Albany: State University of New York Press, 1987).

Homberger, E., *The Art of the Real* (London and Toronto: Dent, 1977).

Hopkins, G.M., Gardner, W.H., ed., *Gerald Manley Hopkins: A Selection of his Poems and Prose* (Harmondsworth: Penguin, 1953).

Horovitz, M., ed., *Children of Albion: Poetry of the 'Underground' in Britain* (Harmondsworth: Penguin, 1969).

houédard, d.s. (sic), 'Bob Cobbing: Troubadour & Poet' in Mayer, P., ed., *Bob Cobbing and Writers Forum* (Sunderland: Ceolfrith, 1974), p. 27.

Houston, L., 'On Being a Woman Poet', in Wandor, M., ed., *On Gender and Writing* (London: Pandora Press, 1983), pp. 42–50.

Hulse, M., Kennedy, D. and Morley, D., eds., *The New Poetry* (Newcastle upon Tyne: Bloodaxe Books, 1993).

Jameson, F., 'Postmodernism and Consumer Society' in Foster, H., ed., *Postmodern Culture* (London and Sydney: Pluto Press, 1985), pp. 111–25.

Jameson, F., *Marxism and Form* (London: Oxford University Press, 1971), p. 111.

Joe Dimaggio, 11, ed. Jeremy Hilton (1974).

Johnson, N., ed., *Foil: defining poetry 1985–2000* (Buckfastleigh: Etruscan Books, 2000).

Joyce, T., 'New Writers' Press: The History of a Project', in Couglan, P. and Davis, A., *Modernism and Ireland: The Poetry of the 1930s* (Cork: Cork University Press, 1995), pp. 276–306.

Jung, C.G., 'Marriage as a Psychological Relationship', in Campbell, J., ed., *The Portable Jung* (New York: Viking/Penguin, 1971).

Jung, H.Y., 'Bakhtin's Dialogical Body Politics', in Mayerfield Bell, Michael and Gardiner, Michael, eds., *Bakhtin and the Human Sciences* (London, New Delhi: Sage, 1998).

Keery, J.,'"Menacing Works in my Isolation": Early Pieces', in Kerrigan J. and Robinson, P., eds., *The Thing About Roy Fisher* (Liverpool: Liverpool University Press, 2000), pp. 47–85.

Kennedy, D., *New Relations* (Bridgend: Seren, 1996).

Kerrigan, J. and Robinson, P., eds., *The Thing About Roy Fisher* (Liverpool: Liverpool University Press, 2000).

Laing, R.D., *The Politics of Experience and the Bird of Paradise* (Harmondsworth: Penguin, 1967).

Larkin, P., *High Windows* (London: Faber, 1974).

Larkin, P., *Required Writing* (London: Faber and Faber, 1983).

Larkin, P., *The Less Deceived* (London: The Marvell Press, 1955).

Larkin, P., *The Whitsun Weddings* (London: Faber and Faber, 1964).

Leech, G.N., 'Foregrounding' in Fowler, R., ed., *A Dictionary of Modern Critical Terms* (London and Boston: Routledge and Kegan Paul, 1973).

Leonard, T., *Reports from the Present* (London: Jonathan Cape, 1995).

Levinas, E., 'Ethics of the Infinite', interview with the editor, in Richard Kearney, ed., *Dialogues with Contemporary Continental Thinkers* (Manchester: Manchester University Press, 1984), pp. 47–69.

Levinas, E., *Otherwise than Being, or Beyond Essence* (The Hague: Martinus Nijhoff, 1981).

Longville, T., ed., *For John Riley* (Derbyshire and Yorkshire: Grosseteste, 1979).

Lowenstein, T., 'Excavation and Contemplation: Peter Riley's *Distant Points*'in Dorward, N., ed., *The Poetry of Peter Riley*, *The Gig*, 4/5 (November 1999/March 2000), pp. 185–95.

Lucie-Smith, E., ed., *British Poetry since 1945* (Harmondsworth: Penguin, 1970; second edition, Harmondsworth: Penguin, 1985).

Lyotard, J-F., 'Discussions, or phrasing "after Auschwitz"', in Benjamin, A., *The Lyotard Reader* (Oxford: Blackwell, 1989), pp. 360–92.

Lyotard, J-F., 'Notes on the Critical Function of the Work of Art' in *Driftworks* (New York: Semiotext, 1984), pp. 69–83.

Lyotard, J-F., *The Differend: Phrases in Dispute* (Minneapolis: University of Minnesota, 1988).

Lyotard, J-F., *The Postmodern Condition* (Manchester: Manchester University Press, 1984).

MacLow, J., *Representative Works: 1938–1985* (New York, Roof Books, 1986).

MacSweeney, B.,'The British Poetry Revival 1965–79', *South East Arts Review* (Spring 1979), pp. 33–46.

MacSweeney, B. (with Clark, Thomas A. and Torrance, Chris) *The Tempers of Hazard* (London: Paladin, 1993).

MacSweeney, B., *Odes* (London: Trigram Press, 1978).

MacSweeney, B., *The Book of Demons*, (Newcastle upon Tyne: Bloodaxe Books, 1997).

MacSweeney, B., *The Boy from the Green Cabaret Tells of his Mother* (London: New Authors, Hutchinson, 1968).

MacSweeney, B., *Wolf Tongue* (Tarset: Bloodaxe Books, 2003).

Mallarmé, S., trans. Bosley, K., *The Poems* (Harmondsworth: Penguin, 1977).

Marcuse, H., *An Essay on Liberation* (Harmondsworth: Penguin, 1969).

Marcuse, H., *The Aesthetic Dimension* (London and Basingstoke: Macmillan, 1978)

Mark, A., *Veronica Forrest-Thomson and Language Poetry* (Tavistock: Northcote House, 2001).

Markham, E.A., ed., *Hinterland: Caribbean poetry from the West Indies and Britain* (Newcastle upon Tyne: Bloodaxe Books, 1989).

Mayer, P., ed., *Alphabetical Poems and Letter Poems: A Chrestomathy* (London: The Menard Press, 1978).

Mayer, P., ed., *Bob Cobbing and Writers Forum* (Sunderland: Ceolfrith, 1974).

McCaffery, S., 'The Scandal of Sincerity; towards a Levinasian poetics', *Pretexts: studies in writing and culture,* vol. 6, no. 2 (1997), pp. 167–90.

McCaffery, S., *Modern Reading, Poems 1969–1990* (London: Writers Forum, 1992).

Middleton, C., 'Ideas About Voice in Poetry', in *Jackdaw Jiving* (Manchester: Carcanet, 1998), pp. 88–101.

Middleton, P., '(Subject) essay on Allen Fisher's *Unpolished Mirrors* & current English Poetry. (Title) *The Poetic Project*, Reality Studios*, 4 (1982), pp. 31–36.

Middleton, P., '80 Langton Street Residence Program 1982/The *L=A=N=G=U=A=G=E* Book', *Reality Studios,* vol. 6 (1984), p. 85.

Migrant, 1, July 1959.

Miller, D. and Soar, G., *Little Magazines and How They Got That Way,* Exhibition Guide, 27 September–25 October 1990, Royal Festival Hall, London.

Milne, D., 'A Veritable Dollmine: Caroline Bergvall, *Goan Atom, 1. Jets-Poupee*', *Quid,* 4 (2000), pp. 6–9.

Milne, D., 'Agoraphobia, and the Embarrassment of Manifestos: notes towards a community of risk', *Parataxis,* 3 (Spring 1993), pp. 25–39.

Milne, D., 'Contributor's Statement' *Angel Exhaust,* 9 (Summer 1993), p. 66; also as 'A Statement on Purpose' in Johnson, N., ed., *Foil: defining poetry 1985–2000* (Buckfastleigh: Etruscan Books, 2000), p. 383.

Milne, D., 'John Wilkinson: Swarf Fever', *Pages* 301–21, pp. 314–19.

Mohin, L., ed., *One Foot on the Mountain: An Anthology of British Feminist Poetry, 1969–1979* (London: Only Women Press, 1980).

Moore, M., *The Complete Poems of Marianne Moore* (London: Faber, 1958).

Morgan, E., 'Into the Constellation: Some Thoughts on the Origin and Nature of Concrete Poetry', *Essays* (Manchester: Carcanet, 1974), pp. 20–34.

Morgan, E., *Selected Poems* (Manchester: Carcanet, 1985).

Morris, P., ed., *The Bakhtin Reader* (London, New York, Sydney, Auckland: Edward Arnold, 1994).

Morrison, B., and Motion, A., eds., The *Penguin Book of Contemporary British Poetry*

(Harmondsworth: Penguin, 1982).

Morrison, B., 'Labour: Continuous' in Astley, N., ed., *Tony Harrison* (Newcastle upon Tyne: Bloodaxe Books, 1991), pp. 216–20.

Morrison, B., 'Speech and reticence: Seamus Heaney's "North"', in Jones, P. and Schmidt, M., eds., *British Poetry Since 1970: a critical survey* (Manchester: Carcanet, 1980), pp. 103–11.

Morrison, B., 'Young Poets in the 1970s', in Jones, P. and Schmidt, M., eds., *British Poetry Since 1970: a critical survey* (Manchester: Carcanet, 1980), pp. 141–56.

Morrison, B., *Seamus Heaney* (London: Macmillan, 1982).

Morrison, B., *The Movement* (Oxford: Oxford University Press, 1980).

Motion, A., *Philip Larkin* (London and New York: Methuen, 1982).

Motion, A., *Philip Larkin: A Writer's Life* (London: Faber and Faber, 1992).

Mottram, E., 'Beware of Imitations: Writers Forum in the '60s', *Poetry Student*, 1 (1975), pp. 6–7, 32–35.

Mottram, E., 'Bob Cobbing's Voice Prints: Introductions', in Cobbing, B., *Voice Prints* (Seaham: Amra Imprint, 1993), n.p.

Mottram, E., 'Conversation with Roy Fisher', *Saturday Morning*, 1 (1976), n.p.

Mottram, E., 'Editing Poetry Review', *Poetry Information*, 20/21 (1979–1980), pp. 154–55.

Mottram, E., '"Every new book hacking on Barz": The Poetry of Bill Griffiths', *Reality Studios*, V, 1–4, 1983.

Mottram, E., 'Inheritance Landscape Location: Data for British Poetry 1977', in Evans, P., ed., *PCL British Poetry Conference – June 1977* (London: Polytechnic of Central London, 1977), pp. 85–101.

Mottram, E., 'Lee Harwood', in 'A Conversation with Eric Mottram, *Poetry Information*, 14 (1975/1976).

Mottram, E., 'Roy Fisher's Work', *Stand*, vol. 11, no. 1 (1969–70), pp. 9–18.

Mottram, E., 'The British Poetry Revival 1960–1974', *Modern Poetry Conference, 1974* (London: Polytechnic of Central London, 1974), pp. 86–117, and revised as 'The British Poetry Revival, 1960–75', in Hampson, R. and Barry, P., eds., *New British Poetries* (Manchester: Manchester University Press, 1993), pp. 15–50.

Mottram, E., 'Writers Forum: A Successful Campaign' in Mayer, P., ed., *Bob Cobbing and Writers Forum* (Sunderland: Ceolfrith, 1974) pp. 15–24.

Mottram, E., *1980 Mediate* (Maidstone: Zunne Heft, 1980).

Mottram, E., *Composition and Performance in the Work of Bob Cobbing: a conversation (1973)* (London: Writers Forum, 2000).

Mukarovský, J., *Aesthetic Function, Norm and Value as Social Facts* (Ann Arbor, Michigan Slavic Contributions, 1979).

Needham, J.D., 'Some Aspects of the Poetry of Roy Fisher', *Poetry Nation*, 5 (1975), pp. 74–87.

Neville, R., *Playpower* (Frogmore: Paladin, 1971).

Nuttall, J., 'Bill Griffiths', *Poetry Information*, 15 (1976), pp. 13–17.

Nuttall, J., *Bomb Culture* (London: Paladin, 1970).

O'Sullivan, M. and Monk, G., *City Limits* (13–19 July 1984), reprinted on Galloping Dog Press flier, Spring 1986.

O'Sullivan, M., 'A Talk Concerning Edges of Her Work (with Adrian Clarke) *Angel Exhaust*, 6 (Winter 1986).

O'Sullivan, M., 'riverrunning (realisations', *West Coast Line*, 17, vol. 29, no. 2 (1995), pp. 62–71.

O'Sullivan, M., *In the House of the Shaman* (London and Cambridge: Reality Street Editions, 1993).

O'Sullivan, M., ed., *Out of Everywhere: linguistically innovative poetry by women in North America & the UK* (London and Saxmundham: Reality Street, 1996).

O'Sullivan, M., *Palace of Reptiles* (Willowdale: The Gig, 2003).

Olson, C., 'Projective Verse', in Allen, D. and Tallman, W., eds., *The Poetics of the New American Poetry* (New York: Grove Press, 1973), pp. 147–58.

Olson, C., 'The Human Universe', in Allen, D. and Tallman, W., eds., *The Poetics of the New American Poetry* (New York: Grove Press, 1973), pp. 161–74.

Olson, C., *The Maximus Poems* (New York: Jargon/Corinth Books, 1960).

Olson, C., *The Special View of History* (Berkeley: Oyez, 1970).

Paulin, T., Letter to *Times Literary Supplement*, 6 November 1992.

Perloff, M., 'After Free Verse: The New Nonlinear Poetries' in *Poetry On & Off the Page* (Evanston: Northwestern University Press, 1998) pp. 141–67.

Perloff, M., 'Cutting-Edge Poetics: Roy Fisher's "Language Book", in Kerrigan, J. and Robinson, P., eds., *The Thing About Roy Fisher* (Liverpool: Liverpool University Press, 2000).

Perloff, M., *Radical Artifice: Writing in the Age of the Media* (Chicago and London: University of Chicago Press, 1991).

Perloff, M., *The Dance of the Intellect* (Evanston: Northwestern University Press, 1996).

Perloff, M., *Wittgenstein's Ladder* (Chicago: University of Chicago Press, 1996).

Perril, S., 'Trappings of the Hart: *Reader* and the Ballad of *The English Intelligencer*', *The Gig*, 4/5 (November 1999/March 2000) ('The Poetry of Peter Riley'), pp. 196–218.

Phillips, T., *A Humument: A Treated Victorian Novel* (London: Thames and Hudson, 1980).

Pound, E., *ABC of Reading* (London: Faber, 1951).

Press, J., *A Map of Modern English Verse* (Oxford: Oxford University Press, 1969).

Prynne, J.H., 'Harwood – Love and "Cold Fear"', *Varsity*, 24/v/69, p. 6.

Prynne, J.H., *Down Where Changed* (Lewes: Ferry Press, 1979).

Prynne, J.H.., *Poems* (Edinburgh and London: Agneau 2, 1982).

Quinn, J., 'The Larkin–Duffy Line', *Poetry Review*, vol. 90, no. 3 (Autumn 2000), pp. 4–8.

Raban, J., *The Society of the Poem* (London: Harrap, 1971).

Rasula, J. and McCaffery, S., eds., *Imagining Language: An Anthology* (Cambridge, MA: The MIT Press, 1998).

Raworth, T., 'Dear Martin', *Joe Soap's Canoe*, 14 (1991), n.p.

Raworth, T., 'The Big Green Day: Tom Raworth talks to Don Watson about British poetry's tottering state', *City Limits* (February 16–23 1989), p. 57.

Raworth, T., *A Serial Biography*, second edition (Berkeley: Turtle Island, 1977).

Raworth, T., *Ace* (Washington: Edge Books, 2000).

Raworth, T., *Ace* (London: Cape Goliard, 1974).

Raworth, T., *Bolivia: Another End of Ace* (London: Secret Books, 1974).

Raworth, T., *Catacoustics* (Cambridge: Street Editions, 1991).

Raworth, T., *Clean & Well Lit: Selected Poems 1987–1995* (New York: Roof Books, 1996).

Raworth, T., *Eternal Sections* (Los Angeles: Sun and Moon Press, 1993).

Raworth, T., *Meadow* (Sausilito: The Post-Apollo Press, 1999).

Raworth, T., *Tottering State: Selected and New Poems 1963–1983*, first edition (Great Barrington: The Figures, 1984); *Tottering State; Selected Poems 1963–1987*, second edition (London: Paladin, 1988); *Selected Early Poems 1963–1983*, third edition (Oakland: O Books, 2000).

Raworth, T., *Visible Shivers* (Oakland: O Books, 1987).

Raworth, T., *Writing* (Berkeley: The Figures, 1982).

Raworth, T., *Big Slippers On*, Solo KO – 01 (1993), Cassette.

Reeve, N.H. and Kerridge, R., *Nearly Too Much: The Poetry of J.H. Prynne* (Liverpool: Liverpool University Press, 1996).

Reznikoff, C., *Holocaust* (Santa Barbara: Black Sparrow Press, 1977).

Ricoeur, P., *Interpretation Theory: Discourse and the Surplus of Meaning* (Texas: Christian University of Texas Press, 1976).

Riley, D., *'Am I That Name!' Feminism and the Category of 'Women' in History* (Basingstoke: Macmillan, 1992).

Riley, J., *Selected Poems* (Manchester: Carcanet, 1995).

Riley, P. and Corcoran, K., 'Spitewinter Provocations: An interview on the condition of poetry', *Reality Studios*, 8 (1986), pp. 1–17.

Riley, P., *Distant Points* (London: Reality Street Editions,1995).

Riley, P., *Passing Measures: A Collection of Poems 1966–1990* (Manchester: Carcanet, 2000).

Rimbaud, A.'Voyelle', trans. Scott Fitzgerald, F., in Steiner, G., *Poem into Poem*, (Harmondsworth: Penguin, 1970), p. 141.

Robbins, J. *Altered Reading: Levinas and Literature* (Chicago and London: The University of Chicago Press, 1999).

Rolo, J. and Hunt, I., *Bookworks: A Partial History and Sourcebook* (London: Bookworks, 1996).

Roszak, T., *The Making of the Counter Culture* (London: Faber, 1970).

Rothenberg, J. and Joris, P., eds., *Poems for the Millennium: The University of California Book of Modern and Postmodern Poetry*, vols. 1 and 2 (Berkeley: The University of California, 1995/1998).

Rumens, C., ed., *Making for the Open: The Chatto Book of Post-Feminist Poetry* (London: Chatto, 1985).

Rushdie, S., *The Satanic Verses* (Dover, DE: The Consortium Inc, 1992).

Scarfe, F., *Auden and After* (London: Routledge, 1942).

Schwitters, K., *Ursonate, original performance by Kurt Schwitters*, WERGO 6304–2, (Mainz, Germany, 1993), CD.

Selerie, G., 'Introduction', *North Dakota Quarterly*, vol. 51, no. 4 (Fall 1983), pp. 5–18.

Shelley, P.B., *The Poetical Works* (London: Frederick Warne), n.d.

Sheppard, R., 'A Note on Performance', *And*, 10, 1998, n.p.

Sheppard, R., 'Bob Cobbing: Sightings and Soundings', in Sheppard, R., *Far Language: Poetics and Linguistically Innovative Poetry 1978–1997* (Exeter: Stride Research Documents, 1999), pp. 61–67.

Sheppard, R., 'De-Anglicizing the Midlands: The European Context of Roy Fisher's *City*', *English*, vol. 41, no. 169 (Spring 1992), pp. 49–70.

Sheppard, R., 'Lee Harwood and the Poetics of the Open Work' in Hampson, R. and Barry P., eds., *New British Poetries* (Manchester: Manchester University Press, 1993). pp. 216–33.

Sheppard, R., 'Linking the Unlinkable', in *Far Language: Poetics and Linguistically Innovative Poetry, 1978–1997* (Exeter: Stride Publications, 1999), pp. 54–55.

Sheppard, R., 'Re-Tooling for the Alternatives', *PN Review*, vol. 23, no. 4 (March–April 1997), pp. 12–14.

Sheppard, R., 'The Poetics of Poetics: Charles Bernstein, Allen Fisher and 'the poetic thinking that results', *Symbiosis*, vol. 3, no. 1 (April 1999), pp. 77–92.

Sheppard, R., 'The Poetics of Writing: The Writing of Poetics', *Proceedings of the 1998 Conference on Creative Writing in Higher Education* (Sheffield Hallam University, 1998).

Sheppard, R., *Far Language: Poetics and Linguistically Innovative Poetry 1978–1997* (Exeter: Stride Research Documents, 1999).

Sheppard, R., *The Flashlight Sonata* (Exeter: Stride Publications, 1993).

Sheppard, R., *Tin Pan Arcadia* (Cambridge: Salt Publishing, 2004).

Sheppard, R., 'Some Aspects of Contemporary British Poetry', PhD thesis, University of East Anglia, 1988.

Shklovsky, V., 'Technique as Device', in Lemon, Lee T. and Reis, Marion J., eds., *Russian Formalist Criticism* (Nebraska: University of Nebraska Press, 1965).

Shklovsky, V., *Mayakovsky and his Circle* (London: Pluto Press, 1974).

Silkin, J., *The Life of Metrical and Free Verse in Twentieth-Century Poetry* (Basingstoke: Macmillan, 1997).

Silliman, R., 'The Politics of Poetry' *L=A=N=G=U=A=G=E*, 9/10 (1979).

Sinclair, I. with Oliver, D. and Riley, D., *Modern Poets,* no. 10 (London: Penguin, 1996).

Sinclair, I., 'Iain Sinclair/Lud Heat/ *The Albion Village Press*: a tracking and an interview by Chris Torrance and Phil Maillard', *Poetry Information,* 15 (1976) pp. 7–12.

Sinclair, I., ed., *Conductors of Chaos: a poetry anthology* (London: Picador, 1996).

Sinclair, I., *Flesh Eggs and Scalp Metal* (London: Paladin, 1992)

Sinclair, I., *Lud Heat* (London: Albion Village Press, 1975).

Sinclair, I., *Suicide Bridge* (London: Albion Village Press, 1979).

Sinclair, I., *The Kodak Mantra Diaries* (London: Albion Village Press, 1971).

Sinclair, I., *White Chappell, Scarlet Tracings* (London: Paladin, 1988).

Soar, G. and Ellis, R.J., 'Little Magazines in the British Isles Today', *British Book News* (December 1983).

Sound Texts/?Concrete Poetry/Visual Texts (Amsterdam: Stedelijk Museum, 1970), LP.

Spender, S., 'Changeling', in Astley, N., ed., *Tony Harrison* (Newcastle upon Tyne: Bloodaxe, 1991), pp. 221–26.

Stevens, W., 'Selections from *Adagia*' in Scully, J., ed., *Modern Poets on Modern Poetry* (London and Glasgow: Fontana/Collins, 1966), pp. 153–58.

Themerson, S., *Collected Poems* (Amsterdam: Gaberbocchus, 1997).

Themerson, S., *On Semantic Poetry* (London: Gaberbocchus, 1975).

Thurley, G., *The Ironic Harvest* (London: Arnold, 1974), pp. 197–207.

Thurston, S., 'Rescale: Method and Technique in Contemporary Poetry and Poetics', PhD thesis, University of Lancaster, 2001.

Thwaite, A., ed., *Selected Letters of Philip Larkin, 1940–1985* (London: Faber and Faber, 1992).

Trotsky L., 'The Limitations of Formalism' in Ellmann, R. and Feidelson, Jnr., eds., *The Modern Tradition* (New York: Oxford University Press, 1965), pp. 340–49.

Tuma, K., ed., *Anthology of Twentieth-Century British and Irish Poetry* (New York: Oxford University Press, 2001).

Tuma, K., *Fishing by Obstinate Isles* (Evanston: Northwestern University Press, 1998).

Turnbull, G., 'A Gesture to be Clean', *Cambridge Opinion,* 41 (October 1965), pp. 18–20.

Turnbull, G., 'Charlotte Chapel, The Pittsburgh Draft Board and *Some Americans*', *PN Review,* 28 (1982), p. 10;

Turnbull, G., *A Trampoline: Poems 1952–1964* (London: Cape Goliard, 1968).

Upton, L. and Cobbing, B., eds., *Word Score Utterance Choreography in verbal and visual poetry* (London: Writers Forum, 1998).

Upton, L., *Wire Sculptures* (London: Reality Street Editions, 2003).

Vološinov, V.N. *Marxism and the Philosophy of Language* (Cambridge MA: Harvard University Press, 1973).

Waldrop, R., eds., *The Vienna Group: 6 Major Austrian Poets* (Barrytown: Station Hill Press, 1985)

Waldrop, R., *The Reproduction of Profiles* (New York: New Directions, 1987).

Waldrop, R., *The Road is Everywhere or Stop this Body* (Columbia, MO: Open Places, 1978).

Wandor, M., 'Masks and Options', in Wandor, M., ed., *On Gender and Writing* (London: Pandora Press, 1983), pp. 1–9.

Ward, G., 'On Tom Raworth', *Perfect Bound*, (unnumbered first issue) (1976), pp. 14–19.

Watson, B.,'The Poet Prynne', *Modern Painters*, vol. 13, no. 2 (Summer 2000).

Watson, B., *Art, Class and Cleavage: A Qunantulumcunque Concerning Materialistic Esthetics* (London: Verso, 1999).

Weatherhead, A. Kingsley, *The British Dissonance* (Columbia and London: University of Missouri Press, 1983).

Wilhelm, R., trans., *The I Ching* (London and Henley: Routledge and Kegan Paul, 1951).

Wilkinson, J., 'Risk, O Risk, O Careless Risk (Reader Inquiry Feature)', *Gare du Nord*, vol. 2, no. 2 (1999), p. 23.

Wilkinson, J., 'The Metastases of Poetry', *Parataxis*, 8/9, p. 49–55.

Williams, E., ed., *An Anthology of Concrete Poetry* (New York: Something Else Press, 1967).

Williams, W.C., 'Measure … a Loosely Assembled Essay on Poetic Measure', *Cambridge Opinion*, 41 (October 1965), pp. 4–14.

Wilson, E., *Axel's Castle* (London: Fontana, 1961).

Wittgenstein, L., *Philosophical Investigations* (Oxford: Basil Blackwell, 1968).

Wittgenstein, L., *Tractatus Logico-Philosophicus* (London: Routledge & Kegan Paul, 1961).

Woods, G., Thompson, P. and Williams, J., eds., *Art without Boundaries 1950–1970* (London: Thames and Hudson, 1972).

Woods, T., 'Memory and Ethics in Contemporary Poetry', *English*, vol. 49 (Summer 2000), pp. 159–60.

Yates, C., *Jumpstart: Poetry in the Secondary School* (London: The Poetry Society, 1999).

Young, A., 'Three "neo-moderns": Ian Hamilton Finlay, Edwin Morgan, Christopher Middleton', in Jones, P. and Schmidt, M., eds., *British Poetry since 1970* (Manchester: Carcanet, 1990), pp. 112–24.

Ziarek, K., *Inflected Language: Toward a Hermeneutics of Nearness* (Albany: SUNY Press, 1994).

Zukofsky, L., 'An Objective' (1930, 1931) in *Prepositions: The Collected Critical Essays of Louis Zukofsky* (California: The University of California Press, 1981), pp. 12–18.

Zurbrugg, N., 'Four Years After: fragments from "typographical problem" questionnaire', *Second Aeon*, 15 (1972), pp. 37–43.

Index